CW01332737

DONCASTER
TOWN OF TRAIN MAKERS
1853-1990

PHILIP S. BAGWELL

DONCASTER BOOKS

First published in 1991 by Doncaster Books

Copyright © 1991 Philip S. Bagwell

ISBN 0 906976-37-5

All rights reserved. No part of this publication may be reproduced, stored in a retrieval system, or transmitted in any form or by any means, electronic, mechanical, photocopying, recording or otherwise, without the prior permission of the copyright holder.

British Library Cataloguing-in-publication Data
Bagwell, Philip. S. (Philip Sidney), 1914–
Doncaster. Town of train makers 1853–1990.
1. South Yorkshire (Metropolitan County) Doncaster
I. Title
625.261094

Typeset by P&M Typesetting Ltd, Exeter, Devon

Printed and bound in Great Britain by BPCC Wheaton

DONCASTER BOOKS
Official Publisher to Doncaster Metropolitan Borough Council

An imprint of Wheaton Publishers Ltd
A member of Maxwell Communication Corporation plc

Wheaton Publishers Ltd
Hennock Road, Marsh Barton, Exeter, Devon EX2 8RP
Tel: 0392 411131 Fax: 0392 425274

SALES
Direct sales enquiries to Doncaster Books at the address above

CONTENTS

	Introduction	
	List of Illustrations	
1	Doncaster before the Coming of the Railway	1
2	Two Key Decisions for Doncaster	3
3	The Establishment of the Plant Works at Doncaster, 1851-55	7
4	The Regime of Archibald Sturrock 1850-66	11
5	The Regime of Patrick Stirling 1866-95	16
6	H.A. Ivatt and the 'Atlantics'	27
7	Working Conditions in the Plant Works before 1914	35
8	The GNR Locomotive Sick Society	42
9	The Plant Works in the First World War	46
10	The Inter-war Years 1919-39	53
11	The Plant Works in the Second World War, 1939-45	65
12	From Nationalization to the Beeching Plan, 1948-62	74
13	From Beeching to British Rail Engineering Ltd, 1962-70	91
14	Reorganization and Privatization, 1970-90	99
15	Conclusions	109
	Appendices	113
	Notes and References	114
	Bibliography	131
	Index	135

Photographs

The author and publishers wish to thank the National Railway Museum, York and British Rail for the use of photographs in this book. Thanks are also due to the National Motor Museum, Beaulieu, Hants (33a); La Vie du Rail, Paris (33b); Mrs Olive Booth (42); M. J. Collingwood (57); Mrs Hilda Eastwood (40); Mr J. Finney (69); Mrs D. Harrison (39); Mrs Nancy Sullivan (38); Peter Tuffrey (68).

The publishers have made every effort to trace the copyright holders of all the photographs.

About the author

Philip S. Bagwell is Professor Emeritus in History at the Polytechnic of Central London. He is a leading authority on transport and labour history, and on these subjects he has been consultant to the BBC for schools' history TV broadcasts. His previous books include *The Railwaymen: A History of the NUR* (Allen and Unwin, 1963: Volume 2 1982) *End of the Line?* (Verso, 1984) *Outcast London: A Christian response 1887–1987* (Epworth Press, 1987) and *Britain and America 1850–1939: A Study of Economic Change* (co-author with G.E. Mingay: Routledge and Kegan Paul: 2nd edition 1987).

LIST OF ILLUSTRATIONS

1 Edmund Becket Denison, 1787–1874
2 London to York Communication
3 Doncaster Station, St Leger Day 1849
4 St James' Church (the Plant church), opened 1858
5 Plan of Doncaster Plant works, 1855
6 Archibald Sturrock, Chief Mechanical Engineer, 1850–1866
7 Patrick Stirling, Chief Mechanical Engineer, 1866–1895
8 Design for a Stirling locomotive
9 The first Doncaster built engine, 1866
10 Stirling 8ft single
11 Crimpsall shops, showing engines awaiting repair
12 Brass finishers, upper turnery, 1887
13 Carriage building shop
14 Interior, Prince of Wales' saloon, 1875
15 Carriage works, showing overhead crane
16 Foremen, managers and superintendents, 1890
17 Great Northern Railway Works, Doncaster – General Plan 1892
18 Henry Alfred Ivatt, Chief Mechanical Engineer, 1895–1911
19 Ivatt's Large Atlantic, 1902
20 Great Northern Atlantic on display
21 Turnery, late nineteenth century
22 Crimpsall shops, June 1900
23 Interior of heavy wagon repair shop
24 Carr wagon works, 1908
25 Member's National Insurance Book, 1912
26 Sir Nigel Gresley, Chief Mechanical Engineer, 1911–1941
27 Carriage works c. 1915
28 Turnery, 1916 (Chief Foreman F. Trescoe in bowler hat)
29 Women carriage cleaners, First World War
30 Plan of Plant works 1919
31 *Flying Scotsman*, 1923
32 *Mallard* near Hexthorpe Bridge
33 International interdependence in technology
  (a) The Bugatti Royale motorcar 1926
  (b) Bugatti railcar, Paris–Deauville service from the summer of 1933
  (c) A4 Pacific *Silver Link*, 1935
34 Carr wagon works, inter-war period
35 Carr wagon works, inter-war period
36 Edward Thompson, Chief Mechanical Engineer, 1941–6
37 Carriage varnishing, Second World War
38 Mrs Nancy Sullivan, who worked as a driller in D2 shop, with Queen Elizabeth and Mr Arthur Peppercorn
39 Mrs Harrison and her fellow workers
40 Mrs Hilda Eastwood and fellow paint shop workers
41 Manufacture of glider wings, Second World War
42 Mrs G. Stephenson talking to King George VI
42 Arthur Henry Peppercorn, Chief Mechanical Engineer 1946–9
44 Carriage body shop after fire, December 1940
45 Rebuilding new body shop, carriage works, 1947
46 View of works from power house, 1946
47 General view of iron foundry (left) and boiler shop (right) 1946
48 The main shops of the Plant
49 Location of the carr carriage and wagon shops
50 New erecting shop, locomotive works, 1948
51 Spring shop, locomotive works, 1948
52 Carriage building shop 1949 (became wagon shop 1964)
53 Royal Mail and other carriages under construction, 1949
54 West carriage shop 1951
55 Another view of west carriage shop, 1951
56 Aerial view of Plant works, 1951
57 Deltic locomotive repairs, late 1950s
58 Pacific locomotive being lifted
59 2000th locomotive built at the Plant works
60 The Workshop Plan 1962: the location of the works to be continued and those to be closed
61 Pacific locomotive A2 Class *Blue Peter* in new erecting shop before repair and painting 4 April 1969
62 Smith's shop, locomotive works 1966
63 Thompson locomotive being broken up in the 'Goliath' area, early 1960
64 Last steam locomotive repair, 1963
65 Women employed in fitting asbestos crinoline to a boiler barrel in the Second World War
66 Apprentices' training school, 1966
67 Class 58 locomotive no 58020 Doncaster Works, 1984
68 Railfreight Class 58 locomotive, early 1980
69 Demonstration against workshop cuts, Derby, 10 August 1984
70 British Rail Engineering Works, Doncaster 1987
71 Doncaster Depot
72 Visit of British Rail Chairman to Doncaster Depot, 10 March 1989

To Sue and Richard

INTRODUCTION

Those who travel by train become aware of the important jobs done by booking clerks, station cleaning staff, drivers, ticket collectors, buffet staff and trackmen. They do not see the work which goes on behind the scenes in the railway workshops and maintenance depots. These establishments have for many decades employed about one fifth of all railway labour. In 1970, for example, of the 250 776 employed by British Railways, 55 262 were occupied in the construction or maintenance of locomotives and rolling stock. The fact that workshop and maintenance staff are out of sight of the travelling public and that their work is less glamorous than that of drivers or signalmen may help to explain why so little has been written about this branch of railway activity. Although a number of workshop towns have been the subject of articles in learned journals or have been commemorated in centenary booklets the only books that have been published are Alfred Williams: **Life in a Railway Factory** (1915: reprinted 1969) about Swindon, and W.H. Chaloner's classic account of Crewe: **The Social and Economic Development of Crewe, 1780-1923**, which appeared in 1950.

This book is therefore intended to fill a part of this gap in our knowledge about British railway history in the nineteenth and twentieth centuries. Its aim is to show how vital to the growth of the town of Doncaster was the arrival of the Great Northern Railway workshops there in 1853 and how important fluctuations in railway traffic in freight and passengers were to the level of employment, the economic activity, and the social welfare of the town.

It remains a mystery why from the 1850s, for well over a century, the railway workshops at Doncaster were known as 'the Plant'. In no other railway workshop town was this name adopted. Even in recent years those who worked in the Doncaster railway shops still referred to being employed at 'the Plant'. In 1987, when the business was split into the three parts of the National Store, the privately owned RFS Industries and British Rail Maintenance Ltd – where repair and maintenance of locomotives continues – British Rail headquarters at Euston ceased all reference to 'The Plant Works'. Henceforth the BRML workshops were to be known as the Doncaster Depot. To many of the inhabitants of Doncaster however the area will still be known with affection as 'the Plant'.

I have been indebted to very many people for help in the preparation of this book. John Chapman, Chief Librarian of Doncaster, has given me every encouragement and the benefit of his knowledge of the sources of information which are available. I am grateful to Adrian Gray of the library staff for reading through the typescript and correcting some of the errors it contained. Carol Hill was most helpful in the selection of the illustrations and arranging for their reproduction. Her help was also invaluable in getting in touch with women who were employed at the Plant in the Second World War.

My thanks are due to the Librarian of the Westminster Public Library for agreeing to accept the temporary loan of the records of the Great Northern Railway Locomotive Sick Society.

Ron Price, Depot Manager of the British Rail Maintenance Ltd Depot at Doncaster, was very willing to answer my questions about recent developments and to show me something of the present-day activity at the works. I am also grateful to Hugh Parkin for supplying up-to-date literature about the works.

Albert Meredith of the BR's National Store at Doncaster was most helpful in putting me in touch with former employees of the Plant works and in answering my numerous questions about changes in work patterns over the last twenty years.

Eric Baines, for many years Secretary of the GNR Locomotive Sick Society, was an invaluable source of information on the activities of that Society. He also gave me well informed comments on the character of the work at the Plant. A number of former employees, some of whom had started work in the mid 1920s, granted me the privilege of interviews with them. Their recollections of their working life were invaluable. They included Willie Bangs, Sam Barnett, Frank Cresswell, Stan Lewins, Eric Marshall, George Mellor, Harry Procter, Raymond Selby, Dick Sargeant and Cyril Wright.

Hundreds of women were employed at the Plant during the Second World War. Following an invitation printed in **The Doncaster Star**, the response by women who had worked there during those years was splendid. They wrote to or phoned the library or made personal visits. Some also brought photographs of themselves and their workmates. From these replies it was possible to compile a much more valuable account of women workers' employment during these years than would otherwise have been possible. Special thanks are therefore due to the following: Mesdames Booth, Brandon, Cant, Eastwood, Fisher, Flannery, Freeman, Harris, Harrison, Kemp, Mason, Pilkington, Quarry, Reeve, Roe, Sains, Smith, Sullivan, Welbourne, West and White. Ted Wakefield, who also read the press notice, came to the library to give his recollections of women's work at the Plant when he was employed there during the war.

I am grateful to Phil Dee and the staff of the research department of the NUR at Unity House, London, for making available the files of the Railway Shopmen's National Council and those of the Railway Shopmen's Informal Liaison Committee. To Joe Finney, Editor of **The Transport Review** I am grateful for the photograph of Doncaster shopmen. With him and with Lawrie Harries I had the benefit of informed discussions.

I would like to thank Caroline Bidwell, Jane Simpson, Ralph Mackridge and Liz Evora of Doncaster Books for their help in the preparation of the book for publication.

My greatest debt is to my wife Rosemary. A book about railway workshops with discussions on such matters as locomotive boiler pressures, the tare of wagons and passenger carriage bogies, is not her favourite reading. Yet she not only helped with some of the newspaper research but also typed the entire manuscript and declared she was pleased to do it!

I accept full responsibility for any errors that remain in this work.

DONCASTER BEFORE THE COMING OF THE RAILWAY

There has been a tendency for historians of Doncaster to write down the importance of the town in the years before the arrival of the Great Northern Railway's Plant works in 1853. J. Tomlinson, in one of the standard histories of the town, wrote in 1887 that:

> Until the railways converged to this town, and the Great Northern Locomotive Works found work for thousands of hands, thereby changing the constitution of this very genteel town, it was a common remark that Doncaster depended for its support upon its weekly market and its annual Race meeting.[1]

However, Doncaster, which had its first charter as a borough granted by Richard I in 1194, and was, in 1833, declared to be the fifth oldest borough in the country, was a communications centre of considerable importance long before the coming of the railway.[2] The Corporation Congress Report of 1903 recorded that the number of mails, post chaises, stage wagons and travellers' gigs which passed through the town in the pre-railway age was 'very great'. Many of the inns listed in the West Riding Directory of 1837 were busy coaching stations. The New Angel, the Old Angel, the Ram and the Reindeer, the Black Boy, the White Bear, the Leg of Lamb, the Wellington and other inns were scenes of bustling passenger and parcels traffic with links to all parts of the United Kingdom.[3]

The 1837 Directory also reveals extensive educational provision in the town. Among the sixteen 'educational establishments' listed were the National School, the British School (nonconformist), the Grammar School and the Deaf Institution. There were two subscription libraries: the Subscription Library, founded in 1821 and the Lyceum, founded in 1834.

The markets for corn and wool (which were a very important feature of the life of the borough) obtained their produce from a wide catchment area. Customers often used the rivers Cheswold and Don for transporting their purchases to Sheffield and to ports on the north-east coast. The fish market also depended on centres as far apart as Newcastle and Flamborough for its supplies. The growth of this trade was so substantial that the Corporation in May 1843, resolved to provide a covered market in the Meal Lane area. This was opened in the autumn of 1845 with the result that there was 'a great and extensive increase' in the marketing of produce. These developments had an important impact on the growth of population.

Figures obtained from the national census and from the researches of William Ranger published in his Public Health Report of 1850, show that the population of Doncaster grew from 5697 in 1801 to 8544 in 1821, 10 020 in 1831 and 10 455 in 1841. Although this rate of growth was nothing like as impressive as that of the second half of the nineteenth century when the railway became the biggest employer, it does reveal a town which was gradually growing in importance.

The annual meeting of racegoers and horse lovers for the St Leger Stakes in September greatly helped to increase the importance of the town as a communications and market centre. These races had their origin in the Corporation's decision in 1703 to make a subscription of four guineas a year towards a piece of plate for races to be run on Doncaster Moor. The St Leger Stakes were established in 1776.[4]

The growth in trade and population induced the Corporation in 1827 to decide to have the main streets of the town lit by gas However, civic amenities were unevenly distributed between different parts of the town and different classes. Although in 1836 Doncaster was described as 'one of the most clean, airy and elegant market towns of the Kingdom'[5] this was a very misleading statement in respect of the borough as a whole. Whoever gave this glowing description of the borough must have concentrated attention on different streets to those seen by the compilers of the Public Health Report of 1850 who noted that many of the humbler dwellings were:

> close to manure heaps, pigsties, stables, slaughter houses and stagnant pools of foul water, charged with animal and vegetable matter, many of these dwellings have no outlet of any kind, or opening except in the front opposite to which, and in some cases within a few feet, are standing dead walls forming the back of adjoining premises.[6]

The establishment of the Plant works in 1853 for some years aggravated such problems of overcrowding and insanitation: but it did lead to an impressive augmentation of the wealth of the borough and at least opened up the possibility for an improvement in the standard of living, including housing conditions, for its population.

1 Edmund Becket Denison, 1787–1874

TWO KEY DECISIONS FOR DONCASTER

In early Victorian England the arrival of the railway in a town was generally regarded as a sign that that community was abreast with the times. Measured by such a yardstick Doncaster cannot have been seen as one of the front runners. The railway did not reach the town until 1849 – nearly two decades after the opening of the London and Birmingham Railway in 1830 – while the arrival of the Plant works was delayed another four years, until 1853.

There were two main reasons for the slowness of these developments. For over two and a half years there was intense rivalry between four separate groups of promoters advocating alternative routes from London to the North. Then, once the Great Northern Railway route via Doncaster was finally approved in June 1846, dissension arose as to whether Peterborough, Boston or Doncaster should be chosen as the site for the main engineering works of the company. The resolution of this controversy did not come until 1851 while the movement of the works and staff from Boston did not take place until 1853.

In the long drawn out battle for a main railway route to the North two of the chief protagonists were George Hudson and Edmund Denison. Hudson, a linen draper of York, was known as the 'Railway King' since he was the most outstanding railway tycoon in the period from c.1835–47, and was renowned for his unscrupulous methods of conducting business. At the height of his influence he owned a larger amount of railway property than any other individual. Edmund Denison (1787–1874), who moved to Doncaster from Barnsley in 1818, has been described as 'a single-minded, determined and obstinate man who *was* the Great Northern Railway for the first twenty years of its life'.[1] Following his marriage to the wealthy Maria Beverley in 1814, Denison had ample means at his disposal to advance what he saw as the interests of his adopted town. From 1841–7 and 1848–59 he was one of the MPs for the Yorkshire West Riding constituency which included the borough of Doncaster. In 1835 he brought a deputation to York to meet Hudson to discuss options for a railway route to the North. He came off the worse for this encounter, since Hudson rejected his proposals for a railway via Doncaster in favour of George Stephenson's scheme for a London-Leeds route.[2] Railway events of the next decade were dominated by the rivalry of these two strong characters.

In the early 1840s four options were being canvassed for a main railway route to the North. The one generally backed by the prominent citizens of Doncaster and by Denison was first known as the London and York but eventually emerged as the Great Northern. It produced a new and enlarged prospectus on 11 June 1844. The project was unique both in respect of the length of line proposed to be built – 327 miles – and the initial capital of £4 500 000 to be raised.[3] That same summer the celebrated Jospeh Locke was appointed as consultant engineer and advised to survey what was known as the 'town route', from King's Cross via Hatfield, Grantham and Doncaster to York, rather than the rival 'fens route' further to the east. To strengthen the London and York group's position against some of its rivals, on 30 August 1844, at a meeting at Normanton, the amalgamation with the Wakefield, Lincoln and Boston railway was announced.[4] A casualty resulting from this tactical move was the resignation of Joseph Locke who considered he had not been adequately consulted. Denison took energetic steps to meet this blow. It is reported that in the middle of the night he drove off to the house of William Cubitt on Clapham Common, roused the engineer out of his bed and 'there and then through the window – Cubitt being in his nightcap – arranged with him to undertake the engineering of the line'.[5]

Meanwhile Parliament, increasingly alarmed at the extravagant and wasteful expenditure on rival promotions during this 'railway mania' period, directed the Board of Trade to examine the merits of rival schemes for a main-line railway from London to the north of England and Scotland. A committee of five Board of Trade officials was appointed on 20 August 1844 to carry out this enormous task. To the distress of Denison and the leading citizens of Doncaster, the report of the committee, published on 11 March 1845, pronounced against the London and York scheme on the grounds that an alternative route via Lincoln would be less costly.[6] A meeting of prominent Doncaster citizens was immediately summoned. It resolved 'that they assembled under the most alarming circumstances that ever menaced the prosperity of the town', and that a petition should be sent to Parliament against the Board of Trade committee's decision. The Committee of the London and York Railway was undeterred and defiant: on the very next day following the publication of the report it resolved it would 'go ahead just as if no Board of Trade had existed'.[7] The prolonged struggle with George Hudson, who had mobilized the boards of the Eastern Counties and Midland railway to advance alternative plans (including one for a line via Leicester and Rotherham, as shown on map) to those sponsored by Denison, at last came to an end on 26 June 1846 when the Bill for the Great Northern Railway (as the London and York was now called) received royal assent. This victory ensured not only that the Great Northern Railway would come to Doncaster but also that the town was bound to be an important centre on one of the great through railway routes of Britain.

There is not the least doubt that the arrival of the railway was an event of immense importance to Doncaster. On 8 August 1848 Joseph Cubitt, the Superintendent Engineer of the Line (son of William Cubitt the Chief Engineer) reported to the Great Northern Board of Directors that 'the works are in such a state of forwardness that I have no doubt of their being ready for traffic previous to Doncaster races'.[8] The temporary station, about a quarter of a mile south of the present station, was opened to traffic from the north in September 1848 as Joseph Cubitt had predicted: but the big event came a year later, on 4 September 1849, with the opening of the line from Retford to Doncaster. This was depicted by the artist of the **Illustrated London News** (see figure 3) and reported in glowing terms in the local newspaper:

> Soon after 6 o'clock on Monday, the rolling stock on the Great Northern requisite for the working of the line reached Doncaster from the South. It consisted of first, seven splendid engines and tenders and painted a bright green. Then came vans, horseboxes, trucks, coke wagons, and first, second and third class carriages. The sight, unprecedented in Doncaster, was remarkably imposing. Early in the morning the town in the neighbourhood of the line was all astir to witness the commencement of the Great Northern Railway as far as Doncaster was concerned.[9]

Edmund Denison's influence in securing the establishment of the Great Northern Engineering works at Doncaster was every bit as important as had been his role in ensuring that the main line to the North should pass through the town. This was recognized by the town's principal citizens when in 1848, together with Robert Baxter, the company's solicitor, he was fêted and dined at great expense.[10]

When the first meeting of the Board of Directors of the Great Northern Railway was held on 1 July 1846, within five days of the company's incorporation by Act of Parliament, William Astell, MP for Beds., an East Indian director who had played a prominent part in the activities of the 'London and York' committee, was elected as Chairman.

2 LONDON TO YORK COMMUNICATION

The proposed GNR line (as it was finally developed) and the route via Rugby as provided by the railway companies under Hudson.

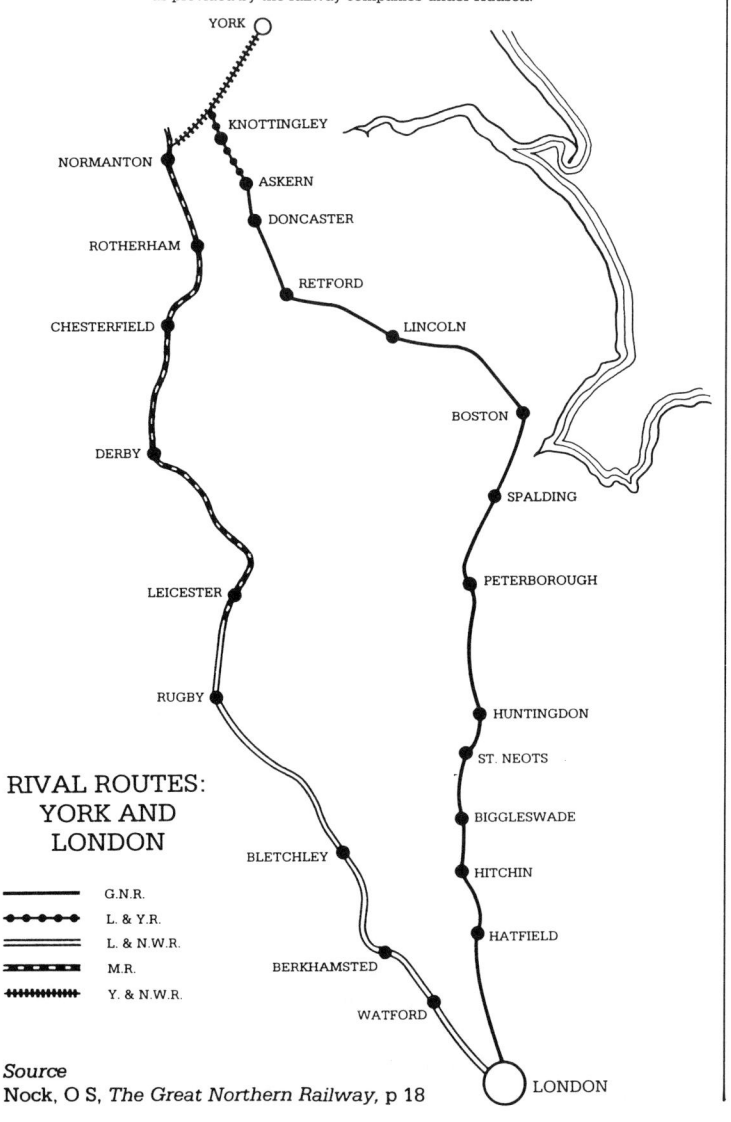

RIVAL ROUTES: YORK AND LONDON

- G.N.R.
- L. & Y.R.
- L. & N.W.R.
- M.R.
- Y. & N.W.R.

Source
Nock, O S, *The Great Northern Railway*, p 18

TWO KEY DECISIONS FOR DONCASTER

3 Doncaster Station, St Leger Day 1849

Edmund Denison was chosen as joint Vice-Chairman, along with Samuel James Capper.[11] Less than a year later, on 30 March 1847, on the death of Astell, he succeeded to the chairmanship. The collapse of the railway mania and the tightening of the money market in the autumn of 1848 led to the Board abandoning many works in progress at the time and to its failure to pay dividends on some of the stock. It is understandable that some of the opprobrium for these set backs should fall on the chairman, and thus at a meeting of the Board on 1 December 1848 Mr W. Packe replaced Denison in that office.[12] Mercifully – from the point of view of the interests of Doncaster – Denison's exclusion was short-lived. On 23 February 1849 a General Meeting of the proprietors of the Great Northern Railway voted 'unabated confidence in the zeal, ability and judgment of Mr Denison', and resolved that 'he should forthwith resume the position of Chairman of the Board of Directors'.[13] It was a momentous decision, since the chairmanship then remained unaltered until December 1864, when at the age of 77, and suffering severely from gout, Denison handed in his resignation both from the chair and from the Board of Directors.[14] By this time, largely through his efforts, the Plant works had been established for more than a decade.

A fortnight after its first meeting the Board of the Great Nothern Railway decided that the firm of Baxter, Rose and Norton should be the principal solicitors for the company.[15] Richard Baxter, the senior partner of this firm, has been described as 'only a little less important to the Great Northern than Denison'. He came from Stoke Golding in Leicestershire, but for many years was a resident of Doncaster. In the course of 1847 he arranged 1200 contracts with landowners.[16] Some of these were referred to euphemistically in the company's plans as 'Station Ground'; but as J.E. Day noted in his account of the history of the works, written in 1953, the quantity of land for which negotiations were completed was 'far greater than would be required for the construction of a station'.[17] That this property was possessed by the company strengthened the case for siting its main engineering works at Doncaster rather than elsewhere.

Five years elapsed between the first meeting of the GNR Board in June 1846 and its decision to establish its chief engineering works at Doncaster. One of the reasons for this long delay was the influence of its locomotive engineers, Edward Bury, February 1848–February 1850, and Archibald Sturrock after April 1850, in the debate on where the works should be sited. Bury, who was appointed on the sudden death of Benjamin Cubitt, held an equivocal position; he was serving the GNR, but he was also a senior partner of the engineering firm of Bury, Curtis and Kennedy of Liverpool which supplied equipment to the railway. In this dual capacity his interest in securing orders for his Liverpool firm took precedence over the need of the Board of the railway to reach a decision on the siting of the main locomotive works. At its meeting on 7 March 1849, therefore, the Board accepted Bury's resignation. Then on 27 March 1850 it appointed Archibald Sturrock, who had been works manager of the GWR at Swindon, the new locomotive superintendent.[18] In the second half of 1850 and in the early months of 1851 the view of Sturrock was that Peterborough, rather than Doncaster, would be the more suitable location for the company's engineering works. On 11 June 1850 the Executive Committee of the GNR instructed the General Manager (Seymour Clarke) and the engineers (including Sturrock) to examine various alternative locations for the works. On 23 July they recommended Peterborough, and the Executive Committee that day resolved:

> That it be recommended to the Board to adopt Peterborough as the site for the permanent locomotive works; and to give instructions to obtain the necessary land, and for the preparation of plans, obtaining tenders for the works.

Sturrock spelt out clearly the reasons for his preference:

> That Peterborough is situated on the GNR at a point which diverges the main lines to York and Great Grimsby. That Peterborough is exactly the distance from London, Doncaster and Great Grimsby to enable your locomotive engineer to run the engines and enginemen to the most advantage, taking into consideration the acknowledged days of work of both, [and] that all the engines from London, Doncaster and Great Grimsby must naturally run into Peterborough once a day, thus affording an opportunity of exchanging an engine for any of those stations without running empty miles.[19]

However, Denison from the chair, persuaded the Board to delay action on the Committee's resolution until further investigation had been made. He knew that the landed interest from the Eastern Counties favoured the engineers' report, but considered that if there was a more widely based enquiry the outcome might be different. Accordingly on 18 February 1851 the directors appointed a Special Committee 'To receive evidence on the necessary arrangements for the repairing shops and for working the line by contract.' The Committee heard the views of famous engineers, including Thomas Brassey, James Nasmyth, E.B. Wilson of Leeds and James Fenton, Chief Engineer of the Midland Railway. Messrs Clarke, Cubitt and Sturrock of the GNR were also examined. At this Special Committee's final meeting on 9 May 1851 it was resolved that:

(a) It is desirable that the work should be concentrated as much as possible and
(b) That the preference be given to Peterborough as the site for the main workshops.

The first resolution was carried unanimously. Mr Parker moved an amendment to the second: 'That Doncaster be substituted for Peterborough.' However, he could find no seconder and the original resolution (b) was then carried.[20]

The report of this Special Committee was considered at the next meeting of the Board on 14 May. Mr Payne moved 'That the Report of the Committee be adopted'. After discussion Mr Parker moved an amendement:

> That the Report of the Committee be adopted with the exception of the resolution giving preference to Peterborough as the locality of the workshops.

When this amendment was put to the vote it was carried by eight votes to three. Finally at the Board meeting on 3 June 1851:

> Mr. Parker, in accordance with notice given, moved, and Mr. Barff seconded, that Doncaster be selected as the place for the erection of the General Repairing Shop.

After this vital resolution had been carried it was resolved:

> That the consulting engineer, the engineer and the locomotive engineer be instructed to prepare and send in, prior to the next Board, the plan they recommend for the workshops at Doncaster.[21]

It had been a long drawn out and close struggle in which the influence of Edmund Denison and Robert Baxter — who had built up close links with the colliery owners in the catchment area of Doncaster — proved decisive. Also influencing the decision was the town's close proximity to the rapidly growing iron industry and its good water communications with the ports of the North East.

When the announcement in favour of Doncaster was made, no wonder the townspeople rang the church bells — in the words of a contemporary account — 'till the wild ear rang giddy with their joy'.[22] In its issue immediately following the Board's decision, the editor of the local newspaper declared that it would give 'great satisfaction to every inhabitant of this town and will be hailed as a new era in the history of Doncaster'.[23]

THE ESTABLISHMENT OF THE PLANT WORKS AT DONCASTER 1851-55

A great deal of preparation was needed before it was possible to move the GNR's engineering works from Boston to Doncaster. Part of the land needed for the new workshops was in the Crimpsall, land over which the freemen of Doncaster and occupiers of freehold houses in Balby and Hexthorpe had grazing rights. The acquisition of these pieces of land involved Robert Baxter, the solicitor, in prolonged negotiations which were not completed until 1852.[1]

In the closing months of 1851 the engineers and architects were engaged in drawing up plans for the consideration of the Board at its meeting on 9 December. Little difficulty was experienced in finding a contractor for the construction of the works. On 3 March 1852 the Secretary's office at King's Cross issued an advertisement inviting tenders for the contract for repairing shops at Doncaster. When the directors met at King's Cross again on 23 March they examined a large number of tenders and at their meeting on 4 May awarded the contract to Messrs A. and G. Holme of Liverpool, who had close links with Messrs A. and C. Brassey, the contractor who had undertaken much of the construction work for the GNR.[2]

The building of the works proceeded in stages, but by the close of 1855 it had taken the shape shown in figure 2. The first section of the plant to open was the smithy and in June 1853 the smiths were the first group of men to make the move from Boston to Doncaster. The Board received periodic reports from Joseph Cubitt the engineer. His hope, expressed on 24 January 1853, that 'all would be completed by the contract time, 31 March', proved over-optimistic. However, on 24 May he wrote:

At Doncaster the work remaining to be done is chiefly fittings and small works of completion – the whole is going on very satisfactorily. The building of the fitting shop and offices, the boiler house, the engine erecting shop and smithy and the iron store are complete. Nothing remains to be done except such as office fittings, baths, machine fixing, completing tanks and such matters. The wagon shop roof is nearly complete. The stationary engine will be ready to try in a few days. The steam hammer, two large lathes, the cylinder boring machine and the fans are fixed and the foundations of other large machines are in hand.

Finally on 9 March 1853 he reported with evident satisfaction:

During the past half year the large establishment of the workshops at Doncaster for building and repairing engines and carriages has been so completed as to admit of its being brought into use, and is now in full operation.[3]

Archibald Sturrock, the locomotive engineer, had the responsibility, subject to the consent of the executive committee, of securing estimates for, ordering, and supervising the erection of, the equipment. On 8 November he estimated that 'the probable cost of additional machinery ... required for the new shops at Doncaster would be about £33 000'. The biggest individual items in this total were the steam engine and boiler £3233; the water heating and gas pipes £2578; four steam hammers £12 943; smith's cranes, and anvils £1500 and tools for carriage repair £2500. The installation of all this machinery gave employment to a large number of skilled craftsmen before the main influx of workshop employees from Boston took place.[4]

An essential and impressive piece of furniture for the new works was the provision of a clock. Edmund Denison, from the chair, suggested to the Board at its first meeting in 1853 'that a clock is necessary for the Doncaster workshops'. At a further meeting on 25 February the directors accepted the offer of J.E. Dent, of the Strand, London, to provide, at a cost of £110, 'a clock of six feet diameter which would strike on a bell of 5 or 6 cwt'.[5]

A further essential was a supply of gas. On 18 February 1853 Archibald Sturrock recommended to the Board the acceptance of a tender from the local gas company to supply sufficient gas for the use of Doncaster station and the Plant works at a price of 2s. 6d. per cubic foot for a period of five years. This tender was accepted and the necessary installation was promptly carried out.[6]

By the end of 1853 the movement of artisans and their families from Boston to Doncaster was complete. An estimated 700 of the total of 949 men employed in the works at that time came from Boston, with serious consequences on the economy and social life of that town. 536 women and 1026 children had moved into Doncaster with their menfolk, so that the population of the borough increased by some 2500 persons in 1853.[7] In the decade 1851–1861 the total number of its inhabitants grew from 12005 to 16406, an increase of 4401, largely due to the establishment and expansion of the Plant works. In 1861 F. Parker, the Superintendent of the Locomotive department at Doncaster, made a careful calculation from which he concluded that 3724 was the 'number of souls of the Plant works had brought into the town in the last ten years'.[8]

In August 1852 a local paper questioned 'whether there would be a sufficient number of dwellings erected in time' to accommodate the big influx of staff due to come to the Plant works. However, just under a year later the same paper noted that a big speculative building programme was under way, particularly in the Balby with Hexthorpe area.[9] In fact, the number of houses in Doncaster rose from 2283 in 1851 to 3594 in 1861, an increase of 1086, some five times the rate of increase in the 1840s.[10]

Edmund Denison, as Chairman of the GNR, felt a deep responsibility for the moral welfare of the hundreds of newly arrived workers and their families. He told the half-yearly meeting of shareholders on 25 February 1854 that he 'could not consent to live day by day seeing the children of the great population brought there in the company's service running about the streets without having, in the week, a school to go to or on Sundays a church in which to worship'.[11] He held these views all the more strongly in the light of the complete destruction of Doncaster's parish church by fire on 28 February 1853.[12] At its meeting in January 1854 the Board of Directors agreed to Denison's proposal that the company should build a church and a school at an estimated cost of £8000. The reaction of the shareholders was decidedly less friendly to the proposal. At their above-mentioned meeting in February the opening motion of the opposition (who all along insisted that it was only the *principle* that they were opposing) was that 'No money be spent by the company for religious purposes until the dividend amounts to 8 per cent'. One speaker questioned whether the organization to which they belonged 'was a railway company or a church extension society'.[13]

Two days after the shareholders had had their say, the House of Commons discussed Denison's Bill which would have allowed the expenditure of the company's funds on erection and endowment of a church. Honourable members, though more polite than the company's shareholders had been, were as firm in their opposition to the GNR Chairman's plan. H. Fenwick, MP for Sunderland, for example, declared that if the Bill was passed the funds of the company would be diverted from the purpose for which they had originally been subscribed. Denison had no option but to withdraw his Bill.[14]

In his history of the Great Northern Railway, O.S. Nock wrote 'Denison won his point about the schools, but the church was never built.' The GNR Board did indeed vote the sum of £1000 for the establishment of a school. However it was not in the character of the chairman meekly to accept defeat in a cause so dear to his heart. Having failed to achieve his objective through official channels of the company and through Parliament, he appealed for voluntary donations. By February 1859 over 650

4 St James' Church (the Plant church), opened 1858

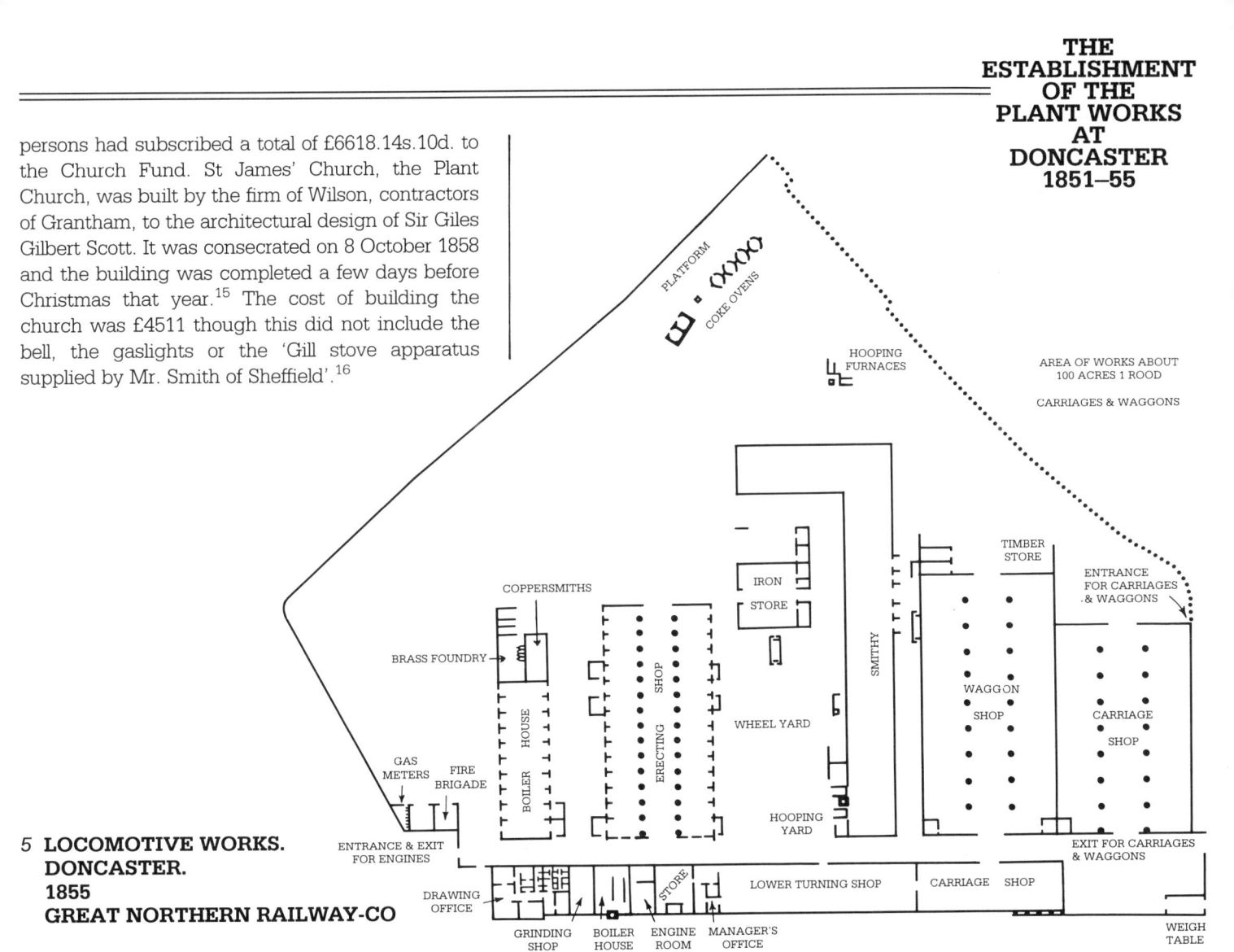

THE ESTABLISHMENT OF THE PLANT WORKS AT DONCASTER 1851–55

persons had subscribed a total of £6618.14s.10d. to the Church Fund. St James' Church, the Plant Church, was built by the firm of Wilson, contractors of Grantham, to the architectural design of Sir Giles Gilbert Scott. It was consecrated on 8 October 1858 and the building was completed a few days before Christmas that year.[15] The cost of building the church was £4511 though this did not include the bell, the gaslights or the 'Gill stove apparatus supplied by Mr. Smith of Sheffield'.[16]

5 LOCOMOTIVE WORKS. DONCASTER. 1855 GREAT NORTHERN RAILWAY-CO

Edmund Denison persuaded the company's directors to allocate a sum of not more than £200 a year for 'remunerating a clergyman for conducting divine service and giving spiritual instruction to the company's servants at Doncaster'.[17] The Revd J. Campion was the first to fill this role and his reports to the Board on the work of the church and his religious instruction in the school were regularly given and informative. Denison took a keen interest in these developments and in February 1859 noted with evident satisfaction that:

> the church has been regularly filled with a good congregation chiefly composed of persons employed by the company and their families.[18]

Edmund Denison was also fully involved with the replacement of the parish church which had been destroyed by fire on 28 February 1853. When he attended the ceremony of the laying of the foundation stone of the new church a year later 'he was received with loud and protracted cheering which continued for several minutes' and proceeded to make 'a long speech which revealed his full involvement with the rebuilding project'.[19] The new Parish Church of St George which, Denison said, cost eight times as much to build as did St James', was completed within a few days of the Plant Church.

Doncaster's population increase of well over 4000 persons in the 1850s, largely due to the GNR's establishment of its workshops in the town, may well have included as many Nonconformists as Anglicans. Certainly in the course of the decade there was a spate of new church building by the different Nonconformist sects. The foundation stone of a new Primitive Methodist Chapel was laid in March 1854 and the Chapel, which had seating for up to 1200 persons, was opened on Sunday 15 October that year.[20] The Independent (Congregationalist) Chapel in Hall Gate opened new Sunday School rooms in August 1856[21] When, in June 1857, the foundation stone of a new Wesleyan Reform Church was laid on a site between the Shakespeare's Head Inn and Camden Street there was 'an audience of about 700, almost entirely composed of workmen employed in the Great Northern Plant Works.'[22]

In May 1854, following the GNR directors allocation of £1000 towards the cost of establishing a school for the children of those employed in the Plant works, they accepted the tender of Messrs Lister and Son, builders of Doncaster, to erect a building on a site nearly opposite St James' Hospital. It was designed to accommodate 500 children. Less than six months elapsed between the signing of the contract and the completion of the building. An opening ceremony took place on 28 December 1854 when the GNR directors provided a free tea to the parents and friends of the children.[23] Classes began in January 1855. The Revd J. Campion, who had oversight of the school on behalf of the directors, reported on 8 August 1855 that although the school had only been open six months the average attendance in the boys' school had been seventy-seven weekly, in the girls' school forty-eight and in the infants 'above a hundred'.

Government inspectors for the district had visited the school and had given approval for the appointment of two pupil teachers to assist in the boys' school and four to assist with the girls and infants.[24] In December 1855 Edmund Denison authorized the extension of the school building at an estimated cost in excess of £200, which he met out of his own resources.[25] When the Revd Campion reported to the directors on 7 February 1859 the average attendance was now eighty-six while that of the infants was 162. In June 1858 Her Majesty's Inspector wrote that 'The boys and girls are intelligently taught and are in fair order' and that 'The Infant School is upon the whole one of the best in Yorkshire.'[26]

The educational provision offered by the GNR did not stop with those of school age. 'At the latter end of 1853' the Great Northern Doncaster Mechanics Institute was founded 'for the accommodation and intellectual improvement of the servants of the company employed in the Plant Works at Doncaster'. The reading room of the Institute was opened in October 1853 and the library in February 1854. By October 1856 the Institute had 208 members, nearly a quarter of the total number of men employed in the works. At that date there were over a thousand books in the library and the reading room was provided with 'all the London daily and weekly journals'. Also in connection with the Institute there were hot and cold baths and showers, a brass band and a drum and fife band. A mechanical drawing class was attended by upwards of thirty members while a writing and arithmetic class attracted double that number.[27]

However, the influence of the establishment of the Plant works in the town was not always regarded as beneficial. Atmospheric pollution increased dramatically in the second half of 1853. In December of that year a memorial signed by most of the borough magistrates and the vicar was sent to the General Board of Health. It noted that 'the town of Doncaster had until lately freedom from the nuisance of engine smoke' but that there had been erected 'many steam engine furnaces within and on the borders of the town which were becoming 'a great nuisance'. The memorialists urged the General Board of Health to submit a Bill to the forthcoming session of Parliament for the application of the Town Improvement Clauses Act to the Borough of Doncaster.[28] The memorial received no satisfactory response. That the problem was a continuing one is evidenced by the fact that on 12 June 1855 the GNR Board received a separate memorial signed by eighteen persons and asking for 'the removal of the nuisance caused by the company's coke ovens at Doncaster' since 'the vapours were injurious to the health of the inhabitants and of the adjoining nursery grounds'. The matter was referred to Mr Sturrock with the suggestion that he should obtain from all complaining parties 'the signature to a document assenting to a chimney as a satisfactory remedy for the annoyance'. On 10 August 1855 Mr Sturrock reported to the Board that he had drafted a document on the lines suggested and had presented it to the petitioners for signature. Some had signed after first adding the words 'and it prove effective to remedy the nuisance', while others had declined to sign. The company went ahead and built the chimney at a cost of £200, but it was far from being a complete solution to the problem.[29]

Environmental contamination continued into the years of the Second World War and after. In January 1940 Mr T.H. Turner, Chief Chemist and Metallurgist of the LNER, in an address given at the Mansion House, Doncaster said:

> If cleanliness is next to Godliness, Doncaster is one of the most ungodly towns, for one cannot have a clean dog, cat or child. One cannot sit on the lawn or pick a flower from one's garden without requiring a wash, and the colour of the duster and of one's handkerchief in the home shows that we live in a dilute atmospheric solution of coal, dust and tar.[30]

The increase in respiratory and other diseases and the problem of industrial accidents made more urgent the need for improvement in medical care. The GNR's first surgeon, Dr Dunn of Doncaster, also agitated for the erection of a hospital in the town. He met with a lot of opposition; but following financial support from his friends among the gentry he succeeded in founding the small St James' Hospital, which was opened at the junction of Cleveland Street and St Sepulcre Gates on 26 January 1852.[31] Meanwhile, on 6 October 1851 the GNR Board decided to establish the Great Northern Railway Provident Society (as it was first named) to support the sick, the old and the widows of its employees. Its role was so important that its history will be dealt with separately in chapter eight.[32]

THE REGIME OF ARCHIBALD STURROCK, 1850-66

For sixteen years from 1850 responsibility for the maintenance and development of the GNR's locomotive power and of its rolling stock rested with Archibald Sturrock, the Locomotive Engineer. Of Scottish birth, Sturrock was thirty-four years of age at the time of his appointment. His early professional experience was much influenced by the famous engineer Daniel Gooch who employed him in his Stirling East foundry before securing his appointment with the GWR as Works' Manager at Swindon.[1]

During Sturrock's tenure of office he was responsible for the design, maintenance and repair of the GNR's locomotives, but not for their construction. In these early years it was the policy of the company to place orders for new locomotives with well established private contractors. In the closing months of 1866 when his period of service was coming to an end, preparations for locomotive building at Doncaster were completed so that his successor, Patrick Stirling, was able from the outset, to adopt the new policy of the company of both designing and building its own locomotives.

In the 1850s Sturrock was acutely aware of the intense competition for main-line traffic to London. He realised that the 2–2–2 locomotives built by Sharp, and the 0–4–0s built by Burys, which he inherited, were incapable of achieving the required speeds and endurance for the long runs to the capital. His conviction was that speed was all important for securing the GNR's ascendancy in passenger and freight traffic and

6 Archibald Sturrock, Chief Mechanical Engineer, 1850–1866

he worked on the principle that 'the power of the locomotive is measured by its capacity for boiling water'. To achieve the higher boiler pressure, which he saw as essential, he designed engines with large fireboxes raised above the level of the boiler. His pioneering locomotive, number 215, built by R.W. Hawthorne of Newcastle on Tyne in 1853, was notable for its 7 feet 6 inches driving wheels and for its boiler pressure of 150 pounds per square inch. It was claimed that this engine would enable the journey from King's Cross to Edinburgh to be completed in eight hours. The claim was not fulfilled, and 215's performance was in many ways disappointing, so that it was withdrawn from service in 1869.[2] As was the case with all early locomotives, it offered no protection to the driver and fireman who were exposed to the vagaries of the weather.

What J.E. Day described as Sturrock's finest express passenger engine was the 2–2–2 of which twelve were built by outside contractors, including Kitson's of Leeds, in 1860–61. These engines had 7 feet driving wheels and a very large firebox. Their performance was as reliable as any designed at that time.

For the coal and general freight traffic Sturrock designed several 0–6–0 goods engines. The wheel arrangement became standard for the goods locomotives of the company for many years.

Sturrock's resourcefulness was revealed in 1863 when he came to the rescue of the Metropolitan Railway, the world's first underground railway, which began operations from Paddington to Farringdon Street on 10 January that year. Because of Parliament's concern about atmospheric conditions in the tunnels, the company's Act required that the locomotives used should consume their own exhaust fumes. The GWR had running powers over the new line and initially Daniel Gooch, that company's engineer, provided engines which were designed to fulfil the Act's requirements. However, a dispute between the two companies resulted in the GWR suddenly withdrawing its engines and rolling stock on 10 August. As it happened, Sturrock had earlier that year conducted experiments on a small 'Sharp' passenger engine to enable the exhaust steam to pass into a tubular condenser fitted in the tender tank. Arrangements had been made for the GNR to work its own underground traffic over the Metropolitan line from 1 September. Faced with the sudden withdrawal of Gooch's engines Myles Fenton, the General Manager of the Metropolitan, appealed to the boards of the GNR and the LNWR. Sturrock then gave an assurance that he would provide the balance of the locomotives by the required date. He requisitioned old engines and the staff at the Plant works used flexible pipes to conduct the exhaust steam into the tender tanks. The GNR lent both these engines and some rolling stock to the Metropolitan until July 1864.[3]

From the start the Plant works was engaged in making and repairing railway and road wagons. A return of the GNR's rolling stock in 1850 showed that the company owned a hundred and forty open goods wagons, a hundred and twenty-two covered goods wagons, sixty-one ballast wagons and six brake vans, and that fifty coal wagons, sixty-five cattle wagons and ten pairs of timber trucks were under construction. Most of the wagons in use had been built by outside contractors but since they were all made of wood and were of small capacity – no more than 8 tons – and dumb-buffered, i.e. the buffers had no springs, they were in need of frequent repair. There was plenty of maintenance work to be done at Doncaster. One of Sturrock's early experiments was to construct a coke wagon with an iron underframe, but the result was deemed too heavy for general introduction in the light of the haulage potential of locomotives then in use.[4]

In the 1850s and early 1860s most of the passenger carriages of the GNR were built by the firm of C. Williams and Co. of Goswell Road, Finsbury, London. The Plant works did not start carriage construction for the company until 1866 although it did undertake repairs and alterations. Under the terms of the Railways Act of 1844 each railway company was obliged to provide third class accommodation at not more than a penny a mile at least once a day in each direction on all its lines. At first most railway companies offered the minimum compliance with the terms of the Act; the third class compartments were little better than cattle trucks, with wooden seats. Sometimes even the seats were omitted! By contrast, the third class carriages supplied by Mr Williams for the GNR were notable as being as good as second class on most lines. The seconds had 'good class windows and cushions on the seats', while the first class were deemed 'as handsome and convenient as any man of the nicest taste or appreciation of comfort in travelling could wish'.[5]

John Griffiths, who was appointed Assistant Carriage and Wagon Superintendent at the Plant works from 1 April 1859, was responsible for designing and supervising the construction of the first passenger carriages built for the GNR at Doncaster. In the early part of 1866 he designed improved third class carriages which were 25 feet long and divided into five compartments, three of which were open to each other in the front part of the carriage, and two behind. The third class passengers welcomed the fact that for the first time a person of average height could stand upright in any part of the carriage and that there was more leg room between the seats.

Later in 1866 Griffiths designed and supervised the construction of a whole train of carriages for the main-line route to Scotland. The train comprised ten firsts, five seconds, two thirds and two brake vans. All were well ventilated – perhaps too well ventilated in the third class – and were more spacious than was generally the case in railway carriages of the sixties. The body of each first class carriage rested on india rubber blocks known as Attocks patent carriage blocks. Pending the later introduction of metal springs, this was the best that could be provided to make for smoother riding.[6]

The lighting of GNR carriages was primitive until a comparatively late date. In Sturrock's time rape oil and paraffin lamps were in general use. It was not until 1891 that there were erected at Doncaster, Holloway and Leeds oil gas works based on Julius Pintch's invention of the 1870s. These works produced gas cylinders which were placed beneath the carriages to provide lighting for approximately forty hours.[7]

In the 1850s and 1860s Queen Victoria and other members of the royal family used the GNR route via Doncaster on a number of occasions when travelling from Buckingham Palace to Balmoral. The first such journey was made on 27 August 1851 when the royal party spent the night at the Angel Hotel in Doncaster.[8] Royal carriages were not constructed in the Plant works during Sturrock's time as locomotive engineer, but in September 1866 it was reported that a new railway carriage for the Prince of Wales was in the carriage sheds – presumably for maintenance work – and that it was 'perhaps the handsomest royal carriage yet turned out by any railway company in the United Kingdom'.[9]

The increase in the work being undertaken at the Plant meant that there was 'an almost continuous process of extension' of the area covered and the number and size of the shops. For example, in 1854 the original smithy was enlarged and in 1866 the erecting shops were extended to make possible the construction of new locomotives.[10] More skilled men and apprentices were also required. In 1863 Mr Sheardown calculated that the number of men and boys employed at the Plant had risen to 2490.[11] This was more than double the number employed ten years earlier.

The rapid growth in the work force increased the need for more accommodation in the town and surrounding villages. The policy of the GNR Board was to provide funds for new housing or extensions for their better paid staff, but to leave the hundreds of craftsmen and their families to fend for themselves. On 11 May 1863 Richard Johnson, the company's engineer, reported to the directors that 'in accordance with a Board order' of March that year, the house occupied by the mineral manager at Doncaster was being enlarged as the existing dwelling 'did not provide sufficient sleeping accommodation for a large family'. On the same date Johnson sent the Board detailed drawings for 'four dwelling houses for station inspectors and foremen porters at Doncaster'. To support the case for the expenditure involved he wrote:

> The station inspectors now live in very old cottages which were acquired by the company when the line was constructed – these cottages are scarcely fit for habitation by respectable men, they are overrun with vermin, and in consequence of their age and bad construction the ordinary means adopted for cleansing ... has not the desired effect.

The Board approved the expenditure of £854 needed for the building of the four houses.[12]

Meanwhile the speculative builders were busy erecting houses for the general work force of the Plant. In July 1864 it was reported that there was 'a general cry in the New Town of the scarcity of houses' and that 'cottage after cottage and row after row have sprung up in rapid succession'.[13]

Although some of the Plant workers could afford reasonably decent accommodation, the many men who were paid under £1 a week were living in the most insanitary conditions. The seriousness of the situation was brought to light in the early 1870s by Dr Thorn, an inspector of the Local Government Board, who found that:

> The amount of filth and refuse, the wretched cottages and the utter want of sanitary regulations in the courts of the town were disgraceful – worse than he had witnessed in any town of equal size.

Since he also found the water supply from the river Don was 'bad in the extreme' it is not surprising that Doncaster's death rate was 24.6 per 1000, compared with an average death rate for healthy districts of 18 per 1000, or that the infantile death rate in the town was 'excessive'.[14]

Extremes of weather brought near destitution and health hazards. In the severe cold of the winter of 1860–61 the **Doncaster Chronicle** reported that 'severe weather and sudden change had an adverse effect on general health' and that sixty-six men – a quite unprecedented number – had been off sick at the Plant works on the last Saturday in January.[15] Dr Vaughan, the Vicar, and other clergymen of the town, raised money for relief kitchens which supplied soup and bread at a half pence a time to over 200 families in the Christ Church district alone in mid-January. Coal was also distributed.[16] When there was a very hot summer there were problems of a different kind. In July 1864 a correspondent of the **Doncaster Chronicle** wrote of a 'horrible stench' coming from sewage running on to the Carr. This was 'too near the town', he protested.[17]

In 1864 the men employed in the workshops, and their families, saw in the creation of a co-operative society a useful means of self-help. In June that year they elected a committee of twelve, 'consisting of representatives from different branches of the Plant works'. On Friday 29 July The Doncaster Co-operative and Industrial Society opened its first shop in St James' Street for the sale of groceries and provisions. A reporter from the local paper noted that 'the heads of the railway departments of the Plant did not object to the formation of the society' and that he understood that 'the goods required would be conveyed on the line free of charge'.[18] The society made slow but steady progress to the end of the 1860s, when it had two hundred members and paid a dividend on members' purchases of one shilling in the pound.[19] On 28 February 1868 a well attended meeting of members was informed that the **Lancet** had recently indicated that nineteen out of twenty food products were adulterated. At the co-op 'goods would not necessarily be cheaper but they would be unadulterated and profits would be shared'.[20] In the 1870s the society expanded rapidly, both in membership and in the range of its activities and near the end of that decade it was estimated that the 1100 members represented a quarter of the households in Doncaster.[21]

During Archibald Sturrock's tenure of office, workers at the Plant looked to local enfranchisement as a means of exercising greater control over the circumstances of their lives. In the run up to the municipal elections of 1861 the **Doncaster Chronicle** noted that:

> Consequent on the large influx of artisan population into the town caused by the establishment of the Plant works at Doncaster ... the last burgers roll shows that the West Ward – in which most of the Plant men reside – contains no less than 500 voters, and we are assured that by another year the roll will be swelled out to almost double that figure.

It went on, somewhat patronizingly, to comment:

> While we rejoice to observe a deeper interest in municipal affairs – yet we were sorry to notice in election proceedings last Friday a disposition to import politics.[22]

Just under a year later there were two hundred claimants for the municipal franchise, 'nearly wholly confined to the West Ward'.[23]

If some concern was expressed over the desire of the artisans to exercise more political muscle, the directors of the GNR gave every encouragement to the growth of recreational activities. Plant workers participated in the cricket match between an eleven of England and twenty-two of Doncaster and district on 7–9 August 1862 (giving the local side double the numbers of the England side was, no doubt, done to provide a better balance of strength). Despite the fact that the first day's play was 'seriously interrupted by rain', the four innings were played out and the Doncaster twenty-two proclaimed victorious by ninety-one runs.[24]

The directors of the GNR were more directly concerned wth the Great Northern Rifle Corps founded in the autumn of 1859. Edmund Denison and Robert Baxter attended the foundation meetings when seventy-five men from the Plant volunteered to join. The cost of the uniforms, £3.10s. per man, was met from a special fund. The first church parade of the Corps was held in the Plant Church (St James') on 20 May 1860, when the chaplain, the Revd J. Campion, preached from Genesis XIV, verse 4:

> And when Abraham heard that his brother had been taken captive, he armed his trained servants, born in his house, three hundred and eighteen in number, and pursued them into Dan.

The reverend gentleman 'showed the necessity as well as the lawfulness of defensive warfare'. There is no evidence that any member of his congregation disagreed with his remarkable interpretation of the Christian gospel.[25]

It was during the 1860s and after that there took place 'the annual treat' of a trip to the seaside, generally Scarborough. The directors charged two shillings per person for the day's outing. On Saturday 6 July 1861 1200 persons boarded trains leaving Doncaster at 5.30 a.m. and arriving at Scarborough at 9 a.m. After 'a pleasant day at the seaside', the return journey was completed at 11 p.m. It is not recorded whether there was a full muster at St James' church the following morning.[26]

Early in the following July the Plant workers took the initiative. They wrote to Archibald Sturrock 'asking for free passes for themselves and their wives to and from London to visit the Exhibition'. On 22 July the Board resolved 'that the workmen be allowed to come up from all points of the line and bring their wives at a uniform fare of three shillings each passenger, and their children at half that rate'.[27]

Early in 1864 Edmund Denison, the Chairman of the GNR, fell ill. That year he did not attend either of the half-yearly meetings of the shareholders. On 17 December he resigned both from the chair and from his membership of the Board. The shareholders, who had cause for satisfaction that the dividend had risen from 2 per cent in 1851 to over 7 per cent in 1864, subscribed £1500 for the purchase of a testimonial. Denison expressed the wish that £1000 should be devoted to building a church at New England, near Peterborough, and the remainder used for the present of a candelabrum.[28] Edmund Denison lived for ten years after his retirement. Just before his death on 24 May 1874, aged eighty-seven, he inherited a baronetcy, dropped the name Denison, and became known as Sir Edmund

Beckett. His son Beckett Denison took his place on the Board, but not in the chair, in 1865.[29]

At a meeting of the Board on 9 January 1866 Archibald Sturrock announced his intention to retire that year from his position of locomotive engineer. While candidates for the post were being considered by the Board he continued at his post; but he handed over responsibility to his successor, Patrick Stirling, on 1 October. He was still only fifty years of age. At a gathering in the erecting shop in the following January he was presented with a plate of £200 value. He reached the ripe old age of ninety-two, dying on 1 January 1909, more than a decade after the death, in harness, of his successor.[30]

5

THE REGIME OF PATRICK STIRLING

7 Patrick Stirling, Chief Mechanical Engineer, 1866–1895

Patrick Stirling, who in 1866 was appointed, first Works Manager, and then Locomotive Engineer of the GNR, was born in Kilmarnock, Scotland, in 1820. He was the son of the Revd Robert Stirling DD who was one of the ministers of the parish but was also a talented mechanic and inventor. Patrick Stirling had a varied experience as a mechanical engineer in his twenties. He served an apprenticeship with an uncle in Dundee and as a journeyman with Messrs Napier and Sons, marine engineers, of Glasgow. After filling a succession of other posts, he was appointed locomotive superintendent of the Glasgow and South Western Railway where he remained for thirteen years before making the move to Doncaster at the age of forty-six. Six feet four inches in height, he was a very distinguished-looking and handsome man who attracted much attention as, each day, he walked from his home,

THE REGIME OF PATRICK STIRLING

8 Design for a Stirling locomotive

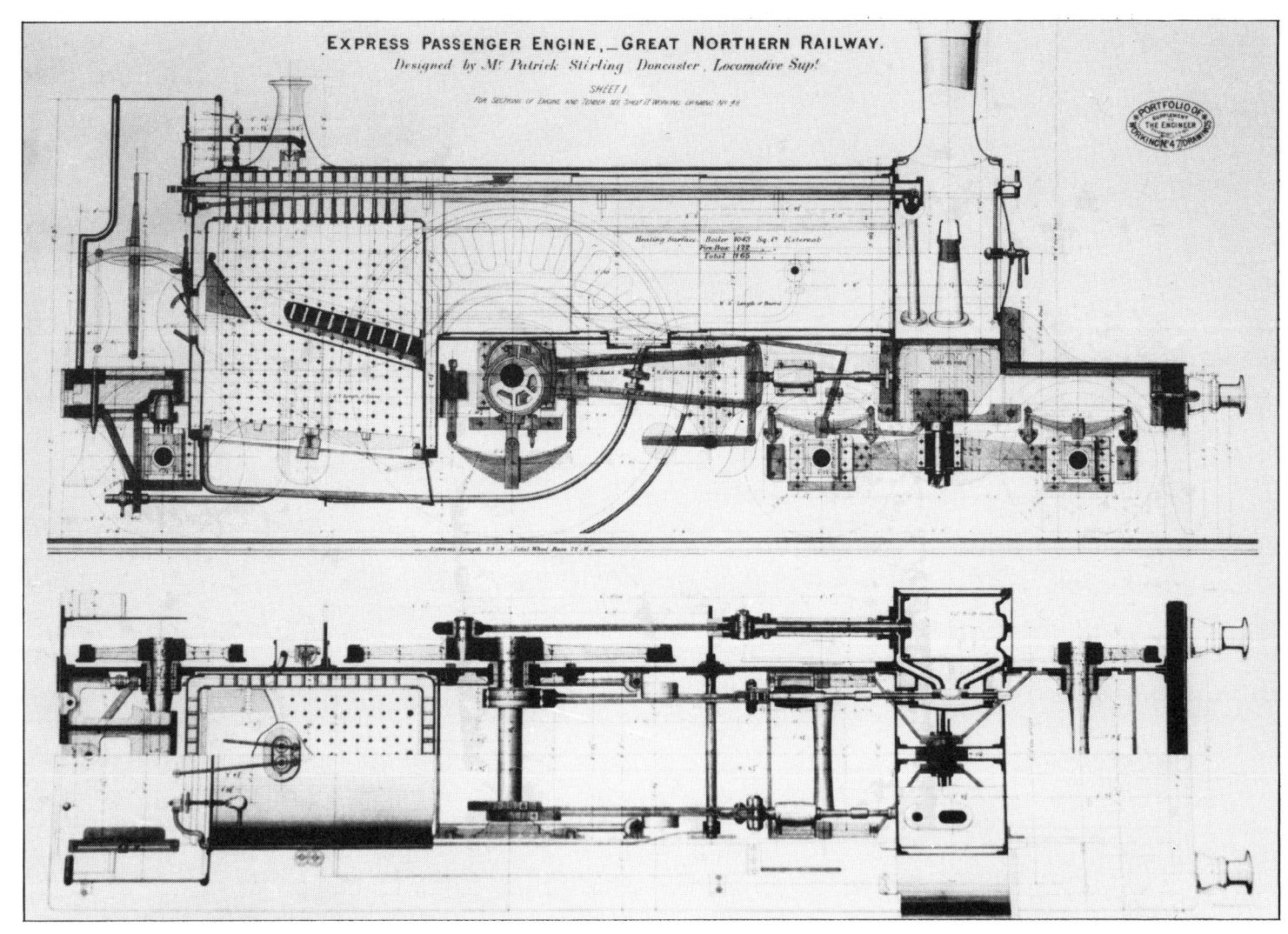

Highfield House, Thorne Road (now the site of the Rectory Gardens) to the Plant works. He was known as a person who spoke his mind, very bluntly on occasions. When he was travelling to the scene of an accident the doctor accompanying him asked whether it might not be possible to drill into an axle to see if the interior was perfectly sound. His terse reply was, 'Doctor, do you look down a man's throat to see if his boots are on straight?'[1]

Since at that time there was no fixed retirement age, Stirling, whose absorbing interest was his work, died in harness on 11 November 1895 in his seventy-sixth year.

The years between 1866 and 1895 when Stirling was in office were a time of rapid expansion of the GNR both in its passenger and its freight services. The business depression of 1879 brought in a period of retrenchment, but the set-backs of that year were short lived.

Some of the outstanding features of these thirty years were the growth of the South Yorkshire coal trade; the fierce competition with the LNWR for the passenger traffic to Scotland, leading to the famous railway races to the North in 1888 and 1895; competition for general merchandise traffic, with business firms expecting quicker delivery times; and the growth of suburban passenger services, particularly in North London. All these developments meant demands for more powerful and faster locomotives, the large scale provision of wagons and the increase in number and improvement in quality of passenger carriages. This spelt a great increase in the volume and range of activities at the Plant works.

To meet these challenges Patrick Stirling introduced a style of locomotive design which, in the view of O.S. Nock, had 'a simple, austere beauty which has never been surpassed'. The engines he designed for the express services from London to York and London to Leeds between 1870–95 hauled the fastest trains operated in Great Britain at that time.[2] His experience as locomotive engineer of the Glasgow and South Western Railway convinced him that large diameter single-wheelers achieved the best results for express work. He once likened a coupled engine to 'a laddie running wi' his breeks doon'. He also displayed great confidence in the power of his express engines. His inflexible rule was 'one train, one

9 The first Doncaster built engine, 1866

10 Stirling 8 ft Single

engine'. Other locomotive engineers might resort to double heading, i.e. two locomotives, where steep gradients had to be surmounted; he believed his best engines could tackle any gradient on the GNR system.

Patrick Stirling's most famous locomotive was the 'No.1 8 foot single' built in the Plant works in 1870 (see figure 10). As the name by which it became famous suggested, it had driving wheels of 8 feet diameter. Its boiler, 11 feet 5 inches long, produced a working pressure of 140 lb per square inch. Since the cylinders were 18 inches in diameter, with a stroke of 28 inches, Stirling considered that it would have been difficult to accommodate them inside the engine without pitching the boiler at an undesirable height. The tender carried 3½ tons of coal and 2700 gallons of water. Thirty-seven of these locomotives were constructed over the twelve years to 1882. These were his favourite engines with which he worked the express passenger trains. The No. 1 8 foot single of 1870 ran under its own steam in the Railway Centenary run from Stockton to Darlington in 1925 and is now preserved in the Railway Museum at York. In 1884 a modification of the original design was produced with a larger boiler, producing a pressure of 160 lb per square inch, and a larger tender which had a capacity of 5 tons of coal and 2900 gallons of water. Ten of these more powerful locomotives were built until 1893. They enabled the GNR to maintain its unrivalled record for speed. Between 1871 and 1883, using these locomotives, the GNR increased its express (i.e. over 36 m.p.h.) mileage by 92 per cent, notwithstanding a simultaneous increase in the weight of trains of at least 50 per cent. At the end of this period sixty-seven daily expresses were run over 6780 miles at an average speed of 46½ m.p.h. By 1884 the 'Manchester Fliers' were working at an average speed of 53 m.p.h. By 1895 GNR trains achieved an average speed of 60 m.p.h. all the way to Aberdeen.[3]

THE REGIME OF PATRICK STIRLING

However, express passenger trains were only a small, though much publicized, part of the total services provided by the GNR. Movement of the freight traffic required many more locomotives and a far greater number of vehicles than did the passenger traffic. During Patrick Stirling's period of service at Doncaster, 899 locomotives were built to his design, 709 of them at the Plant works. The large majority of the total were goods engines. In 1871 he designed a powerful 0–6–0 goods engine which weighed 40 tons, had 19 inch diameter cylinders and was capable of hauling a train of fifty-five loaded wagons with an overall weight of 600 tons. (However, the goods sidings on the GNR network were generally too short to accommodate such lengthy trains.) 229 of these sturdy locomotives were built in the years to 1895.

In 1881, to deal with the growing suburban traffic, Stirling introduced 0–4–0 side tank locomotives with condensing gear and short funnels to enable them to cope with underground working and steep gradients. A modified version of this type of locomotive was produced in 1889. All told twenty-nine side tank locomotives were built at the Plant before the end of 1895.[4]

In addition to providing for the building of new locomotives Stirling carried out a systematic policy of renewal and modification of the locomotives inherited from the Sturrock era. This is made clear in a report by Henry Oakley, the General Manager, to the Board of the GNR made on 8 November, and in a fuller report by Patrick Stirling on 17 December 1877. These provide a valuable summary of what was achieved by Stirling in the first ten years in which he was responsible for the condition of the locomotives and rolling stock of the company. In June 1866 the company's stock of engines numbered 436. By December 1877 the whole of that stock had been renewed or repaired and 168 new engines had been provided. The repairs and renewals were paid for from revenue, while the cost of new construction came out of the capital account. In the course of reconstructing the older engines, advantage was taken of the opportunity greatly to increase their weight and power, in many instances the new remodelled engines having double the power of the original ones. At the same time there was a better organization of the repair work so that in December 1877 the percentage of locomotives under repair was only fifteen compared with twenty-seven in June 1866. In answer to charges that the GNR was not spending enough on locomotive maintenance and renewal, Mr Grinling, the accountant, reported that in the ten years to 1877 the company had spent an average of £252 per engine per year, a figure which compared favourably with the Midland's £239 and the LNWR's £193, but less favourably with the North Eastern's £286 and the Manchester, Sheffield and Lincolnshire's £269. Where the GNR outshone these companies' performance was in revenue earned per locomotive per year, on the average of the years 1866–77, the figures for earnings being taken from total receipts. The GNR's engines earned well over £5000 a year in the years 1872–6 inclusive, a performance none of the other companies could match. These figures reflect both efficient managerial skill and the dedication and skill of the labour force of the Plant works who repaired and renewed an average of forty-one locomotives a year from 1866–77.[5]

11 Crimpsall shops, showing engines awaiting repair

12 Brass finishers, upper turnery, 1887

Surveying the railways' pre-1914 performance in England and Wales, Jack Simmons noted that goods traffic accounted for a consistently higher proportion of total revenue than did passenger traffic. Yet the instruments for carrying the goods traffic were 'notably behind the times in Britian' while 'the passenger service, taken all round, was as good as any in the world'.[6] This generalization about the national situation was also valid for the GNR where, for example, over the period 1866–77, the revenue from the freight traffic exceeded that from the passenger services by over 14 per cent.[7] Simmons found that the great majority of the 1 350 000 wagons which ran on the railways of the UK in 1907 were 'almost identical in design with those that had been in service 50 years before'. Pre-1914 the typical vehicle had a carrying capacity of 9 tons. It was an:

> open, timber-built wagon, rectangular in shape, with doors on its long sides, resting on an iron frame, with a hand brake and with springs to the axles and buffers.[8]

It was also true that the methods of construction and repair of wagons in the Plant works remained basically unchanged before 1914, and even up to railway nationalization in 1948.

On his appointment in 1866 Patrick Stirling inherited 9984 wagons of which 8 per cent were undergoing repair. A disconcertingly large number of these vehicles were of a very low carrying capacity. There were 2908 of them which could carry no more than 6 tons apiece and over 500 more whose capacity was over 6, but under 9 tons. Priority from the beginning of 1867 was therefore given to the conversion of these low capacity wagons to a standard 9 tons. Hence, for the wagon repair staff at the Plant works, 1867 was an exceptionally busy year, with a record of 844 repairs completed. When this conversion programme was virtually completed at the end of 1877, the adaptation of old vehicles had increased the company's carrying capacity by 11 820 tons, while the average age of GNR wagons had fallen to seven and a quarter years. Since 5315 new wagons were added to stock in the period to June 1877 the total number of wagons in the possession of the company had risen to 15 299.[9] However, the ability of the Plant works to meet increasing requirements for repairs and renewals was strictly limited. In 1877 Stirling warned the Board that the 'workshops and siding accommodation for wagon repairs was quite inadequate'. In the following year J. Ramsbottom, the Locomotive Engineer of the LNWR, in an independent report, considered 'that there was not sufficient workshop accommodation' in the wagon department.[10]

THE REGIME OF PATRICK STIRLING

In Stirling's time and after, the largest proportion of new wagons was built at the Plant, the Board at times sanctioning very substantial additions to stock. Thus, on 7 October 1882 the order was for 1000 wagons, while further orders of 1000 each were given on 2 April 1886 and 2 November 1888.[11] These and other orders provided plenty of work for those employed in the wagon shop. But it was also deemed necessary to place orders for new wagons with 'outside' firms such as the 1000 ordered from Messrs Craven Brothers on 6 December 1889.[12] In 1884 wagons were also hired from private companies such as the Midland Carriage and Wagon Company and the Metropolitan Railway Wagon and Carriage Company – a total of 631 wagons at a rent of £6. 10s. per wagon.[13]

The GNR did not provide continuous brakes for its goods trains. There are a variety of reasons why this was the case. The most important reason was that the company, like virtually all railway companies in Britain, allowed privately owned wagons, especially those of colliery companies, to run on its lines in return for the payment of a fee. The owners of these wagons, especially if they were in a small line of business, were reluctant to incur the expense of adapting their vehicles for continuous braking. The railway companies, in turn, were reluctant to put too much pressure on the private wagon owners since they wished to keep their business. Unfortunately the wagons sold to the GNR by the large wagon manufacturing firms were not of uniform design. This was a further obstacle preventing the introduction of continuous brakes.[14] There was also the difficulty caused by dumb-buffered wagons. Under Stirling's direction the wagon stock of the GNR was converted to have spring buffers. However, there was reluctance on the part of management to put pressure on the private owners to make the change. It was not until 1903 that the companies, acting together, told the Association of Private Owners of Rolling Stock that they would not accept dumb-buffered wagons on their lines after 1909. But when war broke out in 1914 the prohibition had still not been enforced.[15]

The result of these failures to introduce basic innovations in wagon design and freight train operation was the long survival of an inefficient system of railway freight transport. When a driver of a freight train approached one of the steeper down gradients on its route he needed to stop the train so that the guard could pass down the line of vehicles applying the hand brake on each of the wagons. The train would then proceed slowly to the foot of the gradient where a further stop was made to allow the guard to release all the brakes. The consequence of the survival of small capacity wagons and the absence of continuous braking on freight trains was that railway companies needed to have a much larger stock of wagons than would have been the case with more advanced methods of wagon construction and freight train operation. Hence, a wagon repairer, employed in the old wagon repair shop in Stirling's early years as Locomotive Engineer, could have visited the much larger Carr wagon repair shops – opened in 1889 – in the latter part of 1913 to find that there was little that was unfamiliar in the materials being used or the end product of the workshop.

Whereas in the last quarter of the nineteenth century there was no major change in the character of the vehicles used and the methods of operation of the freight traffic, it was a very different story in the case of the passenger services. Here there was a change 'from the Middle Ages of railway travel into the beginning of the modern world'.[16] The stimulus for these changes was the competition between the major railway companies to attract customers from the travelling public. In this part of the railway business, although there were plenty of conservative managers who were slow to adopt changing practices, there was no obstacle to innovation comparable to the private wagon owners' dead hand of opposition to change in freight handling methods.

In Sturrock's time it was largely the GNR which led the way in the quality of passenger services provided. In the regime of his successor, however, it was the Midland Railway which pioneered improvements, especially in the third class services. The other companies had, perforce, to follow its example or risk losing their passengers. That company's unprecedented move in 1872 to provide third class accommodation on all its trains was the first of a series of shocks to railway managements

13 Carriage building shop

14 Interior,
    Prince of Wales'
    saloon, 1875

15 Carriage works,
    showing overhead
    crane

throughout the UK. It was followed two years later by the abolition of the second class, the reduction in first class fares, generally to the level of the former second class ones, and the improvement in comfort of third class travel by the padding of the seats. A further Midland innovation was the experimental introduction in 1874 of Pullman cars which ran on bogies and which were provided with lavatories and with heating from hot water pipes.[17]

At first the response of the GNR Board to these challenges was minimal. From 26 October 1872 the issue of free foot warmers was extended to third class passengers for the first time.[18] In a letter to the directors on 26 November 1874 Henry Oakley, the General Manager, wrote that he thought it desirable 'with a view to the settlement of the fares consequent on the alteration of the practices adopted by the Midland Railway, to convene a meeting of all the railways affected'. That meeting resulted in the reduction of ordinary season ticket rates by almost one seventh and the issuance of third class season tickets at reduced rates.[19]

Improvement in the comfort of railway travel required the substitution of eight-wheeled bogie carriages for the six-wheeled variety without bogies. These changes involved extra expense, directly in the construction of the carriages and indirectly in the greater engine power required to draw passenger trains. In 1875 Patrick Stirling resisted these changes. He pointed out that a bogie carriage cost £1030 to build, or £25. 15s. for each seat provided, whereas one running on six wheels without bogies cost £483 or £14. 4s. a seat. He argued that with the eight wheelers 'there was a needless amount of weight per passenger carried and a great increase in the cost of maintenance'. He claimed that 'the bogie system is not likely to make great progress in this country'.[20] However, passengers expressed an ever increasing demand for improved comfort in travel. The riding qualities of Stirling's six wheelers were undoubtedly inferior to those of the bogie carriages. E.L. Ahrons even suggested, with tongue in cheek, that the wheels on Stirling's carriages were octagonal[21] Nevertheless, after the Plant works had turned out the GNR's first bogie carriage in 1875, three more were produced in 1876 and a further batch in 1878–80. These proved very popular with passengers.[22] This led to conflicts between F.S. Cockshott, the Superintendent of the Line – who had more contact with passengers – and Stirling, who was concerned about mounting costs of carriage construction.

In the early 1870s sleeping carriages built by the Pullman Company in the USA became increasingly popular with American travellers. In 1873 the Plant works produced the first sleeping carriage to be made in the UK. It was designed for the East Coast Joint Service (ECJS) to Scotland in which the lines of the Great Northern, North Eastern and North British Companies were used. In fact most of the innovations coming from the Plant works were designed to improve this London–Edinburgh service. At its meeting on 19 November the Board of the GNR instructed Stirling to prepare more plans for sleeping carriages.[23]

The Board was certainly under pressure to improve the standard of accommodation in its third class carriages. On 7 June 1877 Henry Oakley reported that the LNWR intended to stuff the backs of the third class carriages running on the West Coast route. This was in consequence of the action taken by the Glasgow and South Western Railway (GSWR). With some reluctance, at its meeting in January 1878, the Board authorized the General Manager 'in competition with the other companies' route', to improve the stocks up to the same standard adopted by the West Coast companies.[24] On the recommendation of the General Manager further improvements to the third class carriages were endorsed by the Board in 1879. The carriages were to be 'six feet wide, and provided with curtains on rings and stuffed backs with springs'. Although initially it was considered best to put this new work out to tender, it was eventually decided to allocate it to the Plant works.[25]

16 Foremen, managers and superintendents, 1890

On 18 October 1879 the GNR ran for the first time a dining room and a drawing room car from King's Cross to Peterborough. The trial trip left at 12.30 p.m. When the train reached a speed of 65 m.p.h. 'full glasses slopped over and white waistcoats were imperilled'. A Leeds–London run with the same Pullman carriages was made early in the following month.[26]

With a view to retaining the through passenger traffic from London to the North, the first British side corridor coach was built at Doncaster for the East Coast Joint Stock in 1882.[27] On 14 September 1892, F.P. Cockshott wrote to the General Manager that the GNR's third class corridor coaches were 'in great demand' and that the company had not sufficient of them to meet requirements. Shortly afterwards Sir Henry Oakely wrote to the Board endorsing Cockshott's recommendation that more corridor coaches should be built and adding:

> It is almost a desideratum these days to provide lavatory accommodation for passengers travelling a journey of 4 or 5 hours or more.

The Board agreed to these recommendations.[28]

One of the last instructions Patrick Stirling received from the Board was to arrange for the building at Doncaster of third class dining cars for the Yorkshire trains. The Secretary of the GNR had received memorials from both the Halifax and the Dewsbury Chambers of Commerce urging that these new cars should be provided. On 2 October 1895 Sir Henry Oakely wrote to the Board:

> As the Directors are aware, the Midland Company run third class dining cars on their Scottish trains ... There is no doubt that by these facilities they have succeeded in diverting a certain proportion of our Leeds traffic ... I have also been advised of a number of other cases where passengers, more particularly business men, have preferred the Midland route on account of the third class dining accommodation.

The new service of both first and third class dining cars on trains between London and Leeds began on 1 July 1896.[29]

Belatedly, and partly in agreement with the LNWR and NER, the Great Northern followed the example set by the Midland in the 1870s of abolishing the second class. In April 1885 the Board decided that from the following 1st May the use of second class carriages should be discontinued on the Notts, Derbyshire and Lincolnshire lines. Then, following a recommendation of the Traffic Committee, it was resolved that from 1 May 1893 the issue of second class tickets should cease on every part of the system except within the London suburban district. These changes resulted in more work for the carriage department at the Plant, since Patrick Stirling was instructed that 'second class compartments in East Coast and Great Northern main line coaches were to be converted into third class from 1 May 1893'.[30]

Passengers, and eventually the government, demanded safer, as well as more comfortable, rail travel. When Sitrling took office the braking system of passenger trains was as primitive as was that of freight trains. In an emergency the safety of passengers had to depend upon the locomotive's brakes or those fitted to 'brake' coaches which were placed at intervals in the train. The brakesmen sat high up on these vehicles so that they could see lineside signal stops and apply the brakes where necessary. In an emergency the train driver blew his whistle to alert the brakesmen. However, on 21 January 1876 a terrible accident at Abbotts Ripton, seven miles south of Peterborough, underlined the fact that the disaster would not have been as great as it was had a second train which was involved been equipped with continuous brakes.[31] In fairness to the GNR Board it must be pointed out that consideration of improved braking systems had been given before the occurrence of the Abbotts Ripton accident. On 9 April 1875, to help the deliberations of the Royal Commission on Railway Accidents then sitting, it agreed to experiment with Smith's Vacuum brake. This was a system under which the train driver was able to apply a continuous brake to the whole train.[32] Patrick Stirling, after telling George Westinghouse in 1872 that he would not promote his braking system since he was 'not aware of the necessity for continuous brakes on trains', later took a favourable view of the Smith appliance and pressed ahead with its application to the company's rolling stock.[33]

In February 1881 Lord Colville, GNR Chairman, reported that 90 per cent of the company's passenger engines, 88 per cent of the tenders and 85 per cent of the carriages had been fitted with the Smith Vacuum brake.[34] However, as Grinling observed, 'the confidence which Mr Stirling and other eminent locomotive engineers had shown in the simple vacuum brake over the automatic vacuum proved not to have been well founded'. Several accidents might have been avoided.[35] Therefore, on 1 April 1887 the GNR Board decided to adopt the automatic continuous system as quickly as possible on all express trains.[36]

The 'almost continuous process of expansion' of the Plant works which was noted in the 1850s and 1860s was also a feature of the Stirling era between 1866–95. During his early years in office Patrick Stirling was busy carrying out his policy of locomotive conversion to higher boiler pressures. However, by the 1870s extensions of the workshop area gathered momentum as the volume of freight and passenger traffic increased. In October 1873 the Board approved a plan, which Stirling had prepared, for better accommodation. The existing locomotive premises at the back of the down passenger platform were to be abandoned as soon as a new engine shed was constructed. A triangular piece of land on the Carr was purchased and some four additional acres were bought from the corporation and a private landowner in an area known as Thief Lane.[37]

By 1877 there was a severe shortage of accommodation for the efficient construction and repair of wagons and carriages. In August that year Henry Oakley, the General Manager, made an extended visit to the works and recommended further land on the Carr should be purchased for coping with the wagon stock. In the following December Patrick Stirling warned that:

> The workshops and siding accommodation are quite inadequate so that the greatest proportion of repairs have to be done in the open air ... If a suitable wagon shop was built there would be more room given for carriage repairs in the present premises and the repairs could go on independent of the weather or the length of day, and there is no doubt the work would be done much more economically than at present.[38]

The Board heeded this advice and approved expenditure of £20 000 for providing additional accommodation for wagon repairs in the Crimpsall area. The new wagon shop was completed early in 1879.[39]

The construction and repair of wagons and carriages involved the use of large quantities of timber. To provide a more convenient location for the supplies, a large timber drying shed, 300 feet long by 100 feet wide, was erected in 1881–82 between the carriage and wagon shops, at a cost of £6300.[40]

Meanwhile space for the repairing of locomotives was very restricted so that Patrick Stirling wrote to the Board on 28 October 1881 pointing out that it would be 'absolutely necessary to provide more accommodation for building and repairing locomotives and tenders and for the manufacture of boilers'. There had been no addition to the present shops for fifteen years during which time the engine stock had increased by 50 per cent.[41] The directors saw the urgency of this request and on 2 February 1882 voted £8062 for the construction of a large and commodious boiler shop beside the new foundry.[42] On 5 October the following year the construction of a new wheelwright's shop at a cost of £5000 was sanctioned.[43]

The most substantial change at the Plant in Stirling's time was the construction of new wagon shops on the Carr some two miles south of Doncaster in 1888–9. The eventual cost – which was substantially higher than the original estimate because Stirling wanted a larger building than that which was first planned – was £52 386. This huge complex was completed within one year of the Board's authorization of the work.[44] The North Shop at the Carr undertook new wagon construction. It had seven working roads which could accommodate some 140 wagons. The South Shop, with fifteen roads, was responsible for repairs and could house some 220 wagons. The company's horse-drawn drays, vans and other road vehicles were also built there. In the same year as the new Carr wagon shops were opened work started on the construction of a new engine erecting shop and an additional machine shop.[45] The engine erecting shop was divided into three parts, the two outside were used for erecting, while the middle was reserved for the equipment used in building the locomotives.

In view of this impressive catalogue of extensions, it comes as no surprise that in 1893, forty years after the opening of the Plant works, the area occupied by the different shops was more than three times what it had been. The estimate of **The Engineer**, which did not include Carr wagon shops or the station and sidings, was that the works covered 30 acres. A.J. Brickwell, in an estimate which included all the works and the station and sidings, claimed that the area covered in 1894 was 'something like 170 acres'.[46]

Employment in the works – exclusive of those employed in the station or in shunting wagons – reached 3500 in the mid 1890s.[47]

The tradition of an annual works' outing in the summer became even more firmly established in Stirling's time than it was before 1866. The day-long trip was the great event in the lives of the staff of the Plant works, something that was well planned and eagerly anticipated weeks before the actual event. When the company's business was profitable no charge was made to those joining the outing; when dividends were meagre a charge was made, sufficient to cover the cost of the rail transport provided.

In 1868 the directors and the Work's Committee were in an open-handed mood. No charge was made for the trip to Nottingham and back on Saturday 4 July, and whereas previously only the wives and children of employees were permitted to accompany their menfolk, on this occasion, as the **Doncaster Chronicle** noted:

> Even young men who have not yet taken to themselves a partner 'to share their sorrows, double their joys and treble their expenses' – even these were allowed to take a female companion each, without any question being asked as to whether it was their intention, at some future time 'to have this woman as your wedded wife'.

On this occasion some 4000 people filled the four trains of thirty carriages each. The Plant bands accompanied them. Each engine was decorated with flags and flowers with a board on the front inscribed 'GNR Locomotive Free Trip'. In Nottingham the favourite venue was the Arboretum recreation ground where in the afternoon there was dancing on the lawn to the music played by the works bands. It was reported that 'the cases of drunkenness were very rare'. On the Monday following the outing there was a meeting of the Plant workmen in the boiler shop to congratulate the organizing committee, the directors and management.[48]

In 1870, since opinion was divided between favouring Scarborough and Nottingham, trips were organized to both places. The Board made no charge for the rail journeys but the Workmen's committee decided that all those participating should pay 3d. to the funds of the Doncaster Infirmary. Twenty-six pounds was raised in this way.[49] In the following year the alternatives were London and Scarborough, with most favouring the former, even though it involved leaving Doncaster station between 3 o'clock and 3.20 in the morning. Visits were made to the international exhibition at South Kensington and to the Albert Hall, while others joined boat trips on the Thames.[50] The same alternative venues were available in July 1877 when 'a nominal charge was made in each case'. The proceeds did not go to charity. It was not a good year for the company's finances so the directors did not feel justified in contributing to the hospitals, 'under present circumstances'.[51] In 1895, the last year of Stirling's tenure of office, a total of nearly 5000 persons participated in trips to London, Skegness and Grimsby with Skegness the favoured option (3200 visitors), including one woman who gave birth to a baby en route, before leaving the train at Boston.[52]

If the annual works' outing epitomized the continuation of the paternalistic approach of the company's directors, the impressive growth of the Doncaster Co-operative Society revealed the commitment of the Plant workers to a policy of self-help. From a total of 1805 in October 1880 membership of the Society rose to 5217 in October 1895. The dividend on purchases was 2s. 7d. 152 persons were employed in the principal shop in St James' Street and the many branches in the surrounding villages.[53] This growth was indicative of a rising standard of living in the town and neighbourhood reflected in a decline in the death rate from 26 per 1000 in 1876 to an average of 17.2 per thousand in the years 1883–7. Municipal reform and the Public Health Act of 1875, which led to the appointment of medical officers of health and sanitary inspectors in every district, also contributed to the improvement. Nevertheless hundreds of citizens of Doncaster were living near the poverty line. Whenever there was a severe winter the soup kitchens for the relief of distress reappeared. Thus in February 1895 a soup kitchen located at the old library served up to 90 gallons of soup to about 700 persons. A pound of bread was issued with each pint of soup.[54]

17
GREAT NORTHERN RAILWAY WORKS, DONCASTER – GENERAL PLAN 1892

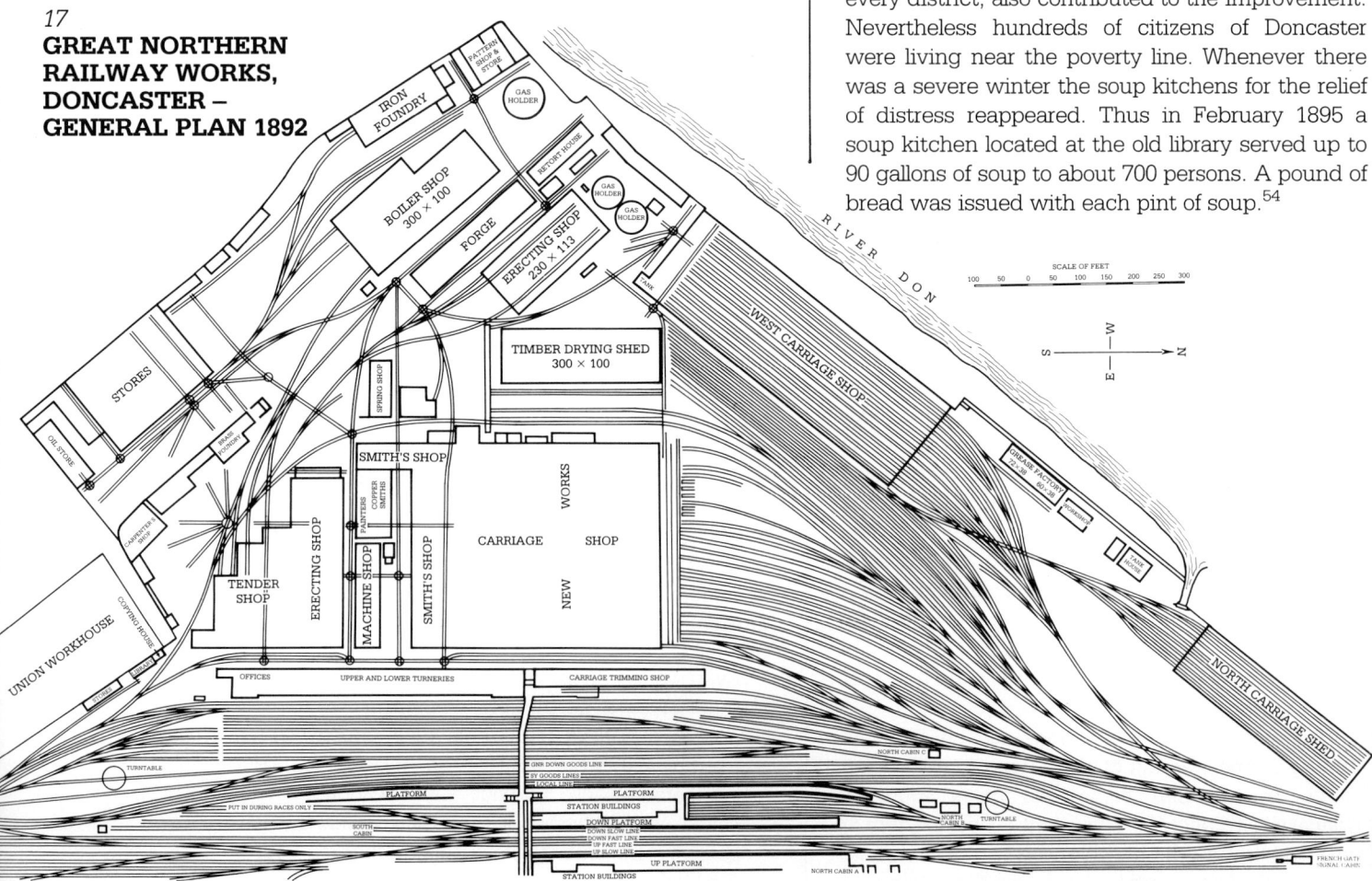

H. A. IVATT AND THE 'ATLANTICS'

Patrick Stirling's successor as Locomotive Engineer was Henry Alfred Ivatt, the eldest son of the Revd A.W. Ivatt, MA, the Rector of Coveny-cum-Manca in Cambridgeshire. 'Harry' Ivatt, as he became known, served his apprenticeship in the late 1860s with the LNW Railway, at Crewe where J. Ramsbottom was in charge of the locomotive works. After further experience with the LNWR at Stafford, Holyhead and Chester, he crossed the Irish Sea to join the Great Southern and Western Railway at Cork. Then in 1886 he was appointed Assistant Locomotive Engineer of that company. This proved to be the most fortuitous move in his career, since he won the high regard of his immediate superior, the engineer, J.A.F. Aspinall.[1] By the summer of 1895 the GNR board was thinking seriously of a possible successor to the septuagenarian Patrick Stirling, and in the autumn Sir Henry Oakley, the General Manager, wrote to Aspinall – who by then had moved to the Lancashire and Yorkshire Railway – asking him whether he thought Ivatt suitable for the post of Locomotive Engineer. Aspinall's confident and succinct reply was 'Indubitably'.[2]

18 Henry Alfred Ivatt, Chief Mechanical Engineer, 1895–1911

The new Locomotive Engineer was both thorough in his methods of working and innovative in his approach. When employed by the LNWR he served for six months as a fireman to familiarize himself with the handling of locomotives. Following a serious accident on the GNR at St Neots in November 1895 in which two people were killed and several seriously injured as a result of the train passing over a fractured rail, he walked the entire length of the track, from Doncaster (in stages!) to King's Cross. He wanted to check the suitability of the permanent way for the heavier trains increasingly coming into use.[3] The outcome of his investigations was that the GNR board agreed to a programme of replacing the light weight (85 lb per yard) rails of the company's main line tracks with the heavier, 92 lb per yard, variety.

In the view of O.S. Nock the locomotive stock which Ivatt inherited from the Stirling era was 'something of an anacronism'.[4] The '8 foot Singles' had served the company well when trains hauled had carriages which were comparatively light, since they did not run on bogies and were generally without corridors or many embellishments. However, the drawbacks of Stirling's opposition to coupled driving wheels and to bogies were already apparent in 1895. To haul the heavier loads, trains were having to be double-headed, with consequent extra expense of operation. In the last few years of Stirling's management, corridor coaches, sleeping cars and dining cars, even in third class coaches, were being built to meet the challenge presented by rival companies. These changes inevitably meant heavier trains, requiring greater tractive power than could be provided by the 8 foot singles.

If Ivatt's objective was clear – to build more powerful locomotives to accommodate the rapidly expanding freight traffic and to haul heavier passenger trains at fast speeds – the constraints on the locomotive designer were also apparent. These were clearly described in a contemporary railway journal:

> Bigger trains require larger engines, but the height and width to which the engine may extend is limited by bridges, platforms, etc., so that increased length is the only direction in which there is room for expansion. Here again increased size is limited by the provision necessary for getting round curves and also by the average strength of a fireman's arms. A firebox so long that it cannot be properly fired is manifestly out of the question.[5]

During his fifteen years at Doncaster Ivatt designed ten types of locomotives. But he achieved fame with the 4-4-0 express passenger locomotives known as 'Atlantics'. The name came from the USA. In 1895 W.P. Henssey, a partner of the American firm of locomotive builders which later became the Baldwin Locomotive Company, designed an engine for the Philadelphia and Reading Railroad, which on the run between Camden and Atlantic City achieved some of the fastest times yet recorded. Both Ivatt and his former mentor, Aspinall, designed new large express passenger engines which incorporated some of the leading features of Henssey's design; but Ivatt's product included more novel features.[6]

In 1898 the Plant works produced locomotive number 990 named 'Henry Oakley', the first 'Atlantic' type locomotive to appear in Britain. Henry Ivatt, who designed the new engine, accepted Archibald Sturrock's maxim that the power of the locomotive was measured by its capacity for boiling water. The boiler barrel of the '990', therefore, was 14 feet 8 inches in length, while the firebox had the very generous heating surface of 140 square feet. This combination gave the engine a working pressure of 175 lb per square inch. With such a large firebox and boiler the engine needed lots of water and coal. In fact the unusually large tender could carry up to 3670 gallons of water and 5 tons of coal. The total weight of engine and tender was 98 tons 18 cwts. Gone were the days of relying on a single pair of large driving wheels to pull a train. The 990 had two pairs of coupled driving wheels with a four-wheeled bogie at the leading end and a small pair of trailing wheels under the back end of the firebox.[7] After two years of trials, the first order for ten locomotives of this type was placed with the Plant works. Between 1898 and 1903 twenty-one of these small Atlantics were built at Doncaster.[8] The small Atlantics acquired the nickname of Klondikes since they appeared at about the same time as the Klondike gold rush in the Yukon Territory in which the overriding feature was the need for speed to reach the desired objective.

Meanwhile Henry Ivatt was working on the design of an even more powerful passenger locomotive. The first of the larger type Atlantic, No. 251, appeared in 1902. The greatest difference between the two types lay in the employment of an even larger boiler – 16 feet in length – in the 1902 version. With a total heating surface of 2500 square feet, the 251 was a far more powerful machine than the 990. Although the first large order for locomotives of the larger 'Atlantic' class was not placed until 1904, eighty-one of them were produced, all from the Plant works, between 1902 and 1908.

At the beginning of the twentieth century the 'heat balance sheet' of locomotive performance i.e. the overall ratio between the latent energy potential in the coal fire, and the power made available at the drawbar for haulage of a train, was as low as 4 or 5 per cent. Ivatt was by no means the only locomotive engineer to seek means of reducing this great

H. A. IVATT AND THE 'ATLANTICS'

19 Ivatt's Large Atlantic, 1902

20 Great Northern Atlantic on display

inefficiency of operation. In 1900 he read the work of the German engineer Wilhelm Schmidt for the superheating of locomotives. Under Schmidt's system, by heating the steam beyond its temperature of formation in the boiler, its volume was increased and the power of the locomotive augmented. In 1909 Ivatt ordered trials with the fitting of the Schmidt superheater to small Atlantic class engine number 988. It was found that, as a result of superheating, the volume of steam produced was increased by 12 to 13 per cent.[9] This success led to a decision in 1910 to order the building of ten superheated large Atlantic locomotives at the Plant works.[10]

Locomotive engineers also sought alternative ways of saving in the consumption of fuel. One option was by the use of compound engines which, it was claimed, achieved higher steam pressure at the drawbar of the locomotive with the same consumption of coal. In March 1891 Patrick Stirling was asked by the Locomotive Committee of the GNR to allow trial of NER compound engines on the GNR's lines 'to ascertain whether it were possible to effect any saving in the consumption of coal by the addition of the compound principle in our engines'. In reporting back to the committee on 28 September 1891, Stirling claimed that 'the compound engines of the NER were more extravagant in the consumption of coal than were those of the GNR'. He concluded that 'there is nothing at present to be gained by the adoption of the compound principle on the GNR'.[11] In March 1905 the Plant works adapted Atlantic class engine No. 292, which had the standard boiler of the '251' class for compound working. It had a working pressure of 200 lb per square inch instead of the usual 175. It was found that the tractive power was considerably more than that of the non-compounded Atlantic type locomotive.[12]

The great importance of the 'Atlantics' in the development of steam locomotion was recognized on the occasion of the centenary celebrations of the Plant works in 1953. On Sunday 20 September that year nearly 500 persons joined a 'Plant Centenarian' excursion from King's Cross to Doncaster and back. On the outward journey the pilot engine was the small Atlantic No. 990 **Henry Oakley**. The train engine was No. 251, the first of the large Atlantics. Both engines had their GNR livery restored and were afterwards withdrawn for preservation. The return journey of the excursion was made behind the Gresley 'A4' Pacific locomotive No. 60014, **Silver Link**.[13]

A feature of Henry Ivatt's last years at Doncaster was the rapid opening up of the South Yorkshire coalfield. There was consequently a strong demand for more freight locomotives and wagons. The competition for the carriage of coal to London and other markets was keen. Not only rival railway companies but also coastal steamships were eager for their share of the business. John Armstrong has shown that in 1910, nationwide, the ton mileage of freight carried coastwise in the UK exceeded that carried by rail. Coal carried from the North East ports to London was the most important element in the coastwise shipping trade.[14] Ivatt designed freight locomotives with a much greater tractive capacity than was possible with their predecessors. His new engines had eight coupled wheels and a total heating surface – firebox plus tubes – of 1438.84 square feet. In full working order the engines weighed nearly 55 tons. The tender could carry 3670 gallons of water and five tons of coal. The total weight of engine plus tender was 95½ tons, little short of the 98 tons 18 cwts of the small 'Atlantic' passenger engines.[15]

To deal with the rapidly growing freight traffic the GNR Board experimented with the use, and eventually the construction, of bigger capacity wagons. On 6 December 1901 it accepted a tender from Hurst, Wilson and Co for supplying twenty 30 ton bogie wagons at £210 each, and on 3 July 1903 it agreed to the construction at the Plant of 500 '15 ton' open goods wagons.[16] Its biggest venture into larger capacity wagon construction in Ivatt's time came in December 1905 when fifty 35 ton wagons were ordered to be built at the Plant. However, these more imaginative innovations were a mere drop in the ocean compared with the company's total stock of 260 000 wagons, the overwhelming majority of which had a capacity of 10 tons or less. The order for fifty 35 ton wagons, of December 1905, must be set against the much larger order for 500 10 ton wagons placed on the same date. 'Make do and mend' was the policy of the Board in October 1902. It was resolved:

> That as many of the existing 9 ton wagons as can carry 10 tons with safety be plated to carry ten tons. This has already been done to the extent of 6000 wagons which enables an increase of paying load of over 11 per cent. That a board be fitted round the top of a portion of the 9 ton wagons to enable them to carry 10 tons of coal.[17]

Even if all members of the Board had been thoroughly convinced of the advantage of building larger capacity wagons, there were some years in which financial restraints precluded the adoption of such a policy. In both 1907 and 1908 original plans for rolling stock replacements were scaled down because of shortage of funds.[18]

In chapter five it was shown that as a result of the Midland Railway's policy, in the early 1870s, of providing third class accommodation on all its trains and of improving the comfort of third class

21 Turnery, late nineteenth century

travel, other companies felt obliged to follow suit. As a consequence, by 1875, 77.5 per cent of all passenger carryings in the UK were in the third class. In Henry Ivatt's time at Doncaster the predominance of third class travel was even more marked. By the time of his retirement in 1911 the third class percentage had risen to 95.8.[19]

In 1893–5 in Patrick Stirling's final years at Doncaster new dining cars for first and third class passengers were built in pairs, each car being carried on six-wheel bogies for smoother riding and being provided with a clerestory roof for improved natural lighting. In the first year of Ivatt's tenure as Locomotive Engineer a complete corridor train of these new carriages was built for the mid-day King's Cross–Edinburgh trains, and similar trains were built for the service between King's Cross and Leeds. Ivatt, and other officers of the GNR and the NER, visited the USA to learn of the latest developments in carriage construction there.

22 Crimpsall shops, June 1900

Their experience, in C.J. Allen's view, had 'a revolutionary effect on rolling stock' designed for the East Coast Joint services.[20] In particular, it led to the introduction of Gould patent buckeye couplers and short Pullman vestibules which contributed substantially to smoother riding. W. Grinling, who was chief accountant of the GNR at the time these new vehicles were being constructed, noted that 'of the 300 seats provided in each of these new trains no less than 252 were allocated to third class penny-a-mile passengers'.[21] This was a larger proportion of third class seats than was provided, as second class, in British Rail's Inter-City services in 1989. The improved dining carriages were not introduced on the **Flying Scotsman** services until 1900. Before that time hungry passengers who were lucky enough to get served, had the twenty minutes of the scheduled stop at York station 'to affront their digestions by gulping down a hasty meal'.[22]

In the summer of 1896 the carriage works staff at the Plant constructed a new type of sleeping car with berths built across the cars instead of lengthwise.

It has been estimated that in Edwardian times, on the day of the St Leger, over 100 000 passengers arrived at Doncaster, involving the total suspension of the goods traffic and the clearing of all locomotives from the Plant works sidings. Though normal work was interrupted or completely suspended, the arrival of the racegoers did provide the hundreds of artisans and labourers involved a break from the normal routine and an opportunity to earn a few extra shillings by providing for the wants of the visitors.[23]

On 13 November 1888 Robert Wills wrote to the Secretary of the GNR from his North London address that:

> As a season ticket holder on your line, I, with my fellow passengers, have for a long time endured the misery of the present system of oil lighting, and feel that the universal complaint that obtains is just.[24]

Henry Oakley, the General Manager, was well aware of the poor quality of the lighting of the company's carriages. Nearly four years before Mr Wills had written his letter, he wrote to the Board that 'the present system of lighting trains is, to say the least, highly unsatisfactory'. He put some of the blame for the situation on the staff:

> The men who trim the lamps are of the most ordinary description, as no man worth having will be content to stay in the lamp room, and therefore men of the lowest capacity only can be retained.

The oil used was also of variable quality. On 4 December 1884 the Board agreed to a traffic committee recommendation to fit electric lighting to two suburban trains as an experiment. More significant were the experiments carried out on a larger scale for three years from 1887 on the Pennsylvania Railroad in the USA.

Somewhat belatedly, (since a number of other British railway companies had by then installed electric lighting on many of their trains), the directors of the GNR resolved on 1 December 1905, that all new Great Northern carriages, whether built on capital or revenue account 'be fitted with electric light'.[25] From 1907, when Nigel Gresley became Carriage and Wagon Superintendent at the Plant works, new momentum was given to the improvement of carriage lighting.

The need for more wagons to meet the needs of the expanding coal trade and the increased length and sophistication of both locomotives and carriages, all created a demand for more workshop space and more up-to-date machinery.

In January 1897 the Board sanctioned the expenditure of the large sum of £39 945 for constructing a new wagon repairing shop and providing it with the necessary sidings turntable and electric lighting.[26] Just over a year later the Board authorized the construction of a new carriage shed measuring 600 feet by 125 feet adjacent to the river Don. This became known as the west carriage shop and was used for carriage repairs. This enabled the previously existing carriage shop to be used mainly for new construction work.[27] The largest enterprise of all at this time was the acquisition of a large plot of land on the Crimpsall meadows adjoining the Plant. Soon after his arrival at Doncaster Henry Ivatt learned that heavy locomotive repairs were being carried out in running sheds at other locations on the GNR because of inadequate accommodation at the Plant. In July 1899, therefore, the Board accepted the tender of Messrs Arnold and Sons, local builders, for building a new engine repair shop, with two small and four large bays, providing room for some hundred locomotives. The initial tender was for £129 238, but by the time the huge building was completed the cost had increased to £294 000, the largest item of expenditure at the Plant before the First World War.[28] In 1900 there was erected at the west end of the Crimpsall repair shop a new tender shop for the repair of locomotive tenders. A new paint shop and wheelwright shop were also built at this time.[29]

Negotiations for the purchase of the old Doncaster workhouse were prolonged in the 1890s, but in December 1902 the building and land were eventually acquired for £6250. This eased the land hunger of the Plant works, providing space for offices.[30]

In the first decade of the twentieth century

23 Interior of heavy wagon repair shop

hydraulic machinery and electrically powered machines of all kinds were in greatly increased use in the workshops. In 1906 Messrs Arnold constructed a building to house a new hydraulic riveter. An electrically powered traverser for the carriage shop was purchased from the firm of Ransome and Napiers and a three-throw pressure pump for the spring shop and boiler shop were bought from the engineering firm of Fielding and Platt.[31] The new machinery placed heavy demands on power supplies. Two diesel generating plants were therefore installed; one with an output of 300 kilowatts for the old erecting shop and the other, of 240 kilowatts, for the new Crimpsall repair shop.[32]

On the night of 21 October 1895 the main block building of the St James' schools, which had been built at the GNR's expense in the 1850s and subsequently maintained by the company, was destroyed by fire.[33] The school was already too small to provide places for all the children of the staff of the Plant works and negotiations had already been conducted with the corporation of Doncaster concerning the building of an additional school. In November 1894 the Board decided to follow the example of the corporation in making all school places free.[34] Following the fire and the submission of the surveyor's plans, the Board agreed in January 1896 to accept the estimate of Messrs Arnold, the local builders, for the erecting of two schools at a cost of £5200.[35] The company paid a capitation allowance of 5s. 6d. per child per year and contributed £40 a year to the curate fund and £20 a year to the Sunday School Fund. The new school buildings did not remain the responsibility of the GNR for very long. As a result of the passing of the Education Act, 1902, the members of the Board were confronted with two alternatives. The St James' schools could either be classified as 'non provided' in which case the company would have to pay the rent and maintain the premises out of funds other than those provided by the Local Education Authority; or the school could be classified as 'provided', in which case it would be owned and run by the LEA. In January 1903 they

24 Carr wagon works, 1908

decided on the second option.[36] Six months later they decided to sell the freehold of the Stirling Street School – one of the two built in 1896, for £2000 – and to let the St Sepulchre Gate School, the other one erected in 1896, to the Doncaster education committee on a twenty-one year lease at £125 per annum.[37] These changes brought to an end almost half a century of the GNR's involvement in the provision of school education in Doncaster.

When Henry Ivatt took over as Locomotive Engineer in 1895 the Doncaster Co-operative Society had 5217 members and employed 152 staff. By the time Ivatt relinquished office in 1911, membership had shot up to 12644, encouraged by a dividend payment of 2s. 4d. in the pound on purchases. The influx of miners into the community played a large part in this expansion. However, the election of Mr John Gilles, an employee at the Plant works, as president of the Society in 1902 revealed the continuing heavy involvement of GNR employees in its activities.[38]

Henry Ivatt retired in the autumn of 1911 and died at Haywards Heath in Sussex in 1923.

WORKING CONDITIONS IN THE PLANT WORKS BEFORE 1914

Although there are hundreds of boxes and files of documents of the Great Northern Railway at the Public Record Office at Kew, information about the composition of the labour force at the Plant works is very scanty. The nearest approach to a comprehensive statement is to be found in a return which Patrick Stirling sent to the Board of Directors on 15 October 1870.[1] This includes a breakdown of the occupations of the staff in the main departments of the works at that time. The great variety of crafts represented is clearly shown. The 2107 employees listed were split up as follows:

TABLE 1

LOCOMOTIVE SHOPS	LOCOMOTIVE DEPARTMENT	CARRIAGE SHOPS
7 overlookers	7 overlookers	4 overlookers
123 erectors	140 engine drivers	25 machine men
56 fitters	141 firemen	3 smiths
93 tuners	169 engine cleaners	4 tinmen
79 machine men	23 cokemen	47 painters
67 smiths	41 fitters	4 carriage washers and cleaners
53 spring makers	2 turners	5 gas makers
15 boiler smiths	2 machine men	89 carriage woodmen
5 copper smiths	6 smiths	99 wagon woodmen
14 steam hammermen	9 boiler smiths	44 carriage fitters
173 strikers	2 copper smiths	16 carriage trimmers
6 pattern makers	6 strikers	16 carriage examiners
11 joiners	1 joiner	11 sawyers
2 saddlers	1 bricklayer	119 labourers
14 puddlers	7 carriage washers	2 clerks
2 grinders	8 stationary enginemen	5 wagon cover repairers
4 messengers, office boys and cleaners	4 wagon woodworkers	7 grease factors
12 brass moulders	4 carriage fitters	
5 coke burners	32 carriage examiners and greasers	
8 painters	51 labourers	
5 bricklayers	1 timekeeper	
2 gas fitters	2 clerks	
4 stationary engine men	2 harness repairers	
5 gas makers		
28 iron moulders		
120 labourers		
6 time keepers		
5 watchmen		
18 clerks		
4 draughtsmen		
946 Total	**661 Total**	**500 Total**

The 1870 return reveals the importance of individual craft skills in the work of the shops. A majority of the men employed, but especially the fitters, turners, smiths, brass moulders and those employed in the carriage shop, would have undergone a lengthy apprenticeship. The wages they received – between 22s. and 30s. 5d. a week – reflected the scarcity value of their skills, and compared favourably with the 17s. a week paid to the labourers.[2] The fitters and turners have been described as being 'at the heart of the engineers empire'[3] in a work force where there were many gradations of skill. In the carriage shops the elite crafts were the carriage trimmers and greasers whose pay, at 30s. 5d. a week even exceeded that of the fitters in the locomotive department who took home 3d. a week less.

Unfortunately, no return similar in format to that made by Patrick Stirling in 1870 survives for any later year before the First World War. Had one been available for, say, 1895, it would have revealed some substantial changes in the composition of the work force at the Plant. The unskilled workers by then constituted a bigger element of the total. In the early 1890s new machines, including capstan and turret lathes; vertical, horizontal and, later, universal milling machines; external and surface grinders; vertical borers and radial drills, undermined the pre-eminence of the fitters and turners. The new appliances were often manned by machine minders who had not served a craft apprenticeship and who were paid wages below craft standards. Understandably, the skilled men were concerned at the threat to their wage levels, and even to their continued employment, by this 'dilution' of labour.

It has often been claimed that in Victorian and Edwardian Britain railway employment was more secure than was the case in many other occupations. It was said that a job on the railways was 'a job for life'. Certainly, with rare exceptions, as in the years 1867 and 1884, railway employment grew continuously before 1914. However, the jobs of those manning railway stations or engaged in the movement of traffic were more secure than were those of men employed in the workshops. Booms and slumps were as characteristic of the nineteenth as they were of the twentieth century economy. Trade was depressed, with unemployment at about 10 per cent of the country's work force in 1858, 1867, 1879, 1886, 1894, 1906 and 1909. In those years footplate staff, guards, signalmen and shunters were more likely to keep their jobs than were unskilled labourers in the workshops. Even in slack years, passenger timetables were adhered to and freight trains were run. But programmes for new construction of locomotives, carriages and wagons could be suspended and non-essential repair work on rolling stock could be curtailed until an upturn of trade made the resumption of full workshop activity possible.

At Doncaster, whenever there was a slump in the company's business the Locomotive Engineer received instructions from the Board to cut working expenses by reducing the number of carriage and wagon repairs. In June 1869 the train mileage run by the GNR was 319 052 less than in 1868 and working expenses per train mile were 2.72 shillings compared with 2.44 shillings. Unless expenses were cut the dividend on ordinary shares might well have had to be reduced. The Board therefore ordered Patrick Stirling to make urgent economies. On 21 January 1870 Stirling reported that the Locomotive Department had dispensed with 293 men since the previous January and that in 1869 there were fifty-three fewer wagon repairers than there had been in 1868.[4]

The serious economic depression in Britain in 1879 had repercussions on the business of the GNR. At a meeting of the Board on 26 August 1879 it was resolved:

> That having regard to the diminution of the traffic receipts which has already occurred, to the discouraging prospects of harvest and the general depression in the trade of the country, the Board desire the Engineer, the Locomotive Engineer and the General Manager to take immediate steps to reduce the expenditure of their respective departments and to report to an early meeting of the Board the mode and extent to which they can do so, and the probable pecuniary result.

Henry Oakley, the General Manager, reported to the Board on 23 October that no new appointments had been made since 8 September. Mr Ashley, the Goods Manager, was pleased to report a saving 'in men and horses' of £5000 since the receipt of the directors letter! Total savings in two months had been £9664.[5]

In such years of business depression the men the company sacked were generally unskilled labourers. Even when in full time employment, their wages at 17s. a week, were barely sufficient to feed and clothe themselves, their wives and their families. When suddenly dismissed they had few resources to keep them from having to resort to the dreaded workhouse. In the 1890s, therefore, the Board adopted a policy of part-time working in periods of slackness of trade, rather than one of outright dismissals. It was hoped that this would minimize distress. When leaving the works at midday on the Saturday men would be informed that they were not wanted back until the Tuesday morning. In these circumstances they would take home but 12s. 6d. a week and would depend very much on charitable relief. At Christmas 1904, for example, a

WORKING CONDITIONS IN THE PLANT WORKS BEFORE 1914

party for 1000 children, whose fathers were 'out of work or on short time', was put on by 'a number of Doncaster ladies headed by Miss Beckett Denison' (the granddaughter of Edmund Denison).[6] Short time working continued at the Plant from 1895[7] for most of the years up to the First World War; but in 1908 and 1910 the company's trading position was so unhealthy that dismissals of men were again recorded.[8] The **Doncaster Gazette** reported that in January 1908 some 600 children were receiving soup at the Trade Union Club in the town.[9]

Until January 1872 employees at the Plant worked a fifty-eight and a half hour week. From Mondays to Fridays inclusive they started work at 7 a.m. and finished at 6 p.m., being allowed an hour's break from 1–2 p.m. On Saturdays work finished 'early' at 2 p.m. The total fifty-eight and a half hours was made up by shorter mid-day breaks on some days. There was a strong feeling that the finishing time on Saturdays was 'neither here nor there'. In winter months hours of daylight were nearly over by the time a man reached home. Even if he had sufficient energy left to take part in sporting activities he was scarcely able to do this. In the early 1860s the drivers and firemen employed by the GNR petitioned the Board about their long working hours and requested that they should be limited to not more than ten per day. Archibald Sturrock advised the Board against making any such concession. He said it was 'not practical'. When the footplatemen tried again in 1865, the men at the Plant followed suit, requesting that work on Saturdays should finish at noon instead of at 2 p.m. Both these requests were summarily dismissed.[10]

A more favourable opportunity for the reduction of the working day came in the boom years 1871–2, when the level of unemployment was very low and skilled labour was in short supply. By the summer of 1871 other engineering firms in South Yorkshire had already conceded the nine hour day and key craftsmen were leaving the Plant works for more congenial employment in nearby towns. In October 1871 a deputation from the Plant workers saw Patrick Stirling (who was more sympathetic to the men's case than his predecessor had been). He promised to present to the Board the men's request for a reduction of the working week from fifty-eight and a half hours to fifty-four, with a 12 noon finish on Saturdays.[11] At their meeting on 3 November 1871 the Board agreed to these changes. From the beginning of January 1872 the working week was to be reduced to fifty-four hours, with the works closing at 5.30 p.m. Mondays to Fridays and at 12 noon on Saturdays.[12] The men were delighted. They decided to have a demonstration expressing their appreciation of the decision of the members of the Board. To allow them to have their procession at 2.30 on the following Saturday afternoon, Patrick Stirling closed the works at 1 instead of 2 p.m. The

procession was 'of very great length'. It was marshalled in departmental order, headed by members of the Work's Committee wearing white favours. The Plant band led the march, the militia band was placed in the middle while a drum and fife band took up the rear. Flags and banners were numerous, many being 'emblematic of the kinds of work performed'. Behaviour along the route was reported to be 'exceptionally good'. The procession stopped in front of Mr Stirling's house where three hearty cheers were raised and acknowledged. Similar stops were made at the residences of Edmund Denison and the Mayor who 'addressed a few words of congratulation'.[13]

There was no occasion which called for a similar demonstration before the First World War. Coal-miners, rapidly increasing in number in recently opened pits near Doncaster, experienced a shortening of their working day under the Eight Hour Act of 1908, but it was not until 1919 that a further significant reduction in the hours of work was achieved by those employed in the Plant works.

Discipline at the works was strict. A man had to present himself at the checker's cabin by the entrance gate to his department when the works' hooter sounded at the start of the day's activities. He called out his works number to the clerk in the cabin and received in return a metal disc with his number on it. This would be returned at the end of the shift. Every other Friday he was given a brass disc instead of the usual tin one. At the end of that day's shift, in return for his disc, he was given a pay tin containing his wages for the past fortnight. He pocketed his cash and returned the tin box.[14]

Being paid wages only once a fortnight was resented by the staff and especially by those on the lowest rates of pay. They found it difficult to make ends meet by the closing days of the second week. On 21 July 1871 a memorial was handed in, signed by 1124 men employed in the locomotive department 'praying that their wages may be paid weekly instead of fortnightly.'.[15] However, the members of the Board resolved 'That the men be informed that their request cannot be complied with.' Nevertheless, at the height of the labour shortage early in 1872 the concessions of the shorter pay period was granted.

The job of the 'overlookers', listed on Patrick Stirling's return of 15 October 1870, was to enforce good discipline throughout the works. They would ensure that those guilty of disobedience to orders, or found 'dipping' or 'waxing', i.e. stealing materials or tools, were dismissed and sometimes, in addition, prosecuted. Apprentices found loitering were given a good dressing down or suspended from duty for a time without payment. At Swindon the 'overlookers' were called 'watchmen'. A graphic description of the role of the watchman was given by Alfred Williams, who had twenty-two years' experience at the GWR works at Swindon:

> When a new watchman is made it is noised abroad throughout the department; his size, description, and all else that is known of him are passed around the sheds for the benefit of the masses. Developments are anticipated and the results eagerly awaited. Elated at his promotion and great in his own conceit, the newly initiated one, before he is well known and identified by the workmen, slips to and fro in the sheds, eager for surprise captures. Immediately before the hooter sounds for the men's release at meal times he is to be found suddenly opening doors and popping on the scene. If any workmen should happen to have on their coats, or to have gathered near the door ready to rush out, they scatter like wood-pigeons when a hawk has darted in the midst of them. This forms the subject of a report to the shop foreman or to the manager.[16]

The risks of sustaining an accident were almost certainly greater for those employed in railway workshops than they were for those employed in textile mills. This was partly because of the practice of moving heavy metal materials by overhead cranes from one part of the shop to another. It was sometimes necessary for men to move from one location to another in carrying out their tasks. Constant vigilance was needed if injury was to be avoided. The heating of metal in the forges and smiths' shops and the movement of molten metals exposed the workers to further dangers. The great heat to be endured in many parts of the works and the din caused by the stamping machines increased the physical and the mental strain on both craftsmen and labourers.

The GNR Locomotive Sick Society (whose history is recorded in the following chapter) kept records of the number of its members who were killed in accidents between 1865 and 1889 and between 1894 and 1903 inclusive. The overwhelming majority of these accidental deaths occurred in the Plant works. In the first period, 1865–89, 123 deaths from accidents were recorded while in the second period, 1894–1903, there were fifty. These figures may not be complete since some of the employees at the Plant were not members of the society; but they can be taken as reasonably accurate since in the works non-members of the Society were a small minority. There is no clearly discernible pattern of the accidental deaths that occurred. It might have been expected that in busy years, of great activity in the works, such as 1872, more men would have been killed; but the number of fatalities that year was the same as in the depression year 1879. In most years between three and six people met accidental deaths. Exceptional years were 1880, with nine and 1902, with eleven. From the earliest times in the history of the Plant works frequent accounts of gruesome accidents were reported in the **Doncaster, Nottingham and Lincoln Gazete** and the **Doncaster Chronicle**.

One of the commonest forms of accident was the loss of an arm or hand through the limb becoming entangled in the machinery. On 27 September 1855 a young man, John Ellis, ascended a ladder to detach a strap working over the mainshaft when his hand was caught between the strap and the drum. His arm was first twisted round, then fractured in three places and finally torn from his body just below the shoulder, leaving the attached bone exposed to view. However, so skilful was the work of the surgeon, F.C. Fairbank, that Ellis was back at the works at the beginning of November. His workmates gave three cheers for Mr Fairbank 'for his kindness and attention to the sufferer'. A similar type of accident occurred just over a year later, though with less serious consequences, when J. Gillicady got his right hand entangled in a machine and had to have his thumb amputated.[17]

Under the Factory Acts Extension Act of 1867 the GNR was under obligation to fence in any machinery which the factory inspector deemed dangerous. It also was required to give notice to the certifying surgeon of any accident which kept a man off duty for more than forty-eight hours.[18] However, this did not appreciably reduce the number of serious accidents that occurred in the works. On 26 January 1864 'a youth named Hardy' had his arm caught by the machine belt and was violently thrown over the tumbril. His right arm was broken and his upper arm not only broken but also contused.[19] Another victim was J. Lindley, a sawyer, who lost three fingers through getting his hand entangled in a circular saw.[20] Other cases of fingers cut off in the machinery were reported in the **Doncaster Chronicle** in May, September and November 1902.[21]

Second only in frequency to cases of injury to arms were those of injuries to legs, though leg injuries were more likely to prove fatal. One of the earliest severe accidents reported from the Plant occurred on 25 May 1854. An engine cleaner slipped on a greasy floor when the engine passed over him, cutting off both his legs.[22] More typically leg injuries were caused by falling components or equipment. On 6 January 1855 Stephen Sparrow was helping to raise a large wheel to one of the turning lathes when the iron by which it was propelled gave way and the wheel fell to the ground over the legs of the unfortunate man.[23] He survived. Less fortunate was Jonathan Rigby in the boiler plant. One of the boiler plates, weighing 5 tons, fell on him, crushing him to death.[24] Rhodes Fletcher, a

WORKING CONDITIONS IN THE PLANT WORKS BEFORE 1914

labourer in the sawing and timber department, aged 62, was another fatality. On 24 February 1868 a sliding door weighing up to 6 cwt fell on him.[25] Among many other examples that could be cited was the case of A. Hurst whose foot was crushed in July 1902 when some engine fittings weighing 5 cwt unexpectedly fell on him.[26]

The greatest danger for moulders was injury from scalding, as in the case of William Eastwood, who was badly scalded when taking off dross from hot metal on 12 July 1871.[27] Within the months of May and June 1902, there were two cases of painters falling to their deaths from scaffolding.[28] In the carriage department – in an age when the wearing of protective goggles was not compulsory – flying wood splinters could cause serious facial injuries and even blindness. On 29 August 1856 an eighteen-year-old named Holden, employed in the carriage department, sustained severe injury to his face through the ejection of a 6 inch long, 1½ inch wide, piece of wood from a circular saw. Fortunately the efforts of his mates to pull the wood from his face were unsuccessful before the arrival of a surgeon and doctor who treated the case with more circumspection.[29]

One notable accident resulted from the irresponsible bravado of a few men. On Saturday 17 May 1865, building contractors completed the construction of a very tall chimney for the new erecting shops. In accordance with custom, a flag was flown from the top of the chimney. This provided the cue for six men from the Plant works to climb the inside of the chimney early the following Sunday morning, the works being 'out of bounds' that day. The ascent was made by way of a cage worked by a crane. After admiring the view from the top, three men re-entered the cage for the descent. About 18 yards from the base of the chimney the crane slipped and the occupants of the cage were dashed to the ground with great violence. Two of the men were crippled for life.[30]

The Employers Liability Act of 1880 was the first important attempt by Parliament to give a worker a fair claim against his employer for damages arising from accidents at work. However, it proved possible in practice for the employer to 'contract out' of his obligations. In the case of the LNWR, the Midland and a few other large railway companies, they did so by establishing accident provident funds from which compensation to injured workmen or pensions to widows of men killed, were paid. The LNWR fund amounted to the substantial sum of £23236. The GNR had no such fund. Henry Oakley, its General Manager, reminded the Board on 9 April 1888 'that it was the company's practice in cases of accident or illness to make up the difference between the sick pay and full pay during the time a man is disabled'.[31] The company also gave 'spasmodic financial support' to the GNR Locomotive Sick Society and from 1887 (when there was much talk of more stringent legislation on employers liability being in the offing) it made an annual grant of £500 to the Society.[32]

For most of the nineteenth century factory inspectors had no responsibility with respect to cleanliness, ventilation or disease in factories. This was outstandingly the case with railway workshops. For the best part of ninety years sanitary arrangements at the Plant were primitve in the extreme. Frank Cresswell who entered the Plant works in 1933 was told he must 'crap in the box' when he wanted to pay a visit to the lavatory. The operation involved sitting on a wooden beam placed over the box. The 'box', whose stench was unbelievable, was emptied every Friday evening.[33] Alfred Williams found the similar arrangements in operation at Swindon in 1915 'gross and objectionable, filthy, disgusting and degrading' with 'not the slightest approach to privacy of any kind'.[34] All that can be said of the Doncaster situation is that there is no record of any man being *punished* for any mishap that occurred when answering the calls of nature. In June 1873, at the workshops of the LNWR at Crewe, Michael Birks, a riveter, was 'dismissed for falling into a privy'.[35]

It took the circumstances of the Second World War to bring about overdue changes in the Plant works. With the Railway Executive Committee in overall control of Britain's railways, the Board of the LNER resolved on 27 July 1944 to proceed with 'the conversion of twenty-four earth closets in the wagon shop to the water carriage system' and to make similar arrangements for the canteen toilets. With financial help from the government, these and other improvements, including the supply of hand basins and the provision of hot water, were carried out in 1945 at a cost of £6723.[36] Finally on 19 October 1948, ninety-five years after the foundation of the Plant works, the publicly-owned British Transport Commission accepted a Railway Executive recommendation concerning minimum standards for all toilets on RE premises, including workshops. The buildings were to be completely roofed, with minimum ceiling heights of 8 feet 6 inches; there were to be separate WC cubicles for men and women; doors were to be not less than three-quarters length, so that proper privacy could be ensured, and each cubicle was to be fitted with a pedestal pan and tip up horse shoe seat.[37]

In view of the grim conditions often experienced at work the employees of the Plant looked forward avidly to the annual works' trip, usually held in July. The directors were aware of how much store was set by the days outing and were wise enough to continue the paternalistic policy of the founders of the company. Applications to the Board for the continuation of the privilege were deferential in tone and suitable appreciation was expressed to the same gentlemen after the trip had taken place. Thus, in July 1868 a meeting of the employees at the works passed a resolution 'expressing their thanks for the liberality of the Directors in granting them a free trip to Nottingham and back'.[38] There were other special occasions for holidays as on Queen Victoria's Jubilee on 21 June 1887 and the coronations of Edward the Seventh and George the Fifth.

From January 1872 when Saturday work at the Plant finished at noon there were opportunities for the staff to take advantage of the four-in-hand or charabanc excursions to the Dukeries and other places of interest. The local press reported and advertised these trips from the early 1880s onwards. The leading firm providing these amenities was J.G. Steadman, in the late 1980s still in business as Steadman and Sons. The chief rival firm providing excursions from 1888 onwards was Smith and Son. These and other firms were bus operators as well as coach and charabanc proprietors. Their rapidly expanding services in the closing years of Victoria's reign enabled many a Plant worker to take his family to the fresh air of the surrounding countryside.[39]

In 1895 the GNR established its own savings bank. In a letter to the Board written on 3 December, Henry Oakley, the General Manager, wrote that the purpose was 'to encourage thrift amongst their employees and to provide a safe deposit for their money at a fair rate of interest'. Although the bank was open for use by all employees of the company it was well supported, particularly by the better paid workers at the Plant. Interest was paid at 3½ per cent on deposits up to £100 with enhanced interest, on a graduated scale, paid on sums over £100.[40] By 1913 £53 838, or 23 per cent of the total deposited, had been invested and the average credit balance was £62. 19s. per depositor.[41]

In the early years of the twentieth century the Board of the GNR encouraged the staff at the Plant works to attend improvement classes. In 1911 one of the old workhouse buildings near to the works was converted into an additional library and reading room at a cost of £500.[42] That same year when extension of store accommodation for the locomotive running shed was approved it was agreed that some of the extra space should be set aside for the use of the Enginemen's Mutual Improvement class.[43] Outdoor activities were also encouraged. On 6 June 1913 the Board agreed to grant to the Doncaster Plant Works Recreation Club licence to use as a recreation ground spare land near the works that it had available. To carry out the work of preparing the ground a loan of £1000 at 4 per cent interest was made to the club. However, by the time the work was completed early in October 1914 many of the young men who would have been most keen to use the ground had enlisted in the armed forces.[44]

In the thirty years before the outbreak of the First World War the GNR found it increasingly difficult to satisfy, at one and the same time, its customers, its shareholders and its employees. In the 1880s the cost of meeting passengers' demands for more comfortable travel, including restaurant car and sleeping car services, and traders' demands for speedier deliveries, were key elements in increasing expenses. In the 1900s the price of coal – one of the biggest elements in operating costs – rose from an average of 15s. 3d. per ton in 1896–1900 to 17s. 7d. a ton in 1906–10.[45] The price of coal was one of the most important components of the worker's cost of living and led to a demand for higher wages. These were among the more important reasons for the increase in the GNR's working expenses as a proportion of total revenue – a generally accepted pointer to the soundness of a railway company's operations – from 54.5 per cent in 1885–9 to 63.3 per cent in 1905–9.[46] In these circumstances there was strong pressure on the directors from the shareholders to keep down working expenses, especially the cost of labour.

The nineteenth-century directors of the GNR experienced few sleepless nights over any demands made by members of their work force. At the Plant works trade unionism was very weak. Two of the best known 'New Model' style craft unions, the Amalgamated Society of Engineers (ASE) and the Amalgamated Society of Carpenters and Joiners (ASCJ), had a small number of members in the Plant from an early date. The Doncaster branch of the ASE was founded on 27 October 1851. It was reported as celebrating the tenth anniversary by dining together at the Black Bull Inn in the Market Place on 12 August 1861. The seventy members present sat down to 'an excellent and sumptuous dinner, served in very superior style'.[47] On 14 February 1862 a meeting was called by the ASCJ at the Brown Cow Inn, Frenchgate, for the purpose of forming a Doncaster branch of the union. The well-known General Secretary of the Union, Robert Applegarth, came down from London for the occasion and persuaded the members of his audience to join up.[48] A Doncaster branch of the Amalgamated Society of Railway Servants (ASRS) was functioning soon after that union was established in 1872. At a tea party held in the Working Men's Club and Institute, in Cleveland Street, on 30 March 1875 the Mayor of Doncaster took the chair and said that he sympathized with the objects of the Society.[49]

However, all three of these unions and the Boilermakers and other small organizations which had some representation at the Plant, were more in the nature of friendly societies than trade unions determined to exercise their industrial muscle to secure better pay and working conditions for their members. Their philosophy was exemplified by what was said at a dinner of the ASE held in the Reindeer Hotel on 1 December 1877. In moving the toast 'Success to the Great Northern Railway', coupled with the names of Patrick Stirling and John Shotten, Robert Green remarked 'how greatly their interests were interwoven with those of their managers, who by their ability and the workmen's co-operation, helped to make every effort a success to the company'.[50]

The membership of these unions comprised a handful of the elite of the craftsmen at the Plant and Doncaster railway station. The large majority of the employees at the Plant remained untouched by trade unionism until the late 1890s. From then onwards a combination of continued short time working – with take-home pay for hundreds of the unskilled well under £1 a week – and the rising price of coal, food and rents, increased economic hardships. To comply with the necessary bye-laws 5s. was the cheapest weekly rent that could be charged for a decent cottage, but in the first decade of the twentieth century there was a large influx of coal miners into the area able to pay, from their better wages, the rent demanded for the better accommodation. The unskilled workers at the Plant could not afford these rents and were crowded into slum dwellings.[51]

An employee of the GNR at Doncaster, T.R. Steels, was very concerned about the poverty of the lower paid workers at the Plant and attributed their sad condition to the absence of trade union organization. He got himself elected to the executive committee of the ASRS in 1897 and 1898. He joined the newly formed Doncaster branch of the Independent Labour Party (ILP) in 1898 and was a Doncaster councillor 1903–4. While he was on the EC of the ASRS, Steels carried a resolution at its September 1897 meeting initiating an All Grades Campaign.[52] Instead of concentrating on separate campaigns for each of the skilled grades such as signalmen and guards, the union was to follow the sound trade union principle of the strong helping the weak. In its ideology the All Grades Campaign was the forerunner of the National Union of Railwaymen (NUR) in 1913 which had as its object 'the complete organization of all workers employed on or in connection with any railway in the United Kingdom'.

Steels had one other notable achievement. In March 1899 he drafted, for the Doncaster branch of the ASRS, a resolution for submission to the next TUC to be held at Plymouth in September that year. The historic (if long-winded) resolution was worded as follows:

> That this Congress, having regard to its decisions of former years, and with a view to securing a better representation of the interests of labour in the House of Commons, hereby instructs the Parliamentary Committee to invite the co-operation of all the co-operative, socialistic, trade union and other working organisations to jointly co-operate on lines mutually agreed upon, in convening a special congress of representatives from such of the above-named organisations as may be willing to take part to devise ways and means for securing the return of an increased number of Labour members in the next Parliament.[53]

James Holmes, ASRS organizer for Wales and the West Country, moved Steels' resolution at Plymouth. It was carried by 546 000 to 434 000. As a result the Labour Representation Committee, forerunner of the Labour Party (formed in 1906), was established in 1900.

Meanwhile the discrepancy in organization remained between the Yorkshire miners and the GNR employees at the Plant. But just before the First World War the pace of change quickened. In 1913 the newly formed NUR sent round their area organizer William Dobbie, 'for the purpose of raising the spirit of discontent of the men at Doncaster' as he himself admitted. He said that the responsibility for a four day working week and consequent low wages lay firmly on the men themselves. Only 500 of the Plant workers were unionized out of a total work force of 3500 whereas by 1910 1300 of the 1980 miners at Woodlands had been organized in the Yorkshire Miners' Association. This discrepancy in organization was to be changed rapidly in the next ten years.

THE GNR LOCOMOTIVE SICK SOCIETY

As indicated in the preceding chapter, the risks of accidental death, disability and disease were exceptionally high among the workshop employees of the railway companies. This was generally recognized by the directors. Sir Daniel Gooch, Chairman of the Great Western Railway, told a meeting of the Railway Benevolent Institution in 1872 that there were in railway employment 'numberless cases of misery and distress, often by unavoidable accident, sometimes by want of thrift and care'.[1] However, management denied that those injured or killed in the service of a railway company had any legal right to compensation. In 1870 Capt. W. O'Brien, General Manager of the North Eastern Railway, declared that 'servants voluntarily undertook dangerous employment' and that 'servants injured on duty were treated as cases of charity, they had no legal claim'.[2]

Because they recognized that the dangers associated with railway employment were a deterrent to new entrants into the service, the companies viewed with favour the development of provident and friendly societies among their servants. The earliest known example of this kind of organization was the Great Western Railway Provident Society, founded in 1839. By 1871 at least fifty similar societies were functioning. In the case of ten of the largest railway companies, the boards of directors gave subsidies to the funds of such societies.[3] Their motives were not those of undiluted benevolence. To the extent that workers were offered some prospect of compensation in the event of sickness and injury, and in the event of their death, their widows received small grants, railway employment was made more attractive. The companies could get by with paying lower wages than would otherwise have been deemed necessary. The discipline of the workforce could also be more easily enforced. Where, as was generally the case, membership of a society was compulsory, the individual contributor was given a strong incentive to stay loyal to the railway company. If he left the service before he was time-expired he generally lost some of his benefits. If he took part in any 'forward movement' for improved wages and working conditions, he risked both dismissal and the loss of all or some of his previous contributions.

The GNR Locomotive Sick Society was established in 1850 principally for the benefit of footplatemen and workshop staff. In 1853 several small sick clubs within the locomotive department amalgamated with the Society whose headquarters were at Doncaster. Registration as a Friendly Society followed on 4 May 1857.[4]

Meanwhile, following a resolution of the Board passed on 6 October 1851, the GNR Provident Society was established on 23 May 1853. Membership was compulsory for station inspectors, guards, policemen and porters and optional for clerks and officers of higher rank. Thus this body, which was subsidized to the extent of £500 a year from the company's funds, was complementary to, rather than in competition with, the GNR Locomotive Sick Society.[5]

Archibald Sturrock, the Locomotive Engineer of the company, was the first patron of the GNR Locomotive Sick Society (GNRLSS) and helped with the drafting of the rules and with its registration with the Registrar of Friendly Societies, J.T. Pratt. From its inception the Society recruited the majority of its members from the Plant works, but employees were enrolled in the locomotive departments at other centres on the GNR system. In 1899, when membership was at a peak of 9862, the organization was divided into the eight districts of Doncaster, London, Peterborough, Leeds, Boston, Bradford, Colwick and Grantham. Within these districts there were branches which were entitled to elect a member of the central management committee in Doncaster if they had a hundred or more paid up subscribers.[6]

The first meeting recorded in the surviving minute books of the Society was held on 6

November 1867. It is unfortunate that records of the earlier meetings and the book of rules are not available. However, the character of the principal rules can be determined from the minutes of subsequent meetings and from reports in the **Doncaster Chronicle**. Membership of the Society was compulsory for all members of the GNR locomotive department over the age of eighteen. In return for a subscription which was initially 1d. a week, but which was adjusted from time to time, the member was entitled to receive 10s. per week in the event of sickness while the next of kin was entitled to claim a lump sum of £10 after the member's death. When any member sustained an accident which resulted in permanent disablement, such as the loss of a limb or an eye, he was entitled to receive a levy grant. This was raised by each member of the society paying an extra week's subscription (1d.) to the fund. It ensured that the injured member received what was regarded as a substantial lump sum, whilst the rest of the membership made a small contribution which was not burdensome. Thus, T. Challenger who was given a levy grant in 1860 received the sum of £45. 19s. 7d.[7] By the 1890s it became the practice to pay a fixed lump sum levy grant of £100 to the disabled member.[8] Funeral expenses were paid to a member on the death of a wife or husband as well as to a widow or widower following the death of the spouse.[9]

The Society was democratically run. The management committee, secretary, doctors chosen for part-time services, sick stewards and 'watchers' (who checked that those on sick benefit were not violating the rules) were elected by ballot of those attending the AGM and paid for their services.

From the members point of view the greatest advantage of belonging to the Society was the entitlement to 1s. 6d. a day sick benefit. In both 1859 and 1860 more than five hundred members made claims on the funds for this reason. This worked out at an average of eight days a year 'off sick' for each member of the Society.[10]

To guard against fraud, branches of the Society appointed watchers to ensure that the rules regarding sickness benefit were being observed. No member on benefit was allowed to be absent from his home address before 7 a.m. or after 8 p.m. To be gainfully employed while on sickness benefit was also forbidden. The 'watchers' could be appointed on a continuing basis or to investigate the conduct of a suspected violator of the rules. In either case they were paid for their services. The minutes of the Management Committee reveal that on 5 October 1868 Mr Worth was:

> deputed to go to Wath to watch C. Booth a sick member who had got leave of absence to go to Wath and whose real illness is much doubted.

The minutes do not record whether Worth found that Booth was having a high old time at the sick fund's expense, or whether his case was genuine. They do reveal that on 27 October Worth was paid 'one day's time and 6/- for expenses for visiting Wath'.[11]

The most common offence committed by those on sick benefit was that of being 'out after hours'. Most frequently the occasion for the offence was visiting the public house. Those caught by sick stewards or watchers exercised the greatest ingenuity in explaining their situation. A. Stewart who was reported as being in his 'local' at 9.50 p.m. said in his defence that 'his doctor had ordered him to drink a pint of porter a day' and that 'he had no one to fetch it for him'. He was nevertheless fined 1s.[12] The defence of W. McBirnie was more simply put. He had just arrived from York (where he was a non-resident member) and 'he felt the want for some refreshment'.[13]

Others who were on sick benefit were fined for being in gainful employment, contrary to rule. In September 1874 J. Bateman was fined three days' sick pay after he was discovered carrying a bag of bones. He and his wife carried on the business of bone boiling.[14]

Some members' sporting instincts were too strong. In August 1897 F. Tindall was 'charged with playing cricket whilst in receipt of sick pay' and was fined 2s. 6d.[15] In November 1904 E. Harling was fined three days' sick pay for playing football.[16] In April 1898 N. Brunyer took a risk by 'laying

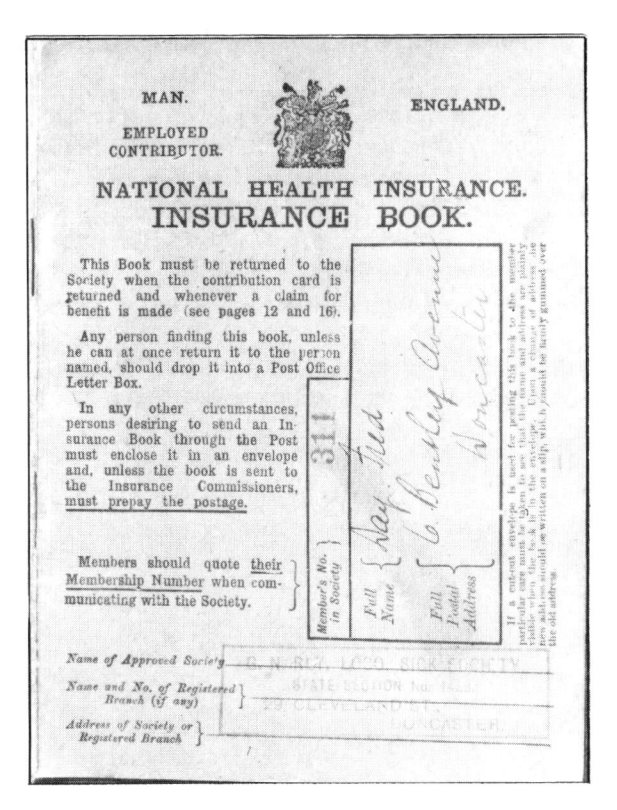

25 Members' National Insurance Book 1912

wagers on the Doncaster course'. He was found out and fined 2s. 6d.[17]

In the inter-war years the Management Committee took a more lenient view of the less serious violations of the rules. There were far fewer punishments. The fine of 1s. imposed on a painter on 19 December 1938 for being out after hours was the first recorded case that year of the punishment of a member on sick benefit.[18]

There were always some cases where, although the rules had been broken, the Management Committee decided it would be unjustifiable to impose a fine. It was sometimes difficult to define what was and was not 'work'. In April 1875 a watcher G. Guthrie charged A.T. Caser 'with doing work while on sick pay by playing the harmonium in Christ Church Parish Room at a tea given to the members of the Bible class who met there'. The Committee hadn't the heart to penalize such a benevolent activity. Mr. Caser was let off without even a caution.[19]

During the years 1865–89 and 1894–1903 the Society kept a register of the causes of death of its members.[20] Although the description and classification of diseases changed over time the register is a valuable guide to the main causes of death over more than three decades. The foremost killer disease through these years was phthisis or, as it was generally known in the twentieth century, consumption. 410 members died from this cause in the years covered. Given the atmosphere of smoke and dust and the extremes of temperature prevalent in the workshops, not to mention unhygienic conditions often found in the home, it is scarcely surprising that the death toll should have been so high. Bronchitis (sometimes classified as lung disease and sometimes simply as 'chest') accounted for 375 deaths. There were 309 recorded as suffering from heart disease, with 117 of that number dying in the four years 1900–1903. Four were classified as dying from cholera in 1865–6, while an epidemic of smallpox carried off 22 persons in 1871–2. Bright's disease was noted in 1876 and from then on was responsible for a steady trickle of one or two deaths annually. In the nineteenth century little was known about the diagnosis and treatment of cancer. The first case recorded in the Society's register was a cancer of the womb in 1872. A total of only seventy-six cases was noted before 1904. Evidence of women being in membership is the record of four deaths in childbirth in 1874–5 and of a further four in 1883–4.

The danger of life in the railway workshops is shown in the steady stream of death from accidents throughout the entire period in which records were kept. There were 171 deaths from this cause in the thirty-five years in which records were kept. The worst year was in 1902 when 11 men were killed in accidents.

During the First World War 161 members of the Society were killed on active service or died of their wounds. The widows or next of kin of these young men were supported from the funds.[21]

On 29 July 1874 the chairman of the Workmen's Trip Committee placed at the disposal of the Management Committee six in-patient and twelve out-patient recommendations for the use of the Society's members in obtaining medical assistance at the Doncaster Infirmary. The Board had allowed free travel for the works outing that summer but the men's committee had charged all those going on the outing 3d. per head, the proceeds to go to the Doncaster Infirmary. This was following the precedent set at the works outing four years earlier. The link with the local hospital was invaluable before the days of the National Health Service.[22]

One notable development in 1916 was the purchase on 6 March of office premises at 29 Cleveland Street, Doncaster with sufficient accommodation for a full time General Secretary and clerical assistants.[23]

The end of the First World War was marked by an intensive membership drive. 815 new members were recruited in the one year 1919.[24] The recruitment campaign continued with the early 1920s bringing the membership to its peak of nearly 12 000 by 1925.[25] Thereafter there was a decline in the depression years 1929–33 with only a trickle of new members in 1931 and 1932. A resolution sumbitted to the Management Committee in 1935 mentioned the 'ever increasing dismissals and re-engagements of workshop staff', giving rise to 'the consequent difficulty of tracing the members of the Society'.[26]

During the Second World War the business of the Society languished. Entries in the minute books often record 'No meeting. Business nil', or 'Officers re-elected unopposed'. In an attempt to stem the tide of apathy posters spelling out the advantages of membership were displayed at all points where workshop staff were employed. A 'procuration' fee of 2s. 6d. was offered to members for each new recruit they enrolled.[27] Since there was some resentment over the fact that membership of the Society was a condition of service the Railway Executive abolished the compulsory membership rule in 1943.

Soon after the end of the Second World War it became necessary to elect a new General Secretary. In voting throughout the Society Eric Baines of the Plant works defeated D. Wood decisively by 1141 votes to 812 on 6 May 1946.[28] Baines' tenure of office, which was the longest in the 131 years of the Society's history, lasted until it was wound up in December 1981. With the new management came a revival of the life of the Society and a reform of many of its rules.

The National Insurance Act was passed by Attlee's Labour government in 1946 and came into operation on 5 July 1948. It established an extended system of national insurance providing pecuniary payments by way of unemployment benefit, sickness benefit, maternity benefit, retirement pension, widows' benefit, guardian's allowance and death grant. Railway workers, members of the GNR Locomotive Sick Society could well be excused for assuming that the new Act of Parliament provided them with comprehensive insurance cover. The line taken by Eric Baines and the Management Committee was that there was a strong case for 'topping up' what the state provided with an additional insurance through the Society. In the Society's 96th Annual Report, published on 31 December 1947 they wrote:

> The National Insurance Act which becomes operative on 5 July 1948 will provide each one of us with a solid foundation, a minimum of security, upon which we can build and consolidate our provisions against sickness and misfortune. To think that this Act will give complete security is a dangerous fallacy however.[29]

This appeal combined with a membership drive resulted in 340 new members joining the Society in 1948 – 'easily the highest figure for fourteen years.'

At the same time it was recognized that membership would have to be made more attractive if numbers were to be kept up. In 1950 a new 'optional' benefit scale was introduced whereby in return for a subscription of 8d. a week, a member was entitled to 15s. a week during incapacity for work. This was known as Scale B to distinguish it from the previously existing scheme, now to be known as Scale A which guaranteed 10s. a week in sickness. Thus if a member joined both scales he could expect to receive 25s. when sick. A second innovation that year was the replacement of the pension of 1s. 6d. a week, payable at the age of sixty-five by a lump sum the value of which was to be calculated by the Society's actuary.[30] More publicity was given to the house purchase scheme initiated before the war. In 1952 it was reported that the total amount of the Society's funds advanced to members was £31 002. 4s. 0d. which was a sum comparable to the pre-war peak[31] Between 1930 and 1960 over 730 members bought their homes more cheaply through the Society's scheme.

As a part of the process of bringing the Society up to date its name was changed to the GNR Locomotive Friendly Society in 1952.

Through all these efforts membership figures were well sustained while railway employment remained at a high level. In 1946 the total was 8881 made up of 7072 'resident' members (i.e. those still in railway employment) and 1809 'non resident' members (i.e. those who had left railway employment but who continued to subscribe). In 1955 the year of the Railway Modernization Plan the total was 8487. Between 1961–63, when Dr Beeching was making his cuts, membership fell from 7122 to 6194. By 1971 it was down to 3187.[32] In 1972 BR announced that the regular grant of £500 to the funds of the Society would no longer be paid. The GNR had started paying this sum on a regular basis in 1887 and the policy had been continued by the LNER and the Railway Executive.[33]

By 1981 with membership down to 2300 the management of the Society took the advice of its actuary 'to dissolve while still in a strong position and able to direct your own destiny'. An application for voluntary dissolution was registered and assets were distributed to members by the end of the year.[34]

Throughout the 131 years of its existence a substantial majority of the membership had come from the Doncaster area. The presence of the 'sick inspectors' in the streets of the borough was for long a familiar sight. After 1981 the men, who were the scourge of the malingerers and who were locally known as the 'Plant Club Bobbies', disappeared from the scene.

9

THE PLANT WORKS IN THE FIRST WORLD WAR

26 Sir Nigel Gresley, Chief Mechanical Engineer, 1911–1941

Changes in the top management of the Plant works came not long before the outbreak of the First World War in August 1914. When the directors of the GNR came to appoint a successor to H.A. Ivatt in the autumn of 1911 they followed the precedent set by previous directors in 1866 and 1896 in appointing the son of a clergyman as Chief Mechanical Engineer.

Nigel Gresley was born on 19 June 1876, the fifth child of the Revd Nigel Gresley, rector of Netherscale, Derbyshire. He could claim descent from the de Toeni family, relatives of William the Conqueror. The name Gresley is taken from that of a village in Derbyshire to which Sir Nigel's ancestors fled at a time of plague in about 1095. Unlike his predecessors in the office of Chief Mechanical Engineer, Gresley was promoted from within the GNR company. It is true that before 1904 he had served his time with F.W. Webb of the LNWR and John Aspinall of the L & Y Railway, but in 1904 he became Assistant Superintendent of the Carriage and Wagon department at Doncaster. In the following year, at the remarkably young age of twenty-nine, he was promoted to Superintendent of that department. Thus when he succeeded Ivatt in 1911 he had already served seven years in the company.[1]

Before the 1920s the changes made by Nigel Gresley in the design of passenger locomotives had been described as 'gradual and unobtrusive'.[2] Pre-1914 improvements in freight locomotives were more substantial. At this time the need for more powerful locomotives to haul the increasingly heavy freight trains was seen as a priority. Superheated 1630 class Mogul engines were built at Doncaster to meet this challenge.

However, since Gresley's outstanding achievements as Chief Mechanical Engineer came in the inter-war years it is proposed to consider these in the next chapter.

Within a month of the declaration of war against Germany on 4 August, the GNR's work force was depleted to the extent of nearly 2000 men. More

46

THE PLANT WORKS IN THE FIRST WORLD WAR

than two-thirds of this number were volunteers, army or navy reservists or territorials.[3] Doncaster railway station and the Plant works contributed nearly 200 to this total. It might, therefore, have been expected that good workmen would be much in demand. This was not the case, at least for some weeks. On 14 August the **Doncaster Gazette** reported that a four day week was in operation at the Plant, the works being closed on Monday and Saturdays. The reason given for this low level of activity was 'inability to get material owing to disorganized transport'. Trains were being used to get men and equipment to the war zones in France. In September the number of men unemployed in Doncaster was double that of the previous month.[4] Since prices of basic materials were rising sharply, considerable distress was caused.

An organization called Doncaster War Relief made allowances to the dependents of servicemen.[5] In addition, from 20 August the GNR made allowances to wives and dependents of men serving in the army or navy at the rate of 7s. a week for the wife and 1s. a week for each child, with a maximum of 10s. per family.[6] However, men who were unemployed or on short time had to depend upon relief administered by the Poor Law Guardians.

Full-time working was restored at the Plant from the middle of October. The NUR newspaper the **Railway Review** speculated as to the reasons:

> What is the secret? Are the company putting down a new fleet of engines and rolling stock in wartime? No. It is rumoured that they are able to do something to assist the government and benefit their employees at the same time.[7]

The rumour was well founded.

At the outbreak of the First World War the 120 separate railway companies of the UK were taken over by the government under the Regulation of the Forces Act, 1871. They were then managed as a single system under the Railway Executive Committee (REC). The organization of railway workshop activity under the REC was undertaken by the Railway War Production Sub-Committee, whose members were the Chief Mechancical Engineers of the larger railway companies.

Just over a month after the declaration of war Gresley received an order from the War Office for 750 ambulance stretchers. Then at the end of September came an order for 80 general service wagons followed, five days later, with an order for 400 more. These were built at the rate of thirty per week by the coachmakers in the carriage department, the wheels being made in the dray shop.

At first it did not dawn upon the War Office that good use could be made of the machinery in the railway companies' locomotive shops. The initiative to bring in the great railway workshops was taken by Sir Frederick Donaldson, Chief Superintendent of Woolwich Arsenal, who wrote personal letters to Nigel Gresley and the Chief Mechanical Engineers of three other large railway companies, asking them to come down to Woolwich 'with a view to rendering assistance in the manufacture of field gun carriages and limbers'. As a result of this visit the GNR, in collaboration with the NER, undertook the manufacture of parts of 150 18-pounder field gun carriages. Gresley later reported to the GNR Board that:

> It was with some diffidence that I undertook the work, realising the extreme accuracy required, involving working to limits of three thousandths of an inch. The class of work was much higher than that required for locomotives, and I was doubtful whether the machinery was sufficiently accurate, or the men sufficiently skilful.[8]

Since the only jigs and gauges capable of doing this work were at Woolwich, they had to be specially made at Doncaster. Both management and craftsmen were keen to meet this new challenge. Though they made some mistakes at first they very soon turned the work out correctly. Gresley received several acknowledgments both from Sir Frederick Donaldson, and from his successors, of the high degree of accuracy and finish of the work performed at the Plant.

Included among the other assignments, requiring great accuracy of workmanship, which were carried out at Doncaster, were the manufacture of 162 outer frames and 62 inner frames for 13-pounder AA guns mounted on motor lorries; fifty complete gun mountings for 18-pounder pedestal guns for the merchant marine; mountings for high angle AA guns; gun cradles and other parts for 8-inch howitzers and the construction of 511 60-pounder BL guns.

Gresley considered that the employment of craftsmen on these very exacting tasks had beneficial effects. There had been 'a raising of the standards of workmanship in the locomotive department' since 'both machine and hand work had to be finished within very fine limits'. He found that an important indirect advantage of craftsmen being employed on the skilled war work was that they 'felt confident they would not be penalized by having piecework rates reduced'. Evidence of this was to be seen in the Crimpsall repair shops. Although the number of men employed there was only 255 in the average of the war years compared with 277 in 1913 the number of heavy repairs to locomotives had increased from 505 in 1913 to a 534 average in 1914–18.

In this same January 1919 report to the Board, Gresley regretted that the impact of the war on the carriage and wagon department was less favourable. After the first year of the war he could secure no munition work for the staff employed there. He tried hard to get work on aeroplanes and ambulance trains but it had been allocated to other companies' workshops. In consequence those employed in that department 'had to be put on inferior work such as carriage repairs and wagon building'. Many of the best workmen had left this part of the Plant works to take up more interesting and better paid 'work of national importance' elsewhere.

Among the more interesting tasks assigned to the Plant works was the equipment of locomotives for military services. In November 1914 orders were received for two armoured engines. Two of the Metropolitan Suburban passenger link engines were selected and were completely armoured with 9/16 inch plates. In December 1916 and early 1917 twenty-three six-wheel coupled goods tender locomotives were sent to France. Twenty of these were fitted with special condensing apparatus to enable them to be worked in advanced military areas.

Three more engines and tenders of the same type were supplied later in 1917.

One consequence of the war was the opening up of employment opportunities for women. In Edwardian times the overwhelming majority of women worked in their own homes, preparing meals, lighting fires, washing clothes, dusting and cleaning. Time was also much taken up in caring for relatives and neighbours. The 1911 census revealed that, out of a total of 12 042 women living in Doncaster, only 937 were in paid employment. Most of these were in domestic indoor service or were day servants.[9]

New opportunities arose when Woolwich Arsenal asked the railway companies to undertake the repair of fired 18-pounder brass cartridge cases. In May 1915, when the request was made, no less than 750 000 of these cases were awaiting repair. The work had been done in Woolwich by skilled coppersmiths but it was evident that following this

27 Carriage works c. 1915

THE PLANT WORKS IN THE FIRST WORLD WAR

procedure would never clear the backlog. Gresley undertook to arrange for the repair of 5000 cartridges a week at the Plant works. At first a number of apprentice lads were employed on the special machinery improvised in the old tender shop, but later women were engaged to do the work. Output was raised to 50 000 repaired cases per week. By the end of the war 4 267 093 of these cartridge cases were repaired at Doncaster at an average cost of 3½d. each.[10] The work was tedious, the women spent long hours standing by their machines and there were hazards from the splinters of metal scattered about the floor of the works. The wearing of clogs was recommended for this reason.

In July 1915, at the urgent request of Lloyd George, Minister of Munitions, Nigel Gresley and other Chief Mechanical Engineers undertook the manufacture of 6-inch high explosive shells. At Doncaster most of the machinery at the south end of the lower turnery was removed and twenty-five new shell lathes and other machines were purchased. The initial output was 250 shells per week but through the introduction of day and night shifts output was increased to 1000 per week by July 1916. As figure 28 shows, the work was done by women. The shell cases were constructed and polished ready for dispatch to the filling factory. The work was conscientiously done. Only 0.17 per cent of the 124 000 shells machined at Doncaster were found to be in any way defective.

28 Turnery, 1916 (Chief foreman, F. Trecoe in bowler hat)

49

PRO RAIL 236/442   TABLE 2

EXPENDITURE INCURRED AT DONCASTER WORKS DURING YEARS 1914 TO 1918 ON MUNITIONS OF WAR FOR GOVERNMENT DEPARTMENTS, RAILWAY CO.S & ARMAMENT FIRMS

Particulars	Principal Work £	Minor Work £	Rolling Stock &c £	Total £
GOVERNMENT DEPARTMENTS				
Ministry of Munitions	357 392	14 061	5 000	376 453
War Office	51 827	266	946	53 039
Woolwich Arsenal	50 778			50 778
Director of Railways and Roads			21 351	21 351
Admiralty	2 794		4 741	7 535
Royal Small Arms Factory, Enfield	3 541	632		4 173
Ministry of Food			4 718	4 718
Director of Inland Waterways & Docks			3 000	3 000
Royal Engineers Stores, Woolwich Dockyard	1 684			1 684
Mechanical Warfare Department		813		813
RAF Training Establishment, Cranwell, Sleaford			350	350
Royal Laboratory, Woolwich		292		292
Royal Aircraft Factory, Farnboro		163		163
Belton Park Camp Railway, Grantham		120		120
Other		2 735		2 735
	468 016	19 082	40 106	527 204
RAILWAY COMPANIES	24 389	7 231	1 118	32 738
ARMAMENT FIRMS	5 312	2 544		7 856
	497 717	28 857	41 224	567 798

This statement does not include the agreed addition of 12½% for Supervision, etc.
It shows Locomotive Department charges only.

7 January 1919
    Doncaster

Much other munitions work was undertaken at the Plant. The drop stampers were very busy turning out hundreds of thousands of noses for shells; 50 000 rifle bodies; 6000 rifle noses and thousands of various parts of gun carriages and tanks.[11]

Although railway trade union membership at Doncaster rose steeply by the closing months of the war – the NUR had 1462 members there in 1918 – not a single day's work was lost through industrial disputes. The main concern of the NUR was that the women employed in such tasks as carriage window cleaning, shown in figure 29, would be treated as cheap labour, undercutting the wages of men. Following representations from the executive of the NUR, in July 1915 the chief railway companies conceded that 'the employment of women would not prejudice in any way any undertaking given by the companies as to the re-employment of men who had joined the colours'.[12] But they would not promise that women would be paid the proper 'rate for the job'.

Table 2 shows that in the years 1914–18, apart from the work carried out for the GNR, staff at the Plant works were fulfilling orders from at least seventeen different organizations. In terms of the money value of the products, the £376 453 worth of orders executed for the Ministry of Munitions completely overshadowed the work done in carrying out all the other commissions. When it is remembered that it was mainly women who had been employed in repairing cartridge cases and

THE PLANT WORKS IN THE FIRST WORLD WAR

manufacturing shell cases and shell noses, the importance of women in Doncaster's war effort is evident.

The paper work involved in connection with war time orders from such a large variety of sources far exceeded that needed in peace time when the Plant works was mainly engaged in meeting the domestic requirements of the GNR. Women clerks were recruited for this work. In June 1915 the GNR Board approved, in principle, the provision of temporary office accommodation for women clerks at Doncaster.[13] This was followed five months later by the acceptance of a tender from the local contracting firm of Arnold and Sons 'for building temporary office accommodation for women clerks in the locomotive department at a cost of £450'.[14]

The Railway Clerks' Association (RCA), as well as the NUR, was concerned about the rates of pay of those women clerks who had replaced men, as well as those who filled new posts, during the wartime emergency. RCA membership rose from 29 394 to 42 654 in the one year 1915,[15] and in June of that year the AGM of the NUR voted to accept women into membership.[16] In July 1916 women clerks in the RCA held a special conference at Leeds where the main demand was that the railway companies should give the same war bonus to their female employees as they had already awarded to the men.[17] The GNR responded to this demand on 3 November 1916 when the Board agreed to award its women clerks a war bonus of 5s. a week, payable from 16 September 1916. Women under eighteen years of age received a bonus of 3s. from the same date.[18]

Wagon building and repair was at a reduced scale between 1914–18 compared with the immediate pre-war period, for the 500 wagons sanctioned to be built in March 1916 were classified as 'renewals' rather than as 'additions to stock'.[19] The need for these renewals would have been considerably less if the Common User scheme which had tentative beginnings in December 1915, but was not very widespread until 1917, had been more effective and had come into use at an earlier date.

Up to 1915 Railway Clearing House regulations stated that all 'foreign' wagons had to be returned to their owners after their freight had been unloaded. This involved a great deal of empty running of rolling stock. To avoid some of this waste

29 Women carriage cleaners, First World War

of resources the regulations were altered in July 1915 to allow most 'foreign' wagons to be loaded for their return journey. It is to the great credit of Nigel Gresley that he entered into negotiations with the Chief Mechanical Engineers of the Great Central and Great Eastern Railways for setting up a common user scheme. From December 1915 all ordinary open goods wagons of these three companies were treated as common stock. The other main-line companies joined the scheme by June 1916.

However, approximately 600 000 wagons – about half the number of those belonging to the railway companies – were privately owned. Despite prolonged negotiations, it proved impossible to bring them into the Common User scheme. Even after a Board of Trade Order (SR and O 1917, number 250) had given the railway companies the power to back-load private owners wagons, less than half of them were in common use by February 1919.[20]

As a result of the gradual introduction of the Common User scheme empty running of wagons was reduced from 60 per cent in October 1913 to 20 per cent six years later.[21] For the GNR the fact that total expenditure on capital account fell marginally in money terms between 1914 and 1918 – from £54 182 309 to £53 684 582 (1 per cent) – while prices of minerals more than doubled in the same period, was in no small measure due to the economies in use of both wagons and passenger carriages in the same period.[22]

Before the war only 20 per cent of the employees at the Plant were organized into trade unions despite the fact that the works had been in existence for sixty years. By 1919 the large majority of workers were unionized, with 2420 of them in the NUR's Doncaster No.3 branch which enrolled workshop members and a further 1858 organized in the four other branches of the Doncaster area.[23] Membership of ASLEF and the craft unions also increased in the war years, but at a very much slower rate since these unions already had members before 1913 and there was far less scope for expansion. Since there were an estimated twenty-eight different craft unions who could claim members at the Plant, and since the majority of them, with the exception of the Amalgamated Society of Engineers (ASE), the Boilermakers Society and the Friendly Society of Ironfounders, were very small organizations, it is impossible to put a figure on their combined membership in 1913 and 1919.

Early in the war it was asserted by Albert Bellamy, President of the NUR, that rates of pay in the railway workshops 'were shillings a week less' than the rates paid in outside industry.[24] In December 1914 J.H. Thomas, MP, Assistant General Secretary of the Union, approached leading railway company directors requesting negotiations over the rates of pay and conditions of service of railway shop workers. The companies declined to include this large group of their employees in the Railway Conciliation Scheme set up in 1907 and modified in 1911. The directors told Mr Thomas that the NUR's claim to speak for shop men 'was disputed by other unions' and that in any case the majority of these workers were not in any trade union.[25]

This experience prompted the NUR to issue a leaflet on 9 July 1915, headed **To Railway Shop workers**. It read (in part):

> Cease your abortive sectional efforts, which can bring you no good, and join with those whose desire is to ensure for all railway workers a proper standard of living ... By joining in you will be joining hands with over 300 000 other railway workers, all employed by a common employer; for the railway companies are as one when dealing with their employees. Railway employees should be as one when dealing with their common employer.

Appeals such as this met with a widespread response, leading to a huge influx of railway shopmen into the NUR – as indicated above. However, the craft unions resented the zealous activity of the NUR's organizers. They accused them of 'poaching' members from their societies. In 1916 and 1917 prolonged discussions took place at the TUC between both sides in this dispute. On 20 July 1917 Mr Thomas proposed that the NUR and the craft unions should be equally represented on a negotiating body to meet with the railway companies to settle the wages and conditions of service of workshop staff. However, the craft unions rejected this plan. They proposed instead that they should have twenty-eight representatives – one for each craft society – and that the NUR should have six. Since the NUR had more workshop members than the combined membership of all the craft unions, it is not surprising that it rejected this proposal. In consequence of this disagreement, the establishment of a negotiating machinery for workshop staff was delayed until well after the conclusion of the war.[26] At Doncaster, therefore, the trade unions had little influence during the war years in determining the conditions of employment of the workers at the Plant.

THE INTER-WAR YEARS 1919-39

After 31 December 1922 the Great Northern Railway ceased to exist. Under the terms of the Railways Act, 1921, the 120 separate railways of 1913 were merged into the four main-line companies familiar to travellers in the inter-war period. On 1 January 1923 the GNR joined the Great Eastern, Great Central, North Eastern, Hull and Barnsley, North British and Great North of Scotland railways, and many smaller concerns, to form the London and North Eastern Railway (LNER). The Report of the Select Committee on Transport in 1918 gave a glowing account of the greater efficiency of railway operation achieved under the single direction of the Railway Executive Committee (REC) during the war years. The acting chairman of the REC, Sir Herbert Walker, declared in 1917, 'I cannot think that our railways will ever again revert to the independent and foolish competitive system.'[1] In 1920 a White Paper outlining the Coalition Government's proposals for railway reorganization advised that 'direct competition between the groups would be as far as possible eliminated'.[2]

Considerable thought was given to the composition of the four railway groupings. The guiding principle was to merge prosperous undertakings with the less prosperous ones, to create new organizations which would be financially viable. In the case of the LNER it was anticipated that the old NER territory, with its booming coal, iron and steel and shipbuilding traffic and long record of profitability, would help to 'carry' the less profitable territories of the Great Eastern, North British and Great North of Scotland railways. As it happened, in the 1920s and 1930s, the situation was the reverse of what had been anticipated. Depression hit the heavy industries of North East England, but an expansion of commuter, agricultural and merchandise traffic increased revenue on the lines of the old Great Eastern and Great Central Railways. However, as one of its distinguished former employees has written, the LNER 'was essentially a freight railway'.[3] The buoyancy of passenger revenues in London's suburbia was insufficient to counter-balance the very heavy decline in coal traffic further north. In 1932 the mineral traffic was only half what it had been in 1924, and in 1938 it was still only 69 per cent of the mid-twenties' volume.[4] Thus the LNER was always hampered by its weak financial position. Not one of its several series of dated first or second preference shares was regularly paid in full, and its ordinary preference shareholders had nothing after 1930. The profitability record of the company was not only poor, it was also uneven. As a result of coal strikes or depression in the heavy industries, 1920-21, 1925-6, 1929-32 and 1937-8 were particularly bad years.

Inevitably the impact of these conditions on railway engineering was serious. The Plant works experienced a 'stop-go' economy in the inter-war years. In June 1925, for example, the locomotive committee decided that 'having regard to the present financial position' the construction of thirty-five locomotives and a hundred and one vehicles would be deferred.[5] However, two summers later there was a shortage of both locomotives and carriages and new building was resumed.[6] In the slump of 1929-32 strict economy was again the order of the day. In August 1932 'owing to the urgent need for further curtailment of expenditure' all new building of carriages was suspended.[7] By November 1934 the legacy of earlier economies was reported as having 'serious disadvantages in the working of the traffic'. There was 'difficulty in maintaining the loads of mineral trains' and a 'substantial loss of excursion business through inability to provide substantial locomotives for haulage purposes'.[8] In 1935-7 the Plant works was busy again carrying out a 'supplementary programme' for the building of more wagons and carriages. There had been 'a definite and continuing increase in the volume of traffic to be handled'.[9]

For the Plant works staff fluctuations in the building and repair programmes for locomotives and rolling stock brought frequent, and sometimes prolonged, periods of short time working, with consequent loss of earnings. In June 1933 15 775 out of 23 927, or 65 per cent of employees in the CME's department of the LNER were working short time. Two years later the figure had fallen to 22 per cent. But it was not until December 1939 that Kenelm Kerr, Assistant General Manager (Staff), was able to report that the number of men on short time working had been reduced 'to a few hundreds'.[10] In most cases being 'on short time' meant no Saturday morning work, but in the worst years, such as 1932–3, men were stood off on other days of the week as well. Hundreds of men were stood off indefinitely in 1932 and 1933.

On 22 February 1923 the locomotive committee of the LNER resolved 'that it be recommended to the Board that Mr H.N. Gresley be appointed Chief Mechanical Engineer at a salary of £4,500 per annum'.[11] The Board, meeting on the following day approved both the appointment and the salary.[12] On 1 January 1934, when there were signs of the company's business improving, the CME's salary was raised to £5000 per annum.[13] By the standards of the time this was generous. However, Nigel Gresley had a very wide range of responsibilities. Besides having to see to the efficient running of the company's locomotive, carriage and wagon departments, he was accountable for the state of machinery used at stations and depots and of all road and other vehicles used by the company.

Gresley's policy was to continue using the best designs of locomotives from the pre-1923 companies and to develop them with his own innovations. He appreciated that improvements in design were urgently needed, particularly in the locomotives serving the Scottish lines. However, it was a huge task. In 1923 the constituent railways merged into the LNER posssssed 7383 steam locomotives and eleven electric ones. Adaptations

30 Plan of the Plant works, 1919

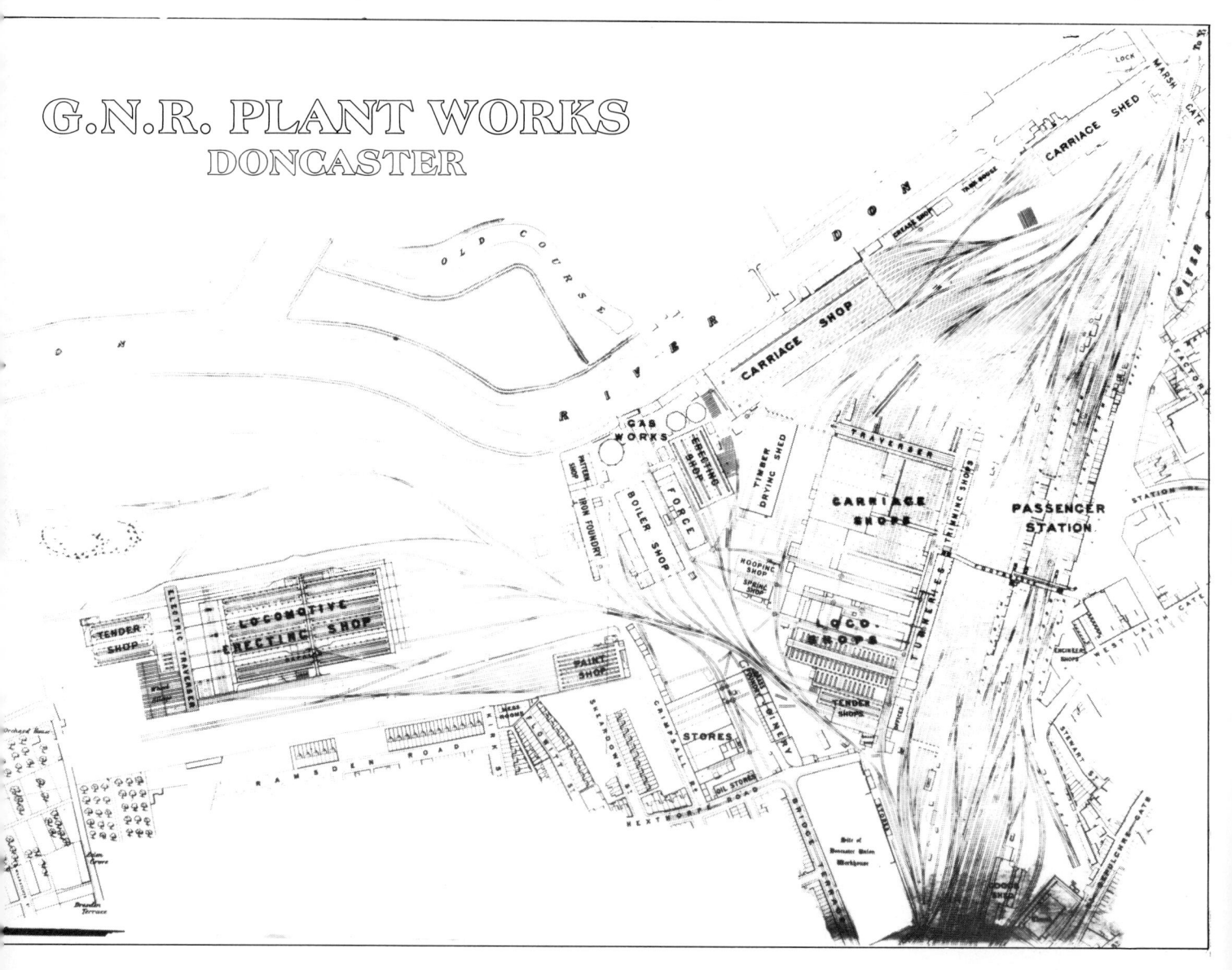

54

THE INTER-WAR YEARS 1919–39

and improvements were carried out through the inter-war years at Darlington, Gateshead, Stratford, Springhead, Cowlais and Inverurie, as well as Doncaster.[14]

Although one of the main ideas behind the grouping of the companies carried out under the Railways Act, 1921, was to eliminate wasteful competition, old rivalries remained. To offset the depression in freight traffic the companies did their utmost to develop their passenger services for businessmen and holidaymakers. This implied improvements in speed and travelling comfort.

At the British Empire Exhibition in Wembley in 1924 the LNER's 'Pacific' locomotive **Flying Scotsman** was exhibited alongside the GWR's smaller and less powerful-looking **Caerphilly Castle**. Because it had a larger boiler, many wiseacres assumed that the Doncaster built Pacific would be the better performer. This could only be proved correct following comparative trials of the two engines in identical conditions. Following conversations between Sir Felix Pole, General Manager of the GWR, and Alexander Wilson, Manager of the LNER Southern Area, the locomotive exchanges between the Pacific class **Victor Wild** and the GWR's **Pendennis Castle** took place in April and early May 1925. Gresley first heard about these trials through reading a press release in his newspaper![15] The outcome of the exchanges was that the Castle class locomotive achieved faster speeds and a lower consumption of coal than did the Pacific. Noting these results, Gresley redesigned valve motions in Pacific locomotives.

Numerous modifications of the Pacific locomotives were made in the mid 1920s. In 1927 locomotive number 4480 was fitted with a new boiler which had a working pressure of 220 lb per square inch compared with the 180 per square inch of the earlier Pacifics. It was also given a larger superheater. The combination of these improvements produced the A3 type Pacifics.

In the late 1920s there was intense competition between the LMS and the LNER for the passenger traffic with Scotland. In 1928 the LMS produced its Royal Scot locomotives which made possible the inauguration of a non-stop run between Euston and Carlisle. Not to be outdone, Gresley retaliated by the introduction of a non-stop run between King's Cross and Edinburgh. This was made possible through the adaptation, at the Plant works, of Flying Scotsman class Pacifics by the construction of a corridor tender. Half way along the 393.8 mile route a driving crew that had been resting in a

31 Flying Scotsman, 1923

special compartment in the front of the train changed places with the crew on the footplate via the corridor tender. The historian of the LNER questioned whether the cost of building twenty of these tenders was justified 'by the prestige of operating, over four months of the year at most, the world's longest non-stop run'.[16]

In his desire to ensure that the LNER provided the fastest train services on the main routes, Gresley kept a watchful eye on developments abroad. In 1933 both the Pennsylvania Railroad in the USA and the German state railways introduced diesel-powered expresses. After riding on the diesel-powered Flying Hamburger between Berlin and Hamburg at an average speed of 77.4 m.p.h., Gresley was so impressed that he gave serious consideration to buying a similar locomotive for use on the LNER. The Board agreed to ask the German manufacturers to prepare a design for a similar locomotive for London–Newcastle runs. However, the best that could be promised for the English run was an average speed of 63 m.p.h. which compared unfavourably with best performances of the A3 Pacifics.[17]

For developments in locomotive design which he introduced between 1935 and 1939 Gresley owed a great deal to Ettore Bugatti, the Italian racing car manufacturer and pioneer in streamlining. In 1928 at Molsheim, Bugatti launched his 'car of kings', the Royale, which was 19 feet long and weighed 3 tons. However, the Wall Street Crash of 1929 hit demand so hard that only three of these vehicles were sold, none of them to a king! He was saved from bankruptcy by a series of contracts from French railway companies anxious to develop faster services to beat off competition from motor vehicles. By the summer of 1933 Bugatti's railcars, powered by his 'Royale' engines were reaching speeds of 113 m.p.h. on runs between Paris and Deauville. Gresley had been experimenting with various forms of partial streamlining since 1929, with the object of achieving faster speeds and devising a way of diverting steam and smoke from the driver's line of vision. After travelling with Bugatti on one of his railcars he was very impressed by the locomotive's wedge-shaped aero-dynamic effect in clearing the fumes from the vision of the driver. So when the LNER Board agreed to the construction at Doncaster of a streamlined train to run between London and Newcastle Gresley had

32 Mallard *near Hexthorpe Bridge*

THE INTER-WAR YEARS 1919–39

the authority to construct the A4 Pacific **Silver Link** locomotive with the Bugatti wedge-shaped front.[18]

The staff at the Plant works were employed 'flat out' to prepare the **Silver Link** for its trial run on 27 September 1935, preparatory to its hauling the **Silver Jubilee** train (in commemoration of King George V and Queen Mary's silver jubilee) that year. On these trial runs speeds of 112½ m.p.h. were attained on two separate occasions. The success of the **Silver Link** was immediate. In 1936 the building of additional locomotives of this type was started at Doncaster. By 1938 a total of thirty-five engines had been constructed, all at the Plant works. Streamlining on the **Silver Link** had resulted in economies in coal consumption as well as better sighting of the track by the drivers. In 1937 it was therefore decided to streamline the locomotives both for the 'Coronation' express between King's Cross and Edinburgh and the 'West Riding Limited' between King's Cross, Leeds and Bradford. On 3 July 1938 the Pacific A4 **Mallard** achieved a top speed of 126 m.p.h. on a test run down Stoke bank – the world's record speed with a steam locomotive.[19]

The craftsmen in the locomotive erecting shop at the Plant were justifiably proud of their achievement in building the mighty A4s. In October 1987, questioned about the **Mallard's** speed record of nearly fifty years earlier, Dick Sargeant, aged 77, stated with obvious and justifiable pride, 'I did the piston job for that run'.[20]

At the same time as these more spectacular events were taking place Gresley was giving attention to the need for improved locomotive designs for the Scottish traffic. The engines inherited from the North British and Great North of Scotland railways in 1923 lacked the power and adhesion to tackle the steep gradients of the

33 International interdependence in technology

(a) The Bugatti Royale motorcar 1926

(b) Bugatti railcar, Paris-Deauville service from the summer of 1933 (above)

(c) A4 Pacific Silver Link, 1935 (below)

57

Highlands. After much experimentation, the Plant works produced by May 1934 Class P2 No.2000 **Cock of the North**. It was a massive engine 73 feet 8 inches in length with eight coupled wheels of 6 feet 2 inches diameter, to give the necessary adhesion when climbing steep gradients. Six of these powerful locomotives were built at the Plant between 1934–6.[21]

Other important locomotives produced at Doncaster between the wars included the J 50 classified shunting engines of which fifty-eight were constructed at the Plant between 1922 and 1939 and the Class VI tank engine, designed primarily for suburban use. Eighty-two of these were built at Doncaster between 1930 and 1939.[22]

The reduction in the LNER's steam locomotive stock from 7383 engines in 1923 to 6467 in 1939 arose from three principal causes. There was a fall in the volume of coal and mineral traffic; more powerful locomotives were employed for the haulage of both passenger and freight trains and there was a significant reduction in the time taken for locomotive repairs.

At the Plant works a major reorganization of the arrangements for heavy repair of locomotives was undertaken at the Crimpsall shops after 1923. In that year it was usual for there to be around a hundred locomotives in the shops at various stages of repair at any one time. There was considerable delay in the completion of repairs owing to the time taken to manufacture new parts or replace unrepairable defective details. It was then decided to reduce the number of locomotives under repair at any one time from a hundred to thirty-six and to concentrate the work in such a way that the movement of both men and materials was minimized.[23] However, according to Willie Bangs, who was employed as a turner at the Crimpsall at the time, the pace of work was increased. More men were placed on piece work and the supervisor would say 'Hurry up: there are plenty more outside' – a reference to the fact that there was a 'reserve army' of craftsmen waiting at the gate.[24]

Throughout the inter-war years, when old equipment was shown to be worn out, Gresley used every opportunity to replace it with up-to-date electrically powered machinery. The locomotive committee minutes record a continuous stream of recommendations for the purchase of new equipment. Frequently the recommendation is buttressed by comments on the saving in wages which would result from the use of the new technology. Two examples may be cited from among the dozens recorded. On 25 July 1929 the purchase, for £1607, of an electrically driven overhead crane for moving engine wheels and tyres was approved when it was pointed out that there would be a saving in wages of £250 per annum.[25] On 9 January 1930, the expenditure of £420. 10s. on a 12 inch stroke electrically driven slotting machine was approved when it was noted that it would replace three old ones and save £50 a year in wages.[26]

In the carriage and wagon department at the Plant the influence of tradition was very strong in the inter-war years. To Michael Harris 'it seemed remarkable that a LNER coach built in 1939–40 'should so closely resemble those made by the GNR in 1906'. The continuity of style was shown by the fact that when it no longer proved economic to build coach bodies completely of teak 'the LNER painted the post-war vehicles in imitation teak finish'.[27] One explanation why the replacement of the GNR by the LNER brought little apparent change was that Gresley had served as the Carriage and Wagon Superintendent on the GNR from 1905–1911 before he was appointed that company's Chief Mechanical Engineer. Thus he had overall responsibility for carriage stock between 1905 and 1941. Even though O.V.S. Bullied was appointed Assistant Carriage and Wagon Superintendent in 1919, with direct responsibility for the condition of the coaches and wagons, the master hand of Gresley was still very much in evidence.

In 1923 the extensive carriage shops of the Plant were essentially wood-working factories. The coach building and repair facilities were grouped in three areas. The offices were in a long building immediately adjacent to the station and the trimming shop continued on from the offices. Behind these buildings was the 384 feet long saw mill. Adjacent was the carriage building shop which was 300 feet by 199 feet and containing twelve roads. The smaller paint shop, 26 feet long and 180 feet wide, was a continuation of the carriage shop. Coach repairs were undertaken in the huge west carriage shop, 593 feet by 182 feet, alongside the river Don. It had space for the repair of 24 bogie coaches and 48 six-wheeler coaches. Finally, varnishing and light running repairs were handled in the north carriage shed.

In 1924, when the reorganization into the LNER had been largely settled, a carriage building programme was agreed. Priority was given to the building of four new train sets for the Anglo-Scottish traffic. Seven hundred new coaches were to be built for the suburban traffic, replacing five hundred four-wheel vehicles which were to be scrapped. Each of the new vehicles was to be fitted with electric lighting and steam heating.[28]

In was Gresley's policy that all express train coaches, as well as many others, should be articulated. In a lecture given in 1928 he explained how the policy came to be adopted. In about 1907, Lord Allerton, Chairman of the GNR, complained of the poor riding qualities of the six-wheeled East Coast route vehicles. It was uneconomic to scrap

THE INTER-WAR YEARS 1919–39

them at the time and so a decision was taken to articulate them. Thenceforward the policy of coach articulation was followed.[29]

One of the early achievements of the coach and wagon department at the Plant in the early days of the LNER was the construction of restaurant cars with electrically powered kitchens for the Flying Scotsman train sets. Power was obtained from Messrs J. Stone and Co.'s dynamos and batteries; but the kitchen car, which was flanked by the first and third class restaurant cars, was also equipped with plugs and sockets to enable electricity to be drawn from local supplies at the stations where the train stopped. This arrangement made possible the provision of hot meals and drinks soon after the 10 a.m. departures from King's Cross and Edinburgh.[30]

After 1928 annual construction of new coaches was divided between York, Doncaster and Dukinfield on the basis 200, 200 and 150. Doncaster specialized in the coaches for what were called, after 1935, the High Speed trains (foreshadowing by many years the BR variety!). The Plant works allocation of coach repairs in the late 1930s was 2722 a year, compared with York's 3566 and Dukinfield's 1806.[31] From the end of May 1939, on Gresley's recommendation, no further repairs were undertaken in the Dukinfield carriage shops, the work being redistributed between York and Doncaster. This reallocation increased the number of vehicles to be maintained in the Plant works from 7600 to 7800.[32]

In the blackest months of the depression some of the staff employed in the Carriage and Wagon Department were glad to be engaged in the manufacture of some new sleeping cars. These were each 66 feet 6 inches long and mounted on two four-wheeled bogies. Interior upholstery was in Stipplex Rexine. Each car had ten sleeping compartments, a shower bath compartment, toilets and a pantry.[33]

From 1929 to 1934 the policy of the LNER was to build new passenger carriages at a slower rate than that of the destruction of old ones. This was done as an economy measure and to save some revenue for dividends. The result in some areas of the rail network was a deterioration in the quality of services. A special committee report of 26 October 1933 revealed that at the end of 1932 there were 1300 fewer carriages and 23 400 fewer seats for passengers than there had been in 1924. The result was that:

> During the summer of 1933 serious difficulties were experienced in the matter of overcrowding in ordinary trains, and a shortage of stock for excursion purposes.[34]

Despite these warnings, on 1 January 1934 Gresley recommended further economies. The break up of carriages continued to exceed new construction. Furthermore 'some carriages were to be built according to modified standards'.[35] Not surprisingly, by late October 1934 it was reported that:

> The need for more carriage stock is being increasingly felt and it is becoming a matter of utmost difficulty to supply stock at busy periods to meet all demands. In many instances business has been turned away for want of sufficient suitable stock and further revenue is also lost.[36]

Meanwhile in the Plant works, Mr Raymond Selby, a skilled coach builder who had served his full seven years apprenticeship, was on a four day week. He was 'stood off' each week from 5.30 p.m. on Fridays to 8 a.m. on Tuesdays. On Monday afternoons in summer, instead of making the carriages the passengers needed, he was practising at cricket for the Plant works team.[37] Many other skilled men were similarly placed.

During the war years 1914–18 the wagon stocks of the railway companies were intensively used. The movement of freight was under the direction of the Railway Executive Committee. A common user scheme was in operation – though imperfectly – and the requirement was that records of the location of wagons had to be kept. Thus when the amalgamation of the railways under the four main-line companies came into effect on 1 January 1923 the whereabouts of all wagons should have been known. This was not the case with the LNER.

In February 1925 the Chief Goods Manager reported that, in connection with the common user scheme of wagons, 'a census had been taken periodically of the number of wagons belonging to each company'. Unfortunately a number of the LNER wagons could not be traced. He went on to confess:

> The number of LNER wagons still undiscovered is 519, of which 106 have not been seen since they were built, while 403 have not been through the shops for a number of years. It was, therefore, recommended that the Chief Mechanical Engineer should be authorised to write off as non-existent all wagons that have not been seen since 1913.[38]

Management shortcomings were not so serious as these figures might suggest. The 'ghostly' wagon element comprised but 0.016 per cent of the total stock of wagons of the LNER!

In addition, the Board of the newly formed company decided early in 1923 to commission Sir Vincent Raven, its Technical Adviser, to prepare a report on the physical assets of the LNER. Sir Vincent was also asked to make recommendations

34 Carr wagon works, inter-war period

35 Carr wagon works, inter-war period

on new building and repair requirements for locomotives and rolling stock in future years. The report revealed that in February 1923 there were 301 354 wagons belonging to the LNER. On the assumption of a twenty-five year life of each wagon, it was recommended that 12 054 vehicles should be built each year. The bulk of these would be built at Faverdale, but Doncaster would be responsible for 2000 of them. Doncaster would also have responsibility for the maintenance and repair of 41 576 of the total stock of wagons, repairing an average of 1653 of them each year. Carrying out this work at the Plant would involve the employment of 102 men in new construction and 411 in repairs.[39]

Sir Vincent Raven's recommendations were made on the assumption that the pattern of the LNER's freight business would continue broadly along the lines of the pre-1914 activity of the separate companies that merged in 1923. This proved not to be the case.

In its foundation year the LNER Board agreed to the building of 16 030 wagons of all types, 10 826 of which were replacements of scrapped vehicles and 4204 were net additions to stock. This substantial programme was justified in the light of the fact that there was very little new building during the war years. A part of the programme was contracted out to wagon building firms, but sufficient of the building was to be 'in house' to 'enable the company's workshops to be fully employed'.[40] By 1925, however, it became apparent that the volume of coal freight was unlikely to recover its pre-war level. Thousands of wagons were lying idle. In October 1925, therefore, the breaking up of 11 690 wagons was authorized, but new building was limited to 7392. The reduction by 4298 in the number of vehicles in service was declared to be justified 'in the existing state of trade'.[41] In 1927–8 there was a further net reduction of 2564 vehicles in the wagon fleet.[42] In 1929 it was again the case that the number of wagons built was less than those broken up: but the building programme included 1300 twenty-ton hopper wagons and other larger than usual capacity wagons, so that there was a net addition to the carrying capacity of 20 469 tons.[43]

These hopeful developments were nipped in the bud by the autumn of 1930 when the LNER began to feel the full brunt of the economic depression. On 22 October Gresley advised the Board that 'in view of the urgent need for economy' the ambitious programme for building larger capacity specialized wagons had been halted. Although work on building the new wagons had started it was not completed. Materials intended for the new programme were 'taken into store and utilized in connection with other wagons as opportunity offered'.[44]

In 1931–2 there were even more drastic reductions. 'Consequent upon the continued depression of trade and the pressing need for economy' the 8595 wagons broken up were replaced by only 2165 of new construction, leaving a net reduction in carrying capacity of 63 981 tons.[45]

By the autumn of 1933, however, there were some signs of economic recovery. Gresley advised the Board that it was essential that the wagon stock 'should not be reduced any further'. He believed that the improvement in merchandise traffic was likely to continue and 'an ample supply of wagons was necessary if the additional business was to be secured to rail in competition with road and water'.[46]

By 1935–7 the ill effects of the drastic reductions in the wagon fleet and carrying capacity of five years earlier were being experienced. 'Increased hiring' of wagons from private wagon firms was recommended in 1935 and in 1936 a supplementary wagon building programme in the LNER works at Doncaster and Faverdale was undertaken.[47]

By the summer of 1936 the Joint Locomotive and Traffic Committee was expressing increasing concern about the threat of road competition. Road hauliers' applications for licences from the traffic commissioners were contested. In recommending to the Board a supplementary programme of wagon building the Committee warned that 'having regard to the urgency of road competition ... it would be fatal to our case if traders were able to point to a shortage of railway wagons as an indication of the need for additional road transport'.[48] A year later the same committee admitted that there had been 'a diversion of traffic to road' in November and December 1936 through 'severe daily shortages of wagons'.[49] For this reason and for the additional reason that the government's rearmament programme was generating more traffic, additional building programmes were authorized in 1937 and 1938.

Right until the creation of the Railway Executive which took over the management of its assets in 1948, the wagon fleet of the LNER comprised an overwhelming majority of small capacity open vehicles. They were listed as 12 ton wagons, but rarely carried more than 6 tons of freight. On the four main-line companies progress in increasing capacity of wagons was extremely slow between the wars. The average wagon load rose from 5.41 tons in 1920 to 5.55 tons in 1938. Rapid progress in this direction only came after 1947 when average wagon loads rose from 6.6 tons to 16.14 tons in 1967.[50] For most workers at the Carr factory in the Plant works the implication was that before the Second World War the character of their employment changed very little. The large majority of the 500 or so employees were engaged either in building or repairing 12 ton wagons. Mechanization took place much more slowly than it did in locomotive building and repair.

George Mellor, who started work at the Plant in 1931 at Carhill, was taken to the vehicle shops in the works train known as the 'Paddy Train'. He believes it was originally so called 'because only Paddies would put up with it'. Working conditions were primitive. They had to supply their own candles. He often worked with a hammer and chisel when an oxy-acetylyne burner would have done the work in a fraction of the time.[51]

There were, however, some innovations. In January 1928 Nigel Gresley reported to the Locomotive and Traffic Committee that the railway companies had recently experimented with the carriage of freight in railway-owned containers of a capacity varying from 2½ to 4 tons. The containers were supplied to traders who forwarded them with their contents by rail to an individual consignee. The advantage of this method was that breakage of bulk would be avoided and the goods could be carried under seal, thus minimizing the risk of theft. With the approval of the Board, the Committee ordered the building of 450 containers in the company's workshops in 1928.[52]

In January 1932 'in order to meet future expansion and to secure the full advantages of the container as a means of competing with road transport', it was decided to build an additional 270 containers and to provide the same number of flat wagons for their conveyance.[53] 300 more containers were built in 1934.[54]

There was some expansion of specialized wagon construction in the later 1930s. To cater for the expanding fish trade 500 refrigerator vans were built in 1935-6. At the same time 400 insulated meat containers were constructed and more special tube wagons were built to carry the increased output from Stewarts and Lloyds British Tube works at Whifflet.[55]

Despite these enterprising responses to new opportunities for merchandise business, the LNER was ill equipped to meet the challenge of road haulage competition. The continuing overwhelming preponderance of small capacity wagons, many not fitted for continuous braking, and the presence on the rails of thousands of privately owned wagons of miscellaneous capacities and fitments, resulted in the average speed of freight trains being well below those of commercial road vehicles. Although the pattern of activity at the Carr shops in 1939 was little different from what it had been, significant and rapid changes were to come there after the Second World War.

As has been shown in chapter nine, only about one fifth of the employees at the Plant were organized in trade unions before the First World War, but that by 1919 the large majority were unionized. In the autumn of 1919 the coalition government decided that the wages of most railway workers – though not those of the footplatemen – would have to be reduced in order to reduce transport costs and make British goods more competitive on world markets. Wage cuts ranging from 1s. to 16s. on weekly wage packets of 55s. to 68s. were announced. When the NUR called a strike on 26 September 1919 most of its more than 3000 members at the Plant withdrew their labour. Clerks and craftsmen belonging to other trade societies carried on working during the nine days of the strike, but gave the NUR an assurance that they would not do work normally undertaken by its members.[56]

The NUR, ASLEF and RCA gained official recognition from the railway companies in 1920. These arrangements were given statutory recognition under the Railways Act 1921. Paragraphs 61 and 63 of the Act also gave statutory recognition of the negotiating machinery through which the working conditions for the large majority of railway workers would be settled. The stages of the machinery were: Local Departmental Committees; Sectional Councils; Central Wages Boards and National Wages Boards. However, these arrangements did not apply to workshop staff. Prolonged negotiations took place between the NUR and the representatives of the Amalgamated Engineering Union (AEU) and the twenty-seven other craft unions with members in the workshops, on what should be the basis of union representation in negotiations with employers. These differences were not settled until 15 August 1927 when an agreement was reached with the four main-line railway companies for the setting up of works and departmental line committees for shopmen, with an established procedure for settling disputes. Under clauses 13 and 14 of the agreement a National Railway Shopmen's Council (NRSC) was established to deal 'with any questions of a national character' concerning shop workers.

In the meantime the NUR had been campaigning for greater standardization of the rates of wages and conditions of service of workshop staff. Failing agreement with the AEU on a programme of action, the NUR applied to the Industrial Court (set up under the Industrial Courts Act, 1919) as arbitrator. In the Arbitration Court Award, Number 728, published on 8 July 1922, it was decided that 'a substantial advance' should be made towards standardization of working conditions. All workshops were classified into five groups and the rates of pay for each of the grades of employees were specified. The working week was to be of 47 hours; night work (between 6 p.m. and 6 a.m.) and overtime on day shifts was to be paid at time and a quarter rates. Overtime on night shifts qualified for time and a half, and Sunday duty, Good Friday and Christmas Day were paid at double rates.[57]

The directors of the LNER were not at first

THE INTER-WAR YEARS 1919–39

prepared to apply Arbitration Court Award No. 728 to the old GNR part of their railway. They exploited the fact that the craft unions advocated the payment of the district rate i.e. the rates of pay prevailing for craftsmen in their part of the country, while the NUR advocated the payment of the nationally agreed rates of the Award No. 728, to decline to pay the rates the Court had laid down. Thus Plant works plumbers were paid 41s. a week instead of the 46s. and cabinet makers 37s.–43s. instead of 46s. On 2 August 1923 C.T.C. Cramp, Industrial General Secretary of the NUR, addressed a crowded meeting of Doncaster railwaymen in the Corn Exchange. A resolution demanding the full application of the Court award was carried with acclamation.[58] Later in 1923 the LNER Board complied with the conditions of the Award.

On the occasion of the General Strike, called by the TUC in support of the miners in May 1926, the **Doncaster Gazette** reported that:

> The railway men came out, almost to a man, as did the workmen at the LNER Plant works, numbering about 6,000.

There had been some doubt as to whether the clerks at the railway station and at the Plant would support the strike call. In the event the booking clerks remained out while a small minority at the Plant defied the pickets.[59]

On Monday 10 May while the strike was still in progress the General Managers of the four main-line companies conferred together and agreed that:

> The railway companies ought not to be put under any general obligation to re-employ persons on strike except as and when they are actually required for the conduct of the business of the companies.[60]

Although this decision, and the other decisions of the meeting were not published at the time, local managers on the LNER were stating that 'the company could not find work for all who came out' and that it would be a requirement of some of those who applied for reinstatement that it would be on condition of a reduction in pay. On 13 May, the day after the official ending of the strike, the joint executive of the three rail unions then called on their members to continue the stoppage. This brought a quick response from the General Managers who met the union leaders that same afternoon and a general settlement of the dispute on the railways was reached on the following day. In the **Doncaster Gazette** R.L. Wedgwood, the General Manager of the LNER, published a denial that the company was either refusing reinstatement of the strikers or planning to reduce their wages.[61] This made possible a return to work at the Plant.

As a result of the sharp fall in mineral traffic and the loss of some merchandise and passenger traffic to the roads, net LNER revenue fell sharply after 1927, apart from the one year 1929. The figures were as follows:

1927 £12 184 478	1930 £11 168 050
1928 £11 277 759	1931 £ 9 424 610
1929 £13 061 250	1932 £ 7 166 858

Preferred Ordinary shareholders received a dividend of 3 per cent in 1929 but this fell to no more than ¼ per cent in 1928 and 1930, and to nothing at all from 1931–3.[62]

The result of this financial crisis of the company was that at the very first meeting of the National Railway Shopmen's Council, the representatives of the trade unions agreed to a 2½ per cent cut in the wages of shop workers from 13 August 1928. In return, the companies undertook to restore full time working wherever possible. Where this did not prove possible, and where full time working would involve extensive dismissals, Saturday working would be suspended.[63] In October 1929 the unions, influenced by that year's improved financial return, proposed the restoration of the cuts. The companies, in reply, claimed that it was premature to take such a step and it was therefore agreed that the cuts should continue until November 1930.[64]

By the autumn of 1930, however, the financial position of the railways had worsened. At a meeting of the RSNC Sir Ralph Wedgwood, for the companies, proposed further reduction in wages. These proposals were resisted by the unions which put forward a demand for twelve days' paid holiday each year for all shopworkers. After prolonged negotiations the RSNC agreed to reductions of 4⅙ per cent to operate from 28 March 1931.[65]

In 1932 the companies' fortunes being at their lowest ebb, Sir Ralph Wedgwood proposed that the 4⅙ per cent deduction should be replaced by one of 10 per cent. The unions refused to accept such a drastic cut in their members' wages.[66]

From the latter part of 1933 there was a marked improvement in the LNER's net revenues and at a meeting of the RSNC in June 1934 the unions demanded the discontinuance of the 4⅙ deduction from wages. However, the abolition of the cuts was a long drawn out process. In September 1934 they were brought down to 3 per cent. From January 1935 they were down to 2½ per cent. Then from June 1936 the 2½ per cent cut was replaced by one of 1½ per cent. It was not until July 1937, with rearmament and a revival of traffic improving the fortunes of the company, that all deductions ceased, eight and a half years after they had first been imposed.[67]

At the Plant works those who kept their jobs in the difficult times of the early 1930s were the relatively fortunate ones, even though their money wages were lower than they were a decade earlier and short time working was the rule rather than the exception. The retail price index fell by 13 per cent between 1929 and 1935 and to that extent it was easier to make ends meet. It was the men and women who were 'stood off' for weeks or months at a time that really felt the pinch. In November 1933 the **Doncaster Chronicle** reported that the erecting shops at the Plant 'had been idle for months'. Its leading article commented:

> For a long time the Plant works have been on short commons. Hundreds of men within recent years, have been dispensed with. For quite a long time the works have been idle on Saturdays.[68]

The consequences for the borough of Doncaster were serious. On 25 April 1932 Mr T. Harry Turner, Chief Chemist and Metallurgist of the LNER, told a meeting of the Rotary Club in Doncaster that he estimated that the railway 'paid nearly half the wages of all who lived in the Doncaster district'. The railway was the largest single ratepayer in the borough.[69] That there were cases of serious poverty in the town was manifested by the occasional sight of children running barefoot in the street, while others were buying 'specked' fruit at a penny a bag from the greengrocers.[70] At the same time there was a strong community spirit in the borough and efforts were made to help the unemployed workers from the Plant and the coal mines. A Doncaster Trades Council Unemployed Association formed by a group of Rotary Club members in August 1932 rapidly recruited over 400 members, including forty women.[71]

With the revival of the LNER's fortunes in the later 1930s the trade unions pressed their demand for some paid holidays for the staff at the Plant. The claim for twelve days' annual holiday with pay was made by the unions as early as 1930 and repeatedly pressed thereafter. Eventually it was agreed at a meeting of the RSNC in August 1937 that:

> After twelve months continuous service, one standard week's leave with pay at ordinary time rates, plus any War Wage, be allowed in respect of each calendar year, commencing 1938, to all employees under shop conditions.[72]

Until that time staff at the Plant works had days off on bank holidays and enforced time off without pay during the St Leger week in September. From 1938 they had two years in which to enjoy the privilege of a week's holiday with pay before the outbreak of war in September 1939.

THE PLANT WORKS IN THE SECOND WORLD WAR, 1939-45

In the autumn of 1938, when war clouds were gathering, the Minister of Transport established the Railway Executive Committee (REC) comprising the General Managers of the four main-line railway companies and the Vice-Chairman of the London Passenger Transport Board. When war was declared against Germany on 3 September 1939 the REC immediately assumed responsibility for the overall direction of railway services in Britain. The REC's functions were never clearly defined; they developed in response to changing circumstances. The objective, however, was to pool the country's railway resources so that they could be used to maximum effect in war time. The LNER Board, which continued to have direct responsibility for operations at the Plant works, was notified of the requirements of the REC, but, in turn, influenced REC decisions by indicating the extent it was able to meet the demands made upon it.[1]

The weaknesses of the legacy of the 'stop-go' economy of the LNER in the inter-war years were exposed under the challenge of war time transport requirements. In the winter of 1940–1 there was a severe shortage of wagons for the movement of essential freight. Two years later there was such a shortage of locomotives, nationwide, that between 1000 and 1500 train services a week were having to be cancelled.

During the war years the railways had to cope with a greatly increased volume of both passenger and freight traffic, without any significant increase in locomotive and rolling stock capacity. Between 1938 and 1944 passenger mileage travelled increased by 68 per cent and freight ton-mileage by nearly 50 per cent.[2]

These increases in demand for rail transport were caused by the necessity of diverting the exposed coastal traffic in coal on the important Newcastle–London route to the LNER rails; of shifting overseas trade outlets from east-coast to west-coast ports; of carrying freight on longer hauls than was normal in peace time and of carrying awkwardly shaped consignments such as aeroplane propellors. In addition it was government policy to reduce to the minimum importation of petroleum for use in motor vehicles and to encourage transport by steam railways supplied with domestically mined coal.

Railway passenger mileage grew through the need to transport evacuees and large numbers of service men and women.

The enlistment into the armed forces of one sixth of the railways' work force and the transfer of skilled craftsmen from the employment of the railway companies to armament factories created further problems. In February 1945 the REC estimated that there was a labour shortage of over 3700 men in the railway workshops.[3]

The pre-eminence of Sir Nigel Gresley as a locomotive engineer was recognized by the General Managers of the four main-line companies when they met in September 1938 for the first time as the Railway Executive Committee. They chose him to be the Chairman of the REC's Mechanical and Electrical Engineering Committee. But the new responsibilities entrusted to the LNER's Chief Mechanical Engineer did not detract from his involvement in the business of the Plant works. Nevertheless, Gresley must have found the restraints imposed by the REC in the early months of the war restrictive of his talents. The Ministry of Transport gave instructions to the REC that only freight or mixed traffic locomotives might be built for the duration of the war.[4] Although this directive was sometimes conveniently forgotten, it was not the only obstacle to the experimentation in locomotive design so dear to Gresley's heart. Materials and skilled labour were in short supply.

'Make do and mend' was the guiding principle for locomotive departments in the early life of the REC. On the day before the declaration of war the Committee recommended 'that plans should be agreed for the reconditioning of 100 condemned locomotives'. It was considered necessary 'to hold these in reserve to meet traffic requirements'. What was envisaged was that extra engine power would be required for operations in France. The LNER's contribution was the reconditioning of twenty-five locomotives previously designated for scrapping, with the promise of more such conversions by the end of 1939.[5] The policy of delaying the scrapping of locomotives as long as possible was continued to the end of the war.

To meet the requirements of the traffic with restricted locomotive power more carriages were added to passenger trains and more wagons to freight trains. The average load per passenger train, swollen by overcrowding as well as by the attachment of extra carriages, was, by 1943, double that of the pre-war level. Over the same period freight train loads per train mile rose from 121.9 tons to 153.6 tons. This more intensive use of locomotives, already employed for a longer than usual life, resulted in 'repairs having to be carried out with the utmost speed, often under very difficult conditions'.[6] The REC calculated that in 1942 locomotives spent 11 per cent more hours in traffic than they did in 1938, yet the number of locomotives available was less than 1 per cent more than it was in that last year of peace. Inevitably heavy repairs of the locomotive stock were one fifth greater than they were in pre-war days and repairs of all kinds took up 90 per cent of the man-hours engaged in all locomotive construction and repair work.

One reason for the acute shortage of engine power on the LNER in the war years was that some of the company's stock had been shipped abroad to work on the Haifa–Beirut–Tripoli line.[7] As early as November 1939 the LNER was asked by the REC to supply three hundred 2–8–0 type locomotives to be delivered in France at the rate of forty engines a month, starting from 1 January 1940.[8]

In August 1939 when war was imminent, the War Office issued instructions that it would require 300 new engines for main-line work. They were to be unpretentious 'work horses' the majority 'suitable for hauling 1000 ton trains over easy gradients at comparatively low speeds'. The LNER allocation was one third of this order. The engines would be of the 02 type 2–8–0s with 4 feet 8 inch driving wheels. When the four companies' representatives met in the REC they had to confess that 'owing to shortage of labour' they could not build the locomotives in their own works but would have to place orders with contractors. However, these new engines 'were built on designs agreed by the LNER'. Too many blue collar workers at the Plant had enlisted with the armed forces or found other armament factory jobs to make locomotive building possible, at least for the time being. But for a while there was plenty of work for the draughtsmen.[9]

Later in 1939 the LNER undertook to build twenty-five of the 2–8–0 type locomotives in their own works, most of them at Doncaster.[10] These wartime 'Austerity' type locomotives embodied the maximum economy in the use of scarce materials as well as simplicity in design and maintenance.

Sir Nigel Gresley's health deteroriated in 1940 and the early part of 1941. He was present at York on 19 February 1941 for the unveiling of the new V4 2–6–2 **Bantam Cock** and the electric locomotive No. 6701, but on Saturday 5 April that year he died suddenly of a heart attack at his home, Walton House, Hertford. He was within three months of his sixty-fifth birthday and within six months of completing thirty years service as Chief Mechanical Engineer, first on the Great Northern and then on the London and North Eastern railways. Sir Nigel lived at Doncaster for eighteen years and always took a keen interest in the Plant works and its staff. By his own request friends who would have sent flowers at his funeral were asked instead to send donations to the Railway Benevolent Institution.[11]

Gresley's successor was Edward Thompson who had spent most of his working life with the NER and then the LNER. In 1909 he was appointed Assistant Divisional Locomotive Superintendent at Gateshead. His later experience included taking charge of the carriage and wagon department at Doncaster as well as of similar departments at York and Shildon. Between 1927 and 1933 he was Assistant Mechanical Engineer at Stratford. This was followed by five years as Mechanical Engineer at Darlington before he succeeded R.A. Thorn at Doncaster in 1938 as Mechanical Engineer, Southern Area (Western) of the LNER.[12]

In some ways Thompson's appointment as Chief Mechanical Engineer of the LNER in 1941 suited the requirements of the time. In contrast with Gresley, whose love of experimentation and innovation could sometimes be regarded as extravagant, Thompson was a careful economically minded man. In the view of C.J. Allen 'everything that would play a part in reducing maintenance costs had always been his aim'.[13] This fitted in well with the War Department's needs for Austerity locomotives which were simple and inexpensive to maintain. However, Thompson had not enjoyed good relationships with his predecessor. It has been said that 'antipathy was mutual, leading to some tense

THE PLANT WORKS IN THE SECOND WORLD WAR, 1939–45

encounters between the two men'. Those employed at the Plant works were amazed to see how much was done after April 1941 to erase the distinctive achievements of Nigel Gresley. All men who had been closely associated with him were removed to other positions. Details of design of the A4 Pacific and other locomotives were altered.[14]

Nevertheless, Thompson ensured that the 2–6–0 mixed traffic engines and the 2–8–0 heavy freight engines built in 1941–3 and much in demand for heavy duty War Office work were produced on time. The position at the end of 1944 was that the LNER had 6609 engines compared with 6470 at the outbreak of war. The small increase was more than accounted for by the addition of a hundred and thirteen mixed traffic engines and fifty-eight of the heavy freight variety.[15]

In addition to the repair work on British-made locomotives which dominated activity at the Plant works, there was the maintenance and repair of the Austerity type locomotives on loan from the USA. The first batch of ninety of these arrived in April 1943.

Soon after the outbreak of war an acute shortage of wagons was experienced on the rail networks contolled by the REC. On 14 March 1940 the secretary of Imperial Chemical Industries (ICI) wrote to the REC in respect of the dispatch of its freight from Billingham, Northwich and Middlewich. He deplored the fact that:

> On very many occasions we have had to cease loading by rail in spite of the fact that we have been in arrears with our orders to the extent of upwards of 5,000 tons at the works concerned and have had to curtail manufacturing output.

Although the government was urging business firms to economize in the use of petrol, ICI had been obliged to collect and deliver freight with its own vehicles.[16] This was just one example of the wagon shortages experienced nationwide.

Wagon shortages were due to the diverson of traffic flows from sea to rail, mentioned earlier in this chapter; to the great increase in demand for freight movement linked with military operations overseas; to the legacy of cut-backs in the depression years of the 1930s and to a Ministry of Transport instruction to the REC in April 1940 that railway workshops should reduce their consumption of steel by a quarter.[17] A further cause of the bottleneck in the supply of wagons was the survival of primitive methods of manufacture and repair of wagons. Frank Cresswell, who was employed at the Carr wagon works in the Plant during the war, complained that he was still using 'hammer and chisel' when machine tools would have enabled him to complete repairs more speedily.[18] When complaints were made at a meeting of the REC about the time taken in repairing wagons in the LNER workshops LNER management responded by ordering new machinery to the value of £743 from Messrs Fullerton, Hodgart and Barclay Ltd.[19]

To simplify wagon use in wartime all private owners wagons were requisitioned by the Minister of Transport. The common user scheme in operation before 1939 was modified to permit the speedier movement of the wagon stock. Individual number-taking at exchange points was replaced by bulk number taking.[20]

To 'squeeze a quart into a pint pot', low capacity wagons were required to take greater loads. In the winter of 1940–41 the staff at the Carr works were busy carrying out an instruction issued by the REC in November:

> Existing 12 ton open wagons, built to 1923 and subsequent specifications, to be up-plated to carry 13 tons.[21]

36 Edward Thompson, Chief Mechanical Engineer, 1941–6

In the war years Doncaster specialized in the construction of covered goods wagons; 13 ton hoppered, bottom door, mineral wagons; 20 ton double bolster wagons and 20 ton plate, or long low, wagons. However, the bulk of the new building was of the traditional 13 ton open goods wagons.[22]

There were a number of reasons why the carriage works were less busy in the war years than they were in 1938. In April 1945 the REC summed up the situation when it reported that 'little new building has been possible'. At the end of the war there were 4575 fewer passenger vehicles in service than there had been when hostilities began. The cut back in restaurant car services was severe. At the outbreak of war all restaurant car services were withdrawn. Shortly afterwards they were restored on a restricted basis, only to be withdrawn completely in April 1944 to release every possible source for the D Day landings. Not surprisingly, by midsummer 1944 only sixty-five restaurant car services were in operation compared with 870 in midsummer 1939. Although new passenger carriage construction came to a halt in the war years, those employed at the Plant had some work, though on a much reduced scale, repairing vehicles and converting some carriages into ambulances.[23]

In the First World War the workshops of the larger railway companies had played a key role in the manufacture of weapons and munitions. It is not, therefore, surprising that those government departments primarily concerned with the war effort from 1939–45 turned to the REC for its co-operation in using the railway companies' equipment and skilled manpower to manufacture the weapons of war.

In the first months of the war the REC considered a request from the Minister of Transport, Ewan Wallace, that the railway companies should make some of their factories available for the production of war materials. The Committee was not to be rushed into any hasty response to the request. It decided that 'the whole question needed some co-ordination'. It was agreed that Sir Ralph Wedgwood, the Chairman, should advise the Minister of Transport that the REC did not propose to proceed to the further allocation of workshop capacity 'until the position had been cleared up'.[24] These hesitations were soon overcome, since a month later, the LNER, through the REC, agreed to make the Dukinfield wagon shops available for the use of the Ministry of Supply.[25] In April the Plant works began the manufacture of tank components and thousands of parts of Hurricane, Spitfire, Tornado and Catalina aircraft.[26] From August 1940, when he was appointed Minister of Aircraft Production, Lord Beaverbrook pressed for the greater use of the railway workshops. In November 1940 the REC expressed its willingness to devote more workshop space to the production of military aircraft.[27] At the Plant works one of the most common early war time tasks was the manufacture of wings and other parts of Horsa gliders which were to be used in D Day landings in France. This work was first allocated in August 1940.[28]

Although in the early weeks of the war the emphasis of activity at the Plant was on the manufacture of tank, gun and aircraft parts, it was not long before the Ministry of Supply was pressing for the production of entire tanks. On 3 July 1940, therefore, the REC agreed to this request 'on condition that essential work on locomotives, wagons and coaches was provided for'.[29] Despite this agreement in principle, it was generally only the hulls of tanks that were erected at Doncaster.

In some cases in the machine shop war work was being done in the same bays alongside railway work. Staff and machines were switched from one to the other use as occasion demanded. Late in November 1942, however, the Board of the LNER agreed to lease to Briggs Motor Bodies Ltd the South Wagon repair shop for the manufacture and repair of aircraft parts.[30]

The demand for labour resulting from war production in the railway workshops increased steadily through 1940 and 1941. The number of established staff of the LNER engaged on war work rose from 9113 on 5 October 1940 to 14 285 on 17 May 1941 when it was more than one fifth of the staff employed by the company. The transfer of skilled or semi-skilled men often left gaps in the workshops' labour force. In June 1941, for example, the company agreed to 'liberate' 750 men to the Ministry of Aircraft Production to work on repairing damaged aircraft.[31]

In July 1940 the REC read letters from the First Lord of the Admiralty and the Ministries of Supply and Aircraft Production pointing out that there was an immediate need for skilled workmen in many factories 'to bring into production plant recently installed or still idle during night shifts'. The directors of the railway companies were urged to 'upgrade men of less experience'. The ministers' letters were passed on to the RSNC which urged that any additional government work should be undertaken in the railway workshops in order to minimize the transfer of skilled men elsewhere. It also advised that:

> To enable the request of the government to be given effect to it was necessary to resort to the employment of women in the railway workshops to a much greater extent than is normally the case.[32]

This policy was followed with vigour. By August 1942 about 28 000 women were on the books of the

THE PLANT WORKS IN THE SECOND WORLD WAR, 1939–45

LNER with 5500 of them employed in the company's workshops.[33] The majority of the workshop women were in unskilled jobs. Nevertheless, with the passing of time more and more semi-skilled and skilled jobs were performed by women. At a Mayoral luncheon held in the Doncaster Mansion House on 9 November 1944, Edward Thompson, the Chief Mechanical Engineer of the LNER, pointed out that in the Plant works machine shop alone 183 of the work force of 585 were women. They were helping the men on the 'highest class machinery'.[34] Far more women were employed in the other shops including the carriage shops, the Carr locomotive shed, the boiler shop, iron foundry, paint shop and stores. Exact figures of these other women employed are not available but it can be estimated that at least an eighth of the LNER's workshop women were working at Doncaster. So many women were involved that in August 1942 the LNER Board decided to set up a Women's Welfare Organization with the appointment for each of the three main areas of the company's network – the Southern, the North Eastern and the Scottish – a Welfare Supervisor. The woman appointed for the Southern Area (which included Doncaster) was Miss C.J. Thallon, MA.[35] Her starting salary was £400 a year; but it may be regarded as an indication of how much her work was appreciated that this was raised to £450 a year in May 1943.[36]

In response to notices placed in Doncaster local newspapers in February 1990 more than two dozen women who had been employed in the Plant works between 1939–45 contacted the Doncaster Public Library to record their work experience in those years. The following paragraphs are based on their accounts which give more life and colour to add to the official records.

Most of the women came to the Plant works because they had received 'call up' papers in which they were offered the alternative of joining the armed forces or doing war work in a factory. Not surprisingly many, like Mesdames Cant, Eastwood, Freeman, Quarry, Sains, Smith, Sullivan, West and White, chose the nearby Plant works with which they were familiar, and which would enable them to keep in touch with their families, rather than the more uncertain future with the armed forces. Some were evacuees from London, as was Mrs D. Mason. Some had moved from other industrial work in the district as had Mrs D. Harrison and L. Roe. Women who had been in jobs which were not classified as of national importance were also obliged to move. Mrs D. Smith had to give up her job in a photographic shop and Mrs M. Sains was not allowed to carry on being an usherette in a cinema.

When they moved into the works they were given jobs in all the different departments and shops. Mrs M.C. Harris was already employed in

37 Carriage varnishing, Second World War

38 Mrs Nancy Sullivan who worked as a driller in D2 shop pictured with Queen Elizabeth and Mr Arthur Peppercorn

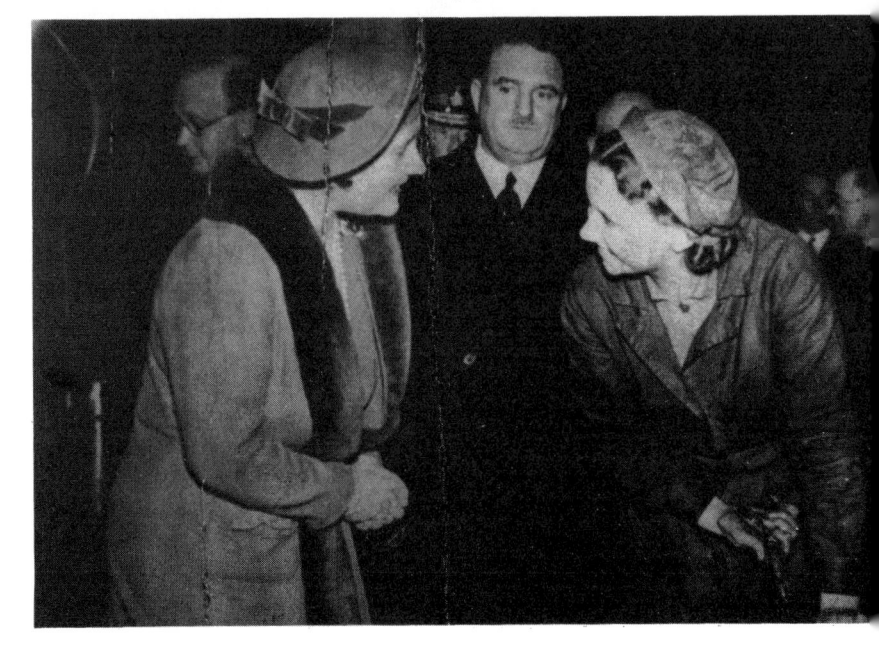

the carriage works as a trimmer and seamstress before the war. She carried on in the same occupation for a time after September 1939, but then made covers out of green waterproof materials for aircraft engines. Mesdames Brandon, Quarry and West worked with drop hammers and steam hammers in the forge. Mrs Hilda Eastwood joined a large group of women in the paint shop and is shown with her fellow workers in figure 40. The boiler shop provided employment for Mrs Irene Fisher as driver of a 12 ton crane, all the movements of which were directed by sign language. Mrs I. Freeman also worked in the boiler shop. She drilled holes in steel tube plates for steam engines, but when she accidentally lost half her hair through it being caught in the drilling machine, and found she would be given no compensation, she asked to be moved to another job. She was transferred to crane driving in the same shop, a task which required great care and accuracy, since it involved lifting sheets of steel over iron rollers to make into the shape of a boiler. Mrs White was also a driver of an overhead crane lifting heavy pistons and other engine parts.

Those who were engaged exclusively on war work included Mrs M. Sains who worked on a bench assembly line making parts of aircraft wings and Mrs Grace Stephenson who was also employed in aircraft assembly. In figure 42 she is shown talking to King George VI when he visited the Plant works in 1942.

Locomotive repairs occupied the largest single group of workers in the Plant during the war years and many women were employed either directly or indirectly in this work. Mrs I. Cant began her war time career in the Crimpsall, doing riveting jobs on engines. Mrs H. Kemp cleaned axle boxes. Mrs D. Mason removed buffers from engines undergoing

39 Mrs Harrison and her fellow workers

40 Mrs Hilda Eastwood with fellow paintshop workers

THE PLANT WORKS IN THE SECOND WORLD WAR, 1939–45

repair. Mrs D. Harrison worked on a capstan lathe making rivets, bolts and other parts for locomotives. Mrs E.M. Welbourne, was similarly employed. Mrs N. Sullivan drilled parts for the repair of engines which had been damaged in raids. Later she drilled armour plating for tanks.

While most women had to learn on the job, Mrs L. Roe attended a one year engineering course at Sheffield before coming to the Carr Loco Sheds where she maintained and repaired engine lubricating systems.

Dozens of women, like Mrs D. Smith, were employed in washing carriages. There were separate gangs for washing carriage exteriors, interior ceilings and woodwork and rexine seats.

Although the work at the Plant was arduous and the surroundings were dirty and noisy, many of the women had a strong sense of purpose. Many, like Mrs Hilda Eastwood, had brothers or husbands who were serving with the armed forces overseas. There was a strong sense of comradeship. Mrs Brandon's job in the forge she described 'as the hardest and heaviest of women's jobs'. But she conceded that 'the time spent there was fun, with a great feeling of friendship.' Mrs Quarry, who also worked in the forge, endorsed these views. She said there was 'great comradeship between the women'. In the B shop working on a lathe machine Mrs E.M. Welbourne found 'there was a great camaraderie'.

Although Mrs I. Fisher found that the man whose crane she worked in the boiler shop objected at first to her taking over his job, there was 'great comradeship among the ladies'. Working in the west carriage shop as a fitter's mate Mrs D. Mason found it 'hard, heavy, dirty work'. She nevertheless enjoyed it.

41 *Manufacture of glider wings, Second World War*

42 *Mrs G. Stephenson talking to King George VI*

71

The women worked twelve hour shifts, many either working a day shift from 6 a.m. to 6 p.m. or a night shift from 6 p.m. to 6 a.m. In the boiler shops the shifts were from 8 a.m. to 5 p.m. but overtime was often worked from 5–7.30 p.m. from Mondays to Thursdays inclusive. Because day shift hours provided few opportunities for shopping, night shift women would help their mates by shopping for them on their way in to work.

There was a canteen in Kirk Street and meals were available at St James' Church Hall. In the lunch hour ENSA concerts were sometimes laid on in these places and whether it was Tommy Handley or Vera Lynn, or less celebrated performers, the entertainment provided was much appreciated. When there was no concert on offer some women such as Mrs Fisher used the brazier fire to boil water for tea and to make toast.

It may be noticed that the women from the paint shop shown in figure 40 were wearing a great variety of overalls. This was because they had to buy their own. The REC had a long drawn out battle with the Ministry of War Transport on which items of workers' clothing were to be regarded as essential for protection against injury and dirt. Eventually, in August 1941 the Ministry conceded that industrial gloves, boiler suits, 'bib and brace overalls of plain or twill weave cotton material', as well as clogs and certain types of headwear could be allowed for purchase without the usual clothing ration tickets. However the main concern of the LNER board was to make sure that station and traffic staff did not have to surrender ration tickets in exchange for their uniforms. There is little evidence that they gave much attention to the needs of the workshop staff for protective clothing.[37]

Mrs L. Roe who was employed at the Carr loco sheds on engine lubrication systems was exceptional in reporting that 'the wages of women employed on this job were equal to the men's'. The women clerks employed at the Plant, in common with others in booking offices throughout the railway network, were paid at less than the men's rate. In an appeal to the Railway Staff National Tribunal (RSNT) in 1942 the RCA had failed to get this practice altered. In January 1944 Reg Sorensen, Labour MP for Leyton West, raised the question in the Commons. On 16 February 1944 the Staff Committee of the REC replied that there was 'no real justification' for equal pay since for many years agreements had been in operation with the unions accepting lower pay for women clerks. Any change in this practice in the war period would 'inevitably result in anomalies'.[38]

The question of the rates of pay of other women taken into the railway service during the war emergency was discussed in the RNSC in August 1940. An agreement made between the AEU and the REC was taken as a precedent and guide. It was decided that where women were employed on work hitherto performed by adult men they might achieve equal pay with men after thirty-two weeks, provided they were able to carry out the work 'without additional supervision or assistance'.[39] Where piece work payments were the rule the same requirement of a thirty-two week 'probationary' period would apply. In his report to the AGM of the NUR in July 1942 John Marchbank the General Secretary, pointed out that some of the women who were employed in the workshops were performing the whole of the duties of the male post after a very short period of training. He contended that 'they ought not to have to wait 32 weeks before receiving the full male rate of pay'. It was also grossly unfair that in some cases after completing their thirty-two week probationary period, they were moved to another job and required to serve a further thirty-two week period of probation.[40] A year later Marchbank's successor, John Benstead, reported that after negotiation the REC had agreed to eliminate the requirement of a second probationary period.[41] There was one respect in which women never caught up with men. In early war time, bonuses, awarded with the intention of offsetting rises in the cost of living, were smaller for women than for men. Later in the war, equal bonus increases were granted to men and women; but at the armistice the total bonus given men was greater than that received by women.

At the Plant a great deal of the repair work especially of wagons took place in the open air and in peace time the sidings and yards were flood lit in the winter months to allow work to continue. The introduction of the blackout at the outbreak of war clearly made the continuation of outdoor repairs far more difficult. In September 1939 Sir Nigel Gresley reported to the REC that 'a number of minor accidents had occurred owing to the absence of light outside the railway workshops'. The REC quickly grasped that this was a serious problem. At its meeting on 5 October 1940 it was agreed that the Minister of Transport be asked to allow Category 'C' lighting to be installed in yards outside carriage and wagon workshops, subject to arrangements being made for adequate control from outside points. The Minister of Transport agreed to these restricted lighting arrangements, Category 'C' lighting being defined as that which should 'not be visible at a distance of more than ten miles on a clear night'.[42]

The introduction of double summer time from Sunday 4 May 1941 also eased conditions for outdoor working.

Apart from the disastrous fire which destroyed the carriage works on 21 December 1940 and which was not due to enemy action, the Plant works

THE PLANT WORKS IN THE SECOND WORLD WAR, 1939-45

suffered little damage from German bombing during the war. But the Germans sent nuisance raiders round the big towns with the object of interrupting production. At first the staff at the Plant took shelter when the 'Alert' signal was sounded and only resumed work at the 'All Clear'. Since this caused considerable disruption of repair and construction work the REC decided on 30 September 1940 that 'staff should continue at work during air raids until danger is imminent', an arrangement to which the trade unions agreed shortly afterwards.[43] However this made more urgent the appointment of aircraft spotters. A notice was displayed at all key points in the Plant asking for volunteers to be trained in aircraft identification but warning that it was a dangerous and hazardous occupation. Fourteen men applied. Mr J. Auckland was sent to London to attend a fortnight's course on aircraft identification and on his return gave a week's instruction to the other volunteers. Sixty feet up on the top of the boiler shop roof an observation post of 1 inch thick steel was built to accommodate the spotters when enemy aircraft were in the neighbourhood.

At that time RAF Hampden bombers from the nearby Finningly airfield were used to intercept enemy 'nuisance' bombers and other aircraft. One bright moonlight night Harry Procter and his fellow 'spotter' sighted a low flying aircraft approaching. Procter's mate shouted 'Hampden bomber' but Procter, who had better eyesight, called out 'Hampden be buggered, it's a Heinkel!'. Shortly afterwards the Heinkel dropped two parachute mines, one of which landed and exploded on a housing estate at the top of Sandford Road near the Tickhill Hospital and not far also from the Carr Loco Sheds. This bomb caused the largest number of fatalities in the Doncaster area in the Second World War.[44]

Some women were employed as air raid wardens and fire watchers. Mrs Eastwood returned to the Plant two nights a week on fire-watching duties. In the Doncaster area as a whole there were 400 women fire guards out of a total for the rota of about 3000. The cost of the scheme was borne by the employer – including the LNER – and the fire-watchers were paid £4 weekly each in 1943.[45]

At 2.41 a.m. on 7 May 1945 the German High Command surrendered to the Allied commanders. The war in Europe was over. On 8 and 9 May the Plant works was closed in celebration. Huge bonfires were lit in many parts of Doncaster. Miraculously shopkeepers produced fireworks to add to the celebrations. Firewatching duties came to an end.[46]

Press advertisements from May 1943 onwards were urging workers as 'a war time measure' to take 'Stay at home holidays'. Readers were advised: 'But do not travel. The railways are already loaded to capacity.'[47] After VE Day such advice was no longer necessary. For the first time since 1937, on 23 June 1945, the LNER ran special trains to Blackpool for Plant workers to start a week's holiday. A man on the platform told one of the women from the paint shop, who was leaning out of the window, that the carriage had a 'magnificent gloss'. She replied that the carriage was not new – she had helped to clean the coaches.[48] Before many more weeks had passed she had to leave the Plant where peacetime activities were gradually restored.

73

12

FROM NATIONALIZATION TO THE BEECHING PLAN, 1948-62

When the war in Europe ended on 12 May 1945 the Prime Minister, Winston Churchill, hoped that by calling an early general election he and his party would secure a handsome Parliamentary majority. In the event, when the people of Britain went to the polls on Thursday 5 July, they voted decisively for the Labour Party which secured 393 seats and a large working majority in the Commons. Evelyn Walkden, of the Railway Clerks' Association, was elected Labour MP for Doncaster with a majority of 23 051.

The Labour Party's election manifesto **Let us Face the Future** promised a policy of 'public ownership of inland transport and co-ordination of services by road, rail and canal'. There was, however, a gap in time of two and a half years before these policies were applied through the Transport Act of 1947 which came into operation on 1 January 1948. During this interim the REC and the four main-line companies continued to function.

During the war an unusually large proportion of the railways' locomotives, passenger carriages and freight wagons had been kept in service long after the usual time for their destruction and replacement. In September 1947 39.3 per cent of the companies' locomotives were over thirty-five years old – the normal age for scrapping. 9.8 per cent of the railway companies' wagons and 50.1 per cent of the privately owned wagons, requisitioned by the REC for the duration of the war, were 'time expired'. Nearly a quarter of the passenger carriages had been built before 1912.[1] These were the grounds for the statement by Christopher Savage that:

The problems of restoration and organisation which faced British inland transport when the war ended were scarcely less formidable than the transport problems encountered in the most difficult war years.[2]

The task of making good the huge backlog in construction and repair work was tackled energetically in 1946 and 1947. In a report to the Ministry of Transport in August 1947 the REC recommended that at least 700 of the over-age locomotives should be replaced in the ensuing five years. It is estimated that, of that total, 352 steam locomotives and 26 diesels (chassis and body only) could be built in the railway workshops and the remainder would need to be provided by 'outside' contractors.[3]

Despite the difficulties caused by a shortage of steel and of skilled manpower, Doncaster made an important contribution to both the construction and repair of locomotives during these two years. In 1946 twelve new 0.6 2–8–0 type and six 4–6–2 type Pacific engines were built while the average weekly rate of repaired locomotives was 10.6 for heavy repairs and 3.2 for light repairs, compared with 9.9 and 3.0 respectively in 1938. New building was stepped up to forty in 1948. On 22 May 1946 the two thousandth locomotive to be built at the Doncaster works passed into traffic. It was the first of the abovementioned A2 Pacifics designed by Edward Thompson and carried his name. He retired later that year to be succeeded by A.H. Peppercorn the last of the LNER's Chief Mechanical Engineers.[4]

Before nationalization the Locomotive Commit-

FROM NATIONALIZATION TO THE BEECHING PLAN, 1948–62

tee of the LNER ordered an enquiry into progress towards standardization of locomotive design. The report, **Standardization of Locomotives of the LNER**, was presented to the Board in February 1946. Shortages of materials and the need to give priority to the backlog of repairs to old engines prevented the implementation of most of these recommendations before the Railway Executive replaced the LNER in January 1948.[5]

In the immediate post-war years domestic householders depended very largely on the supply of coal and its derivatives for the heating of their homes. There was a considerable intensification of this demand in the early months of 1946 and 1947,

43 Arthur Henry Peppercorn, Chief Mechanical Engineer, 1946–9

when there were bouts of exceptionally cold weather. Early in 1947 the Ministry of Transport urged the railway companies to adopt a policy of converting their steam locomotives from coal burning to oil burning. Early in July 1947 the joint Locomotive and Traffic Committee of the LNER authorized the expenditure of £4439 at Doncaster on the necessary equipment for oil fuel installation and the necessary adaptation, over an extended period of time, of coal burning locomotives.[6] A total of ninety-three locomotives, nationwide, had been converted by May 1948 when the Ministry of Transport informed the Railway Executive that the government had decided to abandon the conversion scheme. Balance of payments problems, aggravated by the cost of oil imports, now took precedence over economies in coal consumption. The RE replied that the re-conversion could not be carried out in the busy summer season, but that it could be done in the autumn and winter, provided the government met the costs.[7]

The fuel crisis in February 1947, following one of the harshest winters on record, exposed the severe weaknesses in the wagon supply situation. The total number of railway-owned and requisitioned wagons awaiting repair rose from some 140 000 (11 per cent) at the end of 1946 to 203 000 (16.6 per cent) by September 1947. The crisis in wagon supply was aggravated by the fact that the 544 000 private owners' wagons were 'markedly inferior to the railway's own wagon fleet', with grease, instead of oil, axle-boxes, general absence of fitments for continuous braking, low capacity and a great variety of design.[8] To deal with the emergency a Special Wagon Repairs Committee of the REC was set up in October 1947 under the able chairmanship of R.A. ('Robin') Riddles. It mobilized extra repairs capacity and succeeded in reducing the number of wagons under or awaiting repair by 20 per cent in three months.[9] In 1947 the contribution towards meeting the crisis made by the 1968 strong artisan staff employed in the Carr wagon works and the carriage works was the heavy repair of 2849 wagons and the light repair of a further 19 539.[10]

44 Carriage body shop after fire, December 1940

FROM NATIONALIZATION TO THE BEECHING PLAN, 1948–62

A large part of the carriage building shops at the Plant was destroyed by the fire of 21 December 1940. The body-building shop, sawmill, carriage shop, stores and locomotive joiners shop were complete write-offs. In September 1946 the LNER Board decided to take the advice of the Civil Engineer and Chief Mechanical Engineer and use the opportunity caused by the destruction of the fire to install the most modern equipment such as woodworking machines in the sawmill, cranes and up-to-date machinery in the building shop, hair teaseling and carpet cleaning shops. The sleeping car and bedding shop were housed in a separate building already in existence. Although the estimate for all this work was £247 517 and exceeded the £186 840 insurance paid for the fire damage, it was regarded as worthwhile in order to have up-to-date carriage building and repairing facilities.[11]

In the light of the severe disruption to normal working caused by the aftermath of the fire the achievement of the Carriage Department in completing eighteen heavy and twenty-seven light repairs to carriages of various kinds in 1946 was very commendable. In addition a Post Office van, two bread vans and two buffet lounges were constructed.[12]

In the words of Alfred Barnes, the Minister of Transport in Attlee's government after 1945, the purpose of the Transport Act of 1947 was 'to consolidate the various elements of transport into a single whole which would operate as a non-profit making utility service at the least real cost to trade, industry and the travelling public'.[13] In order to achieve this objective centralized control of the work of the five executives – one each for railways, roads, docks and inland waterways, London Transport and hotels – was regarded as imperative. Under Sir Eustace Missenden, Chairman of the Railway Executive, R.A. Riddles had responsibility for mechanical and electrical engineering and motive power. Riddles was a strong advocate of the policy of standardizing the design and manufacture of locomotives and rolling stock.

45 Rebuilding new body shop, carriage works, 1947

46 View of works from power house, 1946

47 General view of iron foundry (left) and boiler shop (right), 1946

As 1948 was an important turning point in the history of the British railway industry and of the Doncaster Plant works it is worthwhile to take a 'bird's eye view' of the location of the shops and the deployment of the staff to see how well they were placed to meet the new demands which would be made upon them. Figure 48 shows the main shops while figure 49 shows the location of the Carr Carriage and Wagon shops, about a mile and a half to the south of the railway station. Table 3 shows the numbers of persons employed in the main works in December 1948.

TABLE 3

SHOPS	FOREMEN	EXAMINERS	CLERICAL	CHARGE HANDS	ARTISANS	TOTAL
Boiler	8		7	33	537	570
Brass foundry	1		1	1	33	34
Bricklayers	1		1	3	94	97
Electrical	1			4	41	45
Iron foundry	3		1	9	76	85
Joinery	1		2	2	68	70
Loco. repairs	12	9	12	70	1007	1077
Machine	6		7	42	488	530
Millwrights	2		1	7	59	66
New engine erecting			1	3	78	81
Outside material section	1		2		3	3
Paint	1		1	5	41	46
Pattern	1			2	28	30
Smithy	3		2	6	202	208
Tinsmiths	1		3		26	29
Yard	1		2	4	210	214
	43	9	43	191	2991	3182

TOTAL: SUPERVISORY AND CLERICAL .... **95**   TOTAL: BLUE COLLAR **3182**

GRAND TOTAL: 3277

Source: Railway Executive, Report of the Locomotive Works Organization Committee, December 1948 (PRO AN 88/114)

48 THE MAIN SHOPS OF THE PLANT

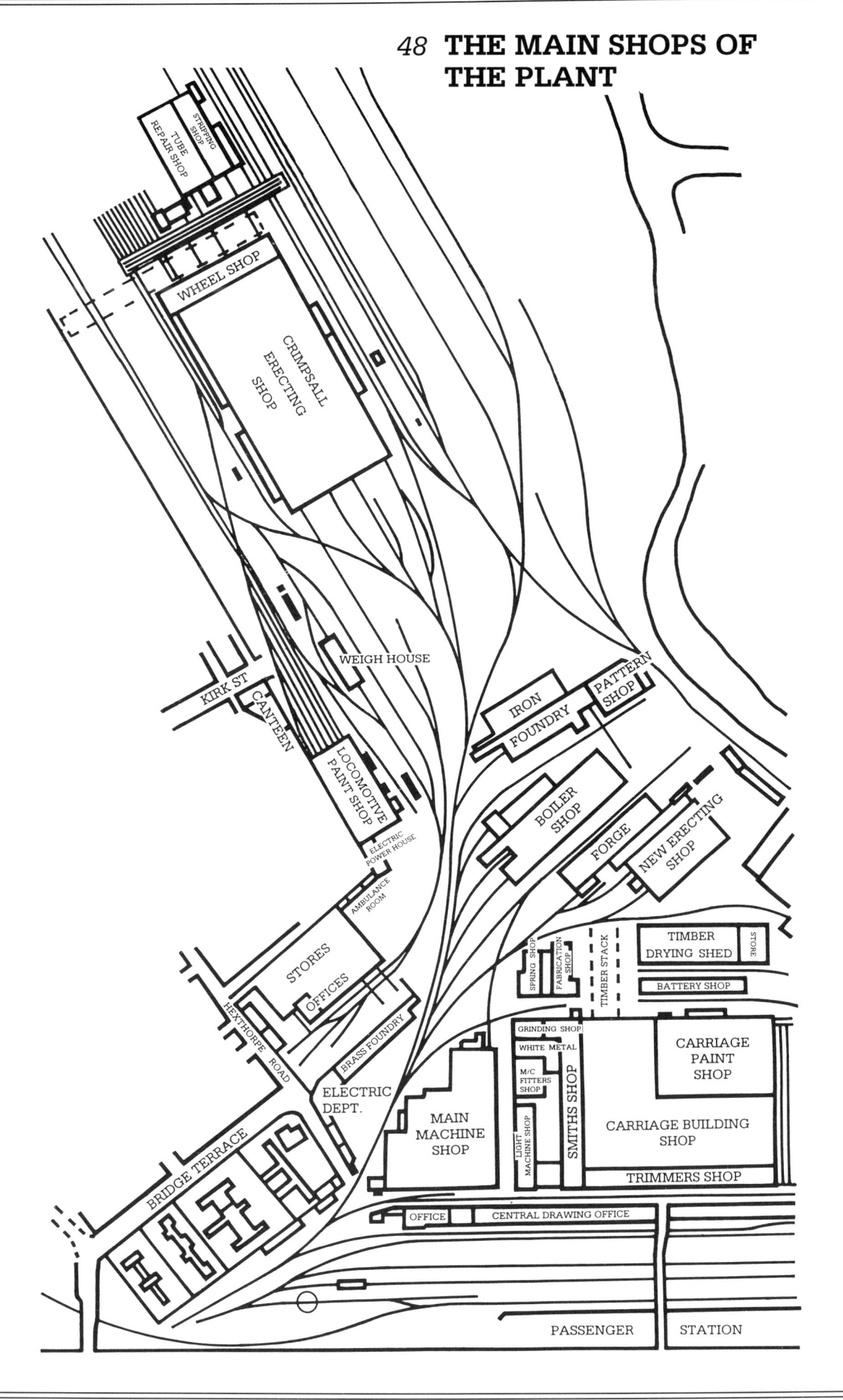

FROM NATIONALIZATION TO THE BEECHING PLAN, 1948–62

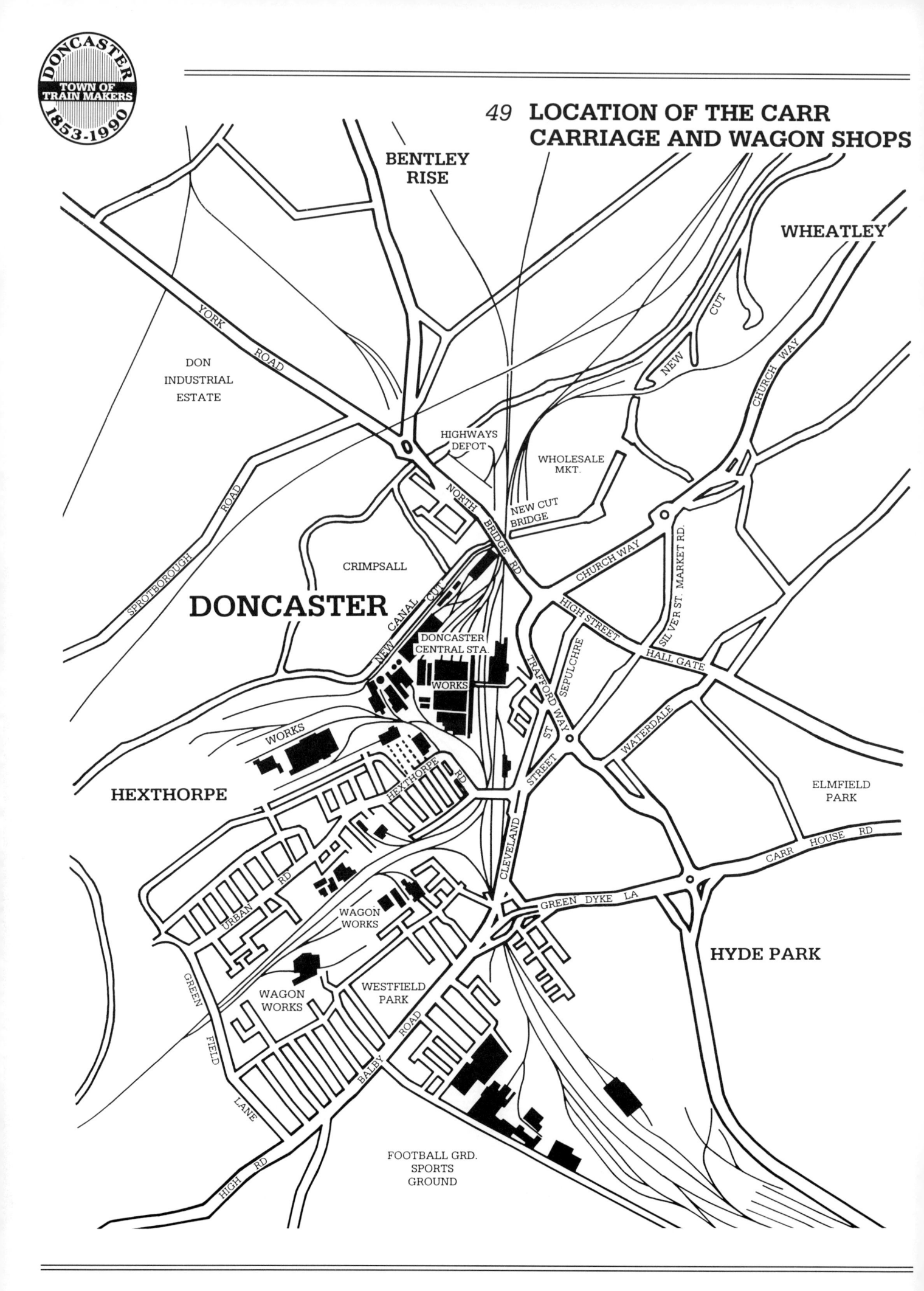

49 LOCATION OF THE CARR CARRIAGE AND WAGON SHOPS

The Report shows clearly the preponderance of locomotive repair in the activity of this part of the Plant works. Those employed in the locomotive repair and boiler shops accounted for just over half of the work force.

There was no comparable breakdown of the staff employed in the Carriage and Wagon Department at this time, but the RE gave the total artisan staff employed in 1949 as 1968.[14] If it is assumed that some fifty clerical and supervisory staff were attached, then the total staff employed at the Carr was around 2000.

Thus at the commencement of public ownership of the railways the Plant was providing work for well over 5000 people. At mid-century, Doncaster employed more people in the railway workshops than did any other town, with the three exceptions of Swindon, with some 10100 workers, Derby with 8800 and Crewe with 7173.[15]

During the first few months of its existence the RE decided to build all new locomotives for British Railways of twelve standard types, with each of the major workshops concentrating on the production of a single type. During 1949 work was begun for the introduction of six of these types for inclusion in the building programme for 1951. The advantage of this plan was that it reduced to a minimum the number of patterns, jigs and tools required. It was also decided to concentrate the manufacture of flanged boiler plates, drop stamping and castings which were needed for more than one design of locomotive in order to effect economies in production.[16] Doncaster was assigned the building of standard Class 4 2–6–0 locomotives of which thirty were produced by 1954. It shared with Derby the production of standard class 5 4–6–0, mixed traffic locomotives, building forty-two to Derby's hundred and thirty. It shared with Brighton the construction of Standard Class 4 2–6–4 tank locomotives, the Plant works being responsible for ten, compared with Brighton's fifteen.[17]

Throughout the post-war period large numbers of locomotives were built by private contractors for supply to British Railways. For many years it was a matter of controversy between the unions and railway management as to whether the numbers ordered from outside contractors might not be reduced and the number built in the railway workshops increased. In the second half of 1950 the Railway Executive made a comparison between the prices charged by leading private contractors, such as the North British Locomotive Company and Robert Stephenson and Company, with the costs of making similar locomotives in its own workshops. The private contractors' prices were invariably higher. In a memorandum to the BTC the RE declared that there was:

> no justification as a matter of policy, for placing orders to outside contractors at the considerably enhanced prices which they quote, so long as capacity exists in our own shops.[18]

The difficulty was that during the lifetime of the RE (i.e. until 1953) the requirements for new locomotives exceeded the capacity of the RE's workshops to build them. Thus, in the two years 1948 and 1949 the railways' workshops produced 660 locomotives but the private contractors were called upon to produce 276.[19] However, locomotives which were constructed by private contractors were maintained and repaired in the railway workshops. The spotlight of attention which has been directed at the manufacture of new locomotives in the RE's workshops has led to an overlooking of the fact that 80 per cent of the man-

50 *New erecting shop, locomotive works, 1948*

51 Spring shop, locomotive works, 1948

45 Carriage building shop, 1949 (became wagon shop 1964)

82

hours worked was on repairs and maintenance and only 20 per cent on new construction.[20] It was the heavy backlog of repair work arising from the war years which limited the workshops' ability to construct more new locomotives.

The RE had formidable problems to tackle in meeting the demand for both passenger and non-passenger carrying coaches from the beginning of 1948. As mentioned earlier in this chapter, nearly one third of the carriages inherited after the war were built before 1912. Their replacement was a matter of urgency.

In a report to the Minister of Transport four months prior to its formal inauguration, the RE estimated that the total requirement for new carriages over the ensuing five years would be 19 100 vehicles. The railway workshops of Britain had a capacity for building 2070 vehicles. It was noted that 'if a full supply of labour and materials were available', the five year programme could be increased to provide 2325 vehicles and the main problems of passenger accommodation could be solved. To achieve this end it was recommended that railway workshops should 'be utilised to their full capacity'.[21] Unfortunately 'the full supply of labour and materials' were not available in the RE's early years. One of the main problems was the shortage of steel. The BTC had to compete with the building trade, shipbuilding, engineering firms and many other trades which could make a good claim on a share of the limited supplies. Early in 1948 Mr Riddles of the RE offered to surrender an allocation of 2500 tons of track steel for each of the next three years in exchange for permission to build five hundred more coaches. Alas, the Ministry of Transport replied that Riddles would have to keep to the same allocations for carriages as had been given the railway companies in 1947.[22] At Doncaster there was the additional obstacle of a shortage of labour for carriage building and repair. In 1955 the complement of staff authorized by the region was 2389 persons: the numbers actually employed was 2292, 97 short of the desired workforce. This deficiency of 4.1 per cent was

53 Royal Mail and other carriages under construction, 1949

explained through the 'better rates of pay in outside industry'. At York, by contrast, where there was a deficiency of only 1.9 per cent, there were few differences between the wages paid in the carriage works and those paid by outside firms.[23]

The inability to reach the desired level of new carriage construction led to a loss of some custom to the roads. The Annual Report of the RE for 1948 noted, with regret, that:

> The reduced stock of passenger coaches had its reactions in a diminution of potential passenger receipts, in a diversion of passengers to passenger road undertakings, including express contract carriages, and in some loss of goodwill amongst the travelling public who used the restricted railway services and amenities.[24]

Despite the continuing obstacles and disappoint-

54 West carriage shop 1951

ments the Doncaster works completed 1002 major repairs and 1941 light repairs of carriages in 1949.[25] By 1954 the major repairs were down to 850 (out of 2840 in the entire Eastern Region). The number of light repairs increased to 1967 out of the regional total of 9324. Doncaster also hosted the Coaching Stock Control Office of the Eastern Region which allocated assignments to one or other of the five main carriage building plants, or placed others with outside contractors.[26] There were always some of these outside orders. In 1949 506 carriages were built by private contractors against 1078 produced in the railway workshops.[27]

The Doncaster carriage works was equipped with up-to-date machinery operated by highly skilled men and women and it turned out a steady flow of standard type carriages. But, partly because of the restricted layout and difficult access, it was generally assigned the more specialist construction work. In 1949–50 six Post Office sorting vans were built for the Newcastle, Bristol and East Anglian regions. Although these vans had full sorting facilities they were not equipped with lineside-net collecting apparatus. Another speciality of the Plant was the production of kitchen cars. In LNER days these had been made with superstructures of teak and were very handsome vehicles. In the more austere immediate post-war years steel body-work replaced the teak from May 1949 onwards. The ten kitchen cars built in 1950–1 were the first British Railways all steel body vehicles to be built. In the mid-1950s Doncaster produced sixty Open First Class carriages of standard British Railways design, having both end and centre doors.

In 1950 the RE set up an 'Ideal Stocks Committee on the design, capacity and types of freight rolling stock'. Its report, published in March 1951, was described by Miles Beevor, Secretary of the BTC, as 'the most important single policy document yet prepared by the executive'.[28] Priorities in policy were to eliminate the loose coupled, unbraked freight train and the low capacity mineral wagon. It was argued that if these vital changes were introduced 'they would contribute more than almost any other single measure to the improvement of the operating efficiency of BR'.

The RE envisaged three main steps by which British Railway's freight services might be transformed. The first step was the 'premature breaking up of all remaining ex-owners wagons'; the second was 'the standardisation of a new all-steel mineral wagon of 24½ tons capacity' and the third was 'the adoption of continuous brakes on all freight wagons and the general use of the instanter coupling in place of the standard three link loose coupling'.[29] Eminently reasonable though these proposals were, the obstacles to their implementation were formidable.

The importance of a greater degree of standard-

55 Another view of west carriage shop, 1951

ization in wagon design to improve the efficiency of the freight services was obvious. In 1950 the RE reported that there were 480 different types of wagon in stock and that, as a first step, it was planning to reduce this number to 150. Good progress in this direction was made in subsequent months.[30]

Progress was also made in the scrapping of time-expired, low capacity, unbraked wagons. In 1950, for example, 41 800 wagons, including 31 000 former privately owned ones, were withdrawn for dismantling. Doncaster had its share of this work and for many employed at the Carr wagon works this was their main task for several years.[31]

The installation of the new standard 24½ ton mineral wagons was far more difficult to achieve. As late as August 1955 only 1.41 per cent of the weekly tonnage carried on British Railways was carried in these larger capacity vehicles. The outstanding reason for this disappointing performance was the shortage of steel. In 1952 the RE reported that 'because of restricted steel supplies, the turn out of new vehicles was the lowest in any of the years 1948–52'.[32] By 1954 inadequate terminal facilities for the handling of the larger capacity wagons was given as 'the most restrictive factor' in preventing their more rapid introduction. It was noted that 'wagon handling appliances at many of the ports and works were not able to handle the 24½ ton wagon, owing to the total height above rail level, the gross loaded weight being too much for the cranes, cradles etc'. At that time only 9 per cent of the collieries could make use of these more economically sized vehicles.[33]

These were among the reasons why the bulk of the work at the Carr in the early 1950s comprised repairing old wagons. The proportion of the stock 'under or awaiting repair' was gradually reduced – it came down from 9.8 per cent to 8.3 per cent between 1948 and 1949. The objective of bringing it down further to 5.5 per cent in the early 1950s was not achieved. The RE reported that:

> Although supervisors and men worked long hours, expectations were not realised owing to the poor condition of the wagons, particularly those privately owned, and the poor quality of the timber now used.[34]

At the same time, workers at the Carr made a contribution to the construction of new 12 and 16 ton wagons, wagon flats and containers.

The General Election of 25 October 1951, resulted in the defeat of Clement Attlee's Labour government and the formation of a Conservative government.

In the run up to the election Conservative

candidates reminded the public that the high speeds of passenger trains in the pre-war days had not been restored by 1951. They ignored the fact that railway resources had been stretched to the limit in five and a half years of war but that, nevertheless, in 1951 net ton miles per total engine hour were 30 per cent higher than they were in 1938.[35] Distrust of the unified control of the BTC was also fostered. Under the Transport Act of 6 May 1953, therefore, the road haulage assets of the Road Haulage Executive of the BTC were sold to private bidders and the Railway Executive was abolished and its responsibilities handed over to six regional boards having a large measure of autonomy. Doncaster's Plant works were placed under the direction of the Eastern and North Eastern boards.

With the new administration in charge at Whitehall the BTC was under pressure to hasten the pace of change. The Modernization Plan, published early in 1955, has been described as 'a belated attempt to rescue the railways from past neglect'.[36] The most important aspect of the Plan from the railway workshops' point of view was the decision to replace steam by electric and diesel traction, though the modernization of freight services and rolling stock were also given prominence. The effects of the Plan on the workshops were foreshadowed in a special report of the BTC in November 1956.[37] During the fifteen years of the Plan's expected life, from 1955–70 new tractive power in the form of electric and diesel main-line locos, diesel shunting locos and EMU and DMU passenger vehicles, would largely replace steam traction. By 1970 it was anticipated that there would be the following locomotives in service: electric 1100; diesel 2500; diesel shunting 1200, making a total of 4800, apart from the anticipated surviving 7500 steam locomotives. For locomotive-hauled passenger vehicles the objective was 24 000 carriages in use by 1970.

56 Aerial view of Plant works, 1951

FROM NATIONALIZATION TO THE BEECHING PLAN, 1948–62

57 Deltic locomotive repairs late 1950s

58 Pacific locomotive being lifted

The biggest reduction envisaged was in the number of wagons. At the time the report was drafted there were still 1 140 000 on the books. Through the introduction of higher capacity wagons and the fitting of continuous brakes, which would make quicker journey times possible, it was hoped to reduce the number in use to 752 000 by 1970.

The implications for the workshops of these changes were spelt out in the report. The workshops would be expected to maintain *all* stock, whatever the type of motive power. They would dispose of all condemned and withdrawn stock; they would build the mechanical parts of new locomotives together with most of the passenger and non-passenger carrying vehicles and wagons as complete units; they would manufacture the component parts for the maintenance of all rolling stock and for stores stock. They would *not* manufacture diesel engines and transmissions. These would be purchased from contractors.

The greatest threat to the traditional role of the workshops concerned locomotive building. There was to be a relatively speedy transition from steam to electric and diesel traction and new building of these locomotives was to be undertaken by outside contractors. The emphasis of policy under the Railway Executive was standardization of construction in the railway workshops with anticipated economies from large scale production. What has been described as a 'somewhat frantic rush' to diesel locomotion meant that instead of some 79 per cent of BR's locomotives being built in the railway's own works, less than half the new generation of diesels were 'in house' products.[38] The change in policy ushered in by the Modernization Plan also undermined earlier attempts to standarize and simplify locomotive design, since the contractors' locomotives were of a greater variety of types. By 1959 the diesel fleet comprised locomotives of forty-one different designs.[39]

Doncaster's last spate of steam locomotive building took place between 1952–7 during which time seventy standard class 4 2–6–0 engines were constructed. Locomotive number 76114 of this class was completed on 14 October 1957 and it was the last steam locomotive to be built at the Plant.

Soon after the publication of the Modernization Plan the BTC appointed a committee to examine the productive efficiency of the carriage and wagon construction and repair facilities in the workshops of the Eastern and North Eastern regions. The committee's report appeared in January 1956. It noted that at Doncaster 1010 staff were employed in carriage and wagon repairs while 426 were employed on new building. Carriage building at Doncaster was carried out in 'cramped conditions' and that 'difficulties were liable to arise in feeding the works with coaching stock'.

The committee found that the equipment in the Doncaster carriage works was 'excellent', but unfortunately:

The space available for building new coaches was less generous, and, in consequence the sequence of movements was not so efficient, the coaches having to be removed from the Building Shop for asphalting of floors and bituminous emulsion spraying. Trimming was fitted in the paint shop.

By contrast, at York, there was 'adequate space and a series of exceedingly efficient layouts were in being'. It was therefore recommended that York should take over all new carriage building from Doncaster.[40]

The sad fact that the building of new carriages was the first of the Plant's activities to be withdrawn was a matter of economics. It had nothing to do with the skill of the carriage builders. With the growth of road passenger and freight competition, British Railways' financial position deteriorated. A small profit of £3.6 million in 1952 was changed to a loss of £156.1 million ten years later. The pressure to increase efficiency of operation was intense. The progressive lay-out of carriage production, being labour saving, resulted in less costly production.

The productive efficiency report of 1956 found that the 707 staff employed on wagon work at the Carr were practically all engaged in either repairs or dismantling. New construction of wagons was concentrated at Shildon where 2259 men were employed. In the Carr works the men operated in gangs under a chargehand and three sub-chargehands. The earnings of all the men were pooled and although this might be considered a disincentive to individual effort, it was not so.

59 2000th locomotive built at the Plant works

FROM NATIONALIZATION TO THE BEECHING PLAN, 1948–62

Earnings had risen 'fairly steeply'.[41] Practically all the staff were employed on piecework.

After 1958 wagon dismantling was guided by a special report of the BTC: **British Railways: Reduction of Wagon Fleet**. The overriding aim was the withdrawal of 100 000 wagons as quickly as possible during 1958. The report was in the form of a book with differently coloured pages for the different regions. The Eastern and North Eastern regions paper was blue. Among the many types of wagons ordered to be broken up were all those life expired by 1959; open merchandise wagons of pre-1925 vintage; wooden hopper wagons of all types, except those LNER built since 1926; pre-1931 cattle wagons built before 1931, and many others. The white section of the book, occupying 162 pages, listed all the private owners and the wagons to be broken up. Before the time of the Beeching Report in 1962 there was plenty of work to do at the Carr since the staff there were employed in dismantling not only railway owned wagons but also those formerly belonging to the private companies.

There was a marked improvement in the conditions of service of the Plant works in the post-war period. From 30 June 1947 the five day week of forty-four hours was brought into operation. Thus the Saturday morning working that had been characteristic of the late 1930s, came to an end.[42] There were some exceptions. Running shed shopmen and outstation repair staff, required to ensure the movement of traffic could be called upon to work at week-ends but could expect to get days off during the week in lieu. Overtime and Sunday working were widespread but not unduly burdensome. In 1954 the *average* Plant worker did one and a half hours overtime and up to two hours Sunday working each week, but the actual experience varied greatly between shops.[43]

In the light of the prevalence of short time working in pre-war days and the sharp variations in earnings which resulted from it, the trade unions had for many years compaigned for the introduction of the guaranteed day and guaranteed week. These were agreed as part of a post-war service settlement between the railway companies and the unions. Under the same agreement railway workers, including shop workers, were granted twelve days' holiday with pay each year, and two of the bank and public holiays which occur during the year. Minimum weekly rates of pay for shop workers in large works, such as Doncaster, were fixed at 85s. per week.[44]

Between the coming into force of the Transport Act, 1947, and its successor of 1953 the shop workers guaranteed week was underpinned by the requirement contained in the earlier Act that the workshops should be kept fully employed. If insufficient railway work was available it might be supplemented by work for government departments. In the course of 1952 the Ministry of Supply placed fourteen separate orders with six of the main workshops, including Doncaster.[45]

As the financial position of the BTC deteriorated in the middle and later 1950s, however, the secure employment situation of the post-war years was undermined. As has been shown, a feature of the Modernization Plan was the rapid substitution of diesel and electric, for steam locomotion. The BTC considered that the railway workshops were not so well equipped to manufacture the new tractive units as were the workshops of private companies. (However, the Plant works did build thirty diesel electric 0–6–0 shunters in 1957–8 and also carried out 'acceptance trials' and maintenance work on electric locomotives). Notwithstanding these facts the Commission pressed ahead wth its plans.

The impact of the changes on the Plant works was forcibly expressed by J.A. Firth, a blacksmith of the Doncaster No.3 branch of the NUR, at his union's AGM on 4 July 1957:

> In the last few years there has been a considerable influx of private contractors into Doncaster works ... we have empty benches in the Carriage Shops which should be actively engaged in making certain component parts which arrive through the medium of private contractors into that department. Further, the influx of private contractors of various types into the Doncaster locomotive department is causing great concern to all the members there ... We have contractors coming in building new units, building new retorts to the electric sub-stations. They are doing train work to a considerable extent.[46]

At that conference, the Doncaster No.3 branch resolution in favour of a forty hour week 'to absorb redundant labour' was set aside in favour of a similar public resolution from the platform. This resolution, which was carried unanimously, coupled the demand for a forty hour week with that for an additional week's winter leave and an insistence for 'the full use of railway workshop capacity in the Modernization Plan'.[47]

A year later at the AGM of July 1958 Mr J.A. Firth was again a delegate. He explained that the unions representing the Plant workers had discussed with management over the previous four years the whole question of possible redundancies. Three to four hundred jobs had been lost, but, by agreement with the management, these had been covered by natural wastage. When the works manager asked for co-operation of the staff, the unions joined with management in forming a **Future Trains Committee**. They were led to believe that, through such working together, redundancy would be avoided. They were, he said, 'led into a false sense of security', since the Regional Staff Officer issued an edict in June 1958 – a month before the AGM met – announcing seventy-five redundancies. It was urgent that the union should negotiate a redundancy agreement with the BTC.[48]

Membership of the Doncaster No.3 branch of the NUR, which catered for the Plant workers, reflected the growth of redundancies. In 1961 it fell below 3000 for the first time since the war.

To make production in the railway workshops more competitive with outside contractors, work-study schemes became more widespread. The aim was to make more effective use of material, plant and manpower. British Railways was at pains to point out that planned productivity through work study was quite different in its implications from earlier, and often discredited 'time and motion' studies. Since work study was often coupled with bonus payments shopmen were frequently happy to accept the new arrangements.

Workshop employment was among the dirtiest of any employment for British Railways. Whether cleaning undercarriages lying on ones back, removing the 'crinolines' of locomotive boilers or axle greasing or oiling of rolling stock, it would be hard to say which job was the filthiest. And yet in the early 1950s there was a long way to go before it could be said that adequate protective clothing was on issue to staff. Even twenty years later Albert Meredith, who, as a storeman, had the job of lifting steel bars from wagons and therefore asked to be issued with gloves, received the reply: 'Gloves, you'll want bloody lipstick next.'[49]

In December 1951 the executive committee of the NUR proposed to the RSNC that:

1 Blacksmiths and strikers, welders, burners and ancillary workers should be supplied with leather aprons and gauntlet gloves, and in some cases burners and welders should have protective clothing.
2 Men dealing with water mains and culverts, piers and docks, engine pits and cesspools should have rubber high boots.
3 Battery attendants and others in contact with acid should have clogs and rubber goggles.
4 Men employed in the spraying and spreading should have rubber knee boots, gloves and goggles.
5 Workers in electrical depots and running sheds or engaged in stripping locomotives and carriage bogies should be supplied with dungaree overalls.

At the time, these demands, which today would be regarded as wholly reasonable, were turned down by the RE which said it was 'not prepared to make any further concessions'.[50] In the event staff had to find many items of protective clothing from their own wages.

In contrast to pre-war days, canteens were available at the Plant where reasonably priced meals could be purchased. However, in the hour break for lunch many preferred to board one of the double decker buses provided and make the short journey home. Hundreds more cycled it each day.

FROM BEECHING TO BRITISH RAIL ENGINEERING LTD.

In the wake of the Conservatives' General Election victory of 8 October 1959 Harold Macmillan, the Prime Minister, appointed Ernest Marples as Minister of Transport in the new government. Following the privatization of the BTC's most profitable arm, the Road Haulage Executive, in 1954, the Commission's finances went increasingly in to the red. In 1958 its deficit exceeded £100 million for the first time. Marples approached his new responsibilities from the viewpoint of a qualified accountant. He saw as his main task the organization of the railways as a strictly commercial business whose operating costs and debt servicing should be covered by its passnger and freight revenues. He rejected any cost-benefit approach to transport policy, whereby the indirect benefits of the railway, such as its environmental advantages, its value as a social service and its importance for reducing the costs of road congestion, are placed in the balance against its immediate financial returns. The new Minister of Transport believed that the future lay in the development of roads rather than railways. He was the founder of the road construction business of Marples, Ridgeway and Partners.[1]

In April 1960 Marples appointed a planning committee under Sir Ivan Stedeford as chairman, to advise on the reorganization of the railway and other services of the BTC. Dr Richard Beeching, a technical director of Imperial Chemical Industries, was appointed a member of the committee. Marples was so impressed with his performance there that in March 1961 he asked him to join the BTC as chairman-designate in succession to Sir Brian Robertson. With the disappearance of the BTC and the Railway Executive under the Transport Act of 1962, Beeching was appointed first chairman of the British Railways Board which began life on 1 January 1963.

The responsibility for axing the rail network, railway services and the railway workshops has often been attributed solely to Dr Beeching. This view is misleading. In February 1959, two years before Beeching's appointment as BTC Chairman, a committee of the Commission's General Staff chaired by the Secretary, Maj. Gen. Lt Wansbrough-Jones, produced a report entitled **Modernisation and Re-equipment of BR; Repair and Production Policy for Locomotives and Rolling Stock**. The report dealt very thoroughly with the eighteen locomotive and nineteen carriage and wagon works taken over from the four main-line companies in 1948. It listed the principal activity of each of the works and the numbers of staff it employed as at 31 December 1957. In the case of Doncaster, it reported new construction of diesel shunting locomotives and electric locomotives, the repair of steam locomotives, the new construction of electric multiple units, and the repair of diesel multiple units, wagons and containers. 2695 people were employed at the locomotive works and a further 2255 at the carriage and wagon works, making a total of 4950.

The report estimated the number of locomotives and the items of rolling stock which would need to be manufactured and repaired in the year 1990. It was calculated that new construction capacity was needed for 250 locomotives (electric or diesel), 1350 coaching vehicles, 13 000 wagons and 2500 containers in any one year. In relation to these requirements there was a large excess capacity and the authors of the report therefore recommended a programme of phased closures spread over the years from 1959–68, with most numerous closures completed by the end of 1960, but the greatest number of staff reductions in the following decade. Doncaster came off relatively lightly in this programme of closures. It was envisaged that carriage building and repair would cease but all other principal activities would continue.[2]

The General Staff plan of 1959 was based on the assumption of the continuation of regional management of the workshops established in 1953

Key
Horwich .... works continuing
Gorton .... works closing down
C .... activity on carriages
L .... activity on locomotives
W .... activity on wagons

An encircled letter indicates that activity is to be discontinued
① .... one works where there were previously two
② .... 2 works closing
2 .... 2 works continuing

60

THE WORKSHOPS PLAN, 1962: THE LOCATION OF THE WORKS TO BE CONTINUED AND THOSE TO BE CLOSED

and the relatively slow disappearance – by 1990 – of steam locomotion. However, when Marples, on the recommendation of Beeching, appointed Sir Steuart Mitchell a member of the BTC with responsibility for the workshops, there was a radical change of policy. Mitchell persuaded the Commission that in the interests of the efficient running of the railway there should be centralized direction of workshop policy and that the transition from steam to diesel and electric traction should be accelerated. Under the Transport Act of 1962 the Workshops Division of the British Railways Board pursued a national plan for the closure or retention of the railway workshops.

The proposals contained in Sir Steuart Mitchell's workshop plan of July 1962 are illustrated in figure 60. They were based on estimated traffic requirements in 1967. The map shows that, under the plan, Doncaster certainly fared better than centres such as Stratford, Gorton and Darlington, though resentment was felt about the proposed cessation of carriage building at the Plant and the transference of the work to York. Under the plan the wage labour force in the nation's workshops was to be reduced from 56 000 to 37 000 and the salaried staff from 7300 to 5800 over the five years to 1967.

On 22 August 1962 Sir Steuart Mitchell met the representatives of all the main trade unions with members in the workshops and spelt out to them the detailed implications of the changes planned for the years 1963–7. Since the total number of locomotives would be 42 per cent lower by 1972, the year in which, it was now planned, steam would disappear from the scene – the manpower needed for the manufacture and repair of locomotives was expected to fall from 28 043 to 17 900. As fewer passenger carriages would be needed, the labour force in the carriage departments would have to fall from 16 343 to 11 300. With fewer, but more durable, wagons in use, the number of heavy repairs to wagons would be more than halved to 70 000 a year. The change to new methods of railway operation and the use of new technologies would create job opportunities for 1850 staff in 1963, 3000 in 1964 and a dwindling number thereafter; but only some of those made redundant by the rundown in use of the old equipment would be suitable for the new jobs. Thousands of redundancies were regarded as inevitable.[3]

In Doncaster the local MP, Mr Anthony Barber, met an eight-strong deputation from Plant members of the Confederation of Shipbuilding and Engineering Unions (CS & EU) on 13 July to listen to their concerns about the impact of the workshops plan on the job situation for skilled workers.[4] Just over two months later a more representative gathering of the Doncaster Plant Shops and Works Committee met in the Kirk Street canteen under the chairmanship of R. Oakes, convener of the AEU loco and carriage works shop stewards. Emerging from the meeting, Mr W.H. Pearce, a coach painter, said that the proposals were 'a blow, especially to some of the younger workers who were married and were paying for their houses'. Although the employees in the carriage department were adversely affected by the plan, staff reductions at Doncaster were modest compared with those in many other workshop towns. It was announced that the Plant would lose fifty workers in 1963, a further fifty in 1964 and a hundred and fifty in 1965, out of a work force which numbered 3740 in 1962. The Mayor of Doncaster, Alderman R. Kelsall, described the news as 'Very gratifying to the town – far better than we had anticipated'.[5]

What is surprising is that protests against the prospect of thousands of job losses nationally were not angrier and more strident. Between 10 and 15 September 1962 the executive of the NUR considered demands for strike action from branches or district councils of the union in Darlington, Liverpool, Derby, Swindon and Glasgow and the decision was taken to call a one day strike on Wednesday 3 October. The stoppage was less complete and effective than it might have been since the support of ASLEF and TSSA was not forthcoming. Nevertheless, at Doncaster there was a 100 per cent response to the strike call among both station and workshop staff. **The Doncaster Chronicle** reported:

> It was such a quiet strike and such a lovely day for it. At Balby bridge the silence and stillness was uncanny. A single figure moving between the lines or on the platforms was the object of attraction.[6]

On 8 April 1963 further plans for industrial action were discussed at a meeting of all the main trade unions with workshop members, but no strike followed. On 1 May ASLEF announced that many of its members were unwilling to participate, and a week later Dr Beeching offered improved redundancy terms including premature retirement to the over 60s with full pay guaranteed up to the normal retirement age of 65. This led to the NUR's abandonment of any further plans for strike action.

The appearance in March 1963 of the much publicized Beeching Plan – **The Reshaping of British Railways** – aroused great concern among those who considered that the retention of an extensive railway network was an essential component of a well-balanced transport system. Although the report did not cover the question of workshop closures its implementation had serious consequences for the level of workshop activity in later years. The closure of 5000 out of 21 000 route miles of line and 2363 out of 7000 stations, envisaged in 1963, was mostly completed by 1967.[7]

At the same time there was a rigorous pruning of unprofitable general merchandize trains and stopping passenger trains, leading to a reduction in demand for the traditional types of rolling stock even beyond that envisaged in the Steuart plan of July 1962.

A glance at figure 60 gives rise to the question, why did Doncaster fare relatively well under Mitchell's Workshop Plan of July 1962? The reasons for the survival of most of the activities of the Plant works can be seen in relation to the situation of the three main areas of construction and repair of railway equipment.

When those who prepared the plan considered locomotive manufacture, they concluded that because of their large size, their geographical location and their outstandingly low cost production, the works at Crewe and Derby had an unanswerable case for being chosen as the centres for new construction work. Although it might have been possible, through intensive shift work, to concentrate locomotive repairs in these two centres as well, it was decided to spread repair work over five other works, besides Derby and Crewe. Considerations of geographical location, cost efficiency and the social consequences of closure were all weighed in the balance. In the Eastern region Darlington, Doncaster and Stratford were all equipped for undertaking locomotive repairs. Doncaster was selected to continue working because its scale of operations was large, its productive efficiency was high and its location near the centre of the region was suitable. The case for Darlington was that closure would bring severe hardship to the town since nearly 15 per cent of the male insured population were dependent upon employment in the railway works compared with less than 9 per cent in the case of Doncaster. However Doncaster's great efficiency and more convenient location carried the day. The other option, Stratford, was rejected on the grounds of higher wage costs and the good opportunities for alternative employment.[8] Doncaster was allowed to retain wagon construction and repair activity because of its large capacity, medium costs and convenient location.[9] It was decided to pass most of the carriage work to York, where the facilities were favourable, but other employment opportunities in the area were not abundant. Doncaster was to retain the maintenance of diesel multiple units; but this could be done in the main workshop area while the carriage works could be closed.[10]

Signs of the Plant work's new lease of life were evident in the early 1960s. In the spring of 1962 new offices, engineering workshop and stores for BR's District Engineer and District Signals Engineer were built with the aim of replacing a series of small outdated workshops and offices in the St Sepulchre

Gate area. The contractors for this £100 000 project were the Doncaster firm of C.R. Price Ltd of Barnsley Road.[11] In 1965 the wagon repair work at the Plant was reorganized. Work previously carried out at Carr Hill was transferred to an area in the Plant which had been used for carriage repairs.[12] Later in the year the Wagon Works area was sold to enable International Harvester to extend its factory production.[13]

In the course of 1965 the Plant works undertook new, more extensive, responsibilities in the repair of diesel locomotives. In August parts of the Carr locomotive sheds were demolished to make way for a major servicing depot for main line diesels.[14] Later in the year a new diesel engine and transmission testing station was fitted up in the works.[15] In 1969 repair and maintenance work on the Deltics was still further entended. A new repair layout was organized to enable the Napier engines of these locomotives, which had previously been maintained in the Napier works in Liverpool, to be overhauled at the Plant. Thus Doncaster was once again responsible for the major repair and maintenance on the powerful engines which hauled the express trains from King's Cross to Liverpool and on other routes.[16]

One reason why this important work was switched from the privately owned firm to the publicly owned one was that the Plant works had very up-to-date equipment. In March 1969 Mr Sydney Jones, a member of the British Railways Board, formally opened a new £83 000 area laboratory on the Hexthorpe Road. The report of the opening ceremony stressed that 'dozens of simultaneous experiments' designed to reduce the operational costs of the railways, would be carried out in the new building. Part of the equipment was a spectrograph, installed at a cost of £7000, and capable of detecting metal fatigue on engines.[17] With an eye to meeting the criticism that the Plant works was a major polluter of the environment a 'trade effluent plant' was installed in the spring of 1969. This enabled 'harmful diesel oil and detergents' to be pumped into the new equipment from all parts of the works from which 'clean effluents were pumped into the river Don'.[18]

Improved workshop layout and the introduction of work study augmented the improvements wrought by new machinery to improve productivity. Sidney Greene (later Lord Greene) in his report to the AGM of the NUR in July 1969 noted that:

> The improvement in the maintenance of the locomotive fleet... coupled with other factors, has reduced the future requirement for locomotive overhaul and repair considerably, and the capacity required will be approximately half of the present capacity by 1974.[19]

This was a trend confirmed by the BR Board's Annual Report in the prevous year which mentioned the introduction of electronic and sequentially controlled machine tools which considerably reduce labour costs.'.[20]

In most workshops management encouraged innovations which reduced operating costs. At Doncaster two Plant workers received money prizes for suggestions submitted in 1969. Ronald Daw received £25 for his method of fitting new keeps on the locks of locomotive cab doors; a device for which he had previously been granted £75. It was estimated that this invention would save BR £3434 over a period of three years. The other employee, Mr Button, received an award of £50 for an idea which 'overcame difficulties in testing axles for fractures, using an ultra sonic signal'.[21]

In the 1960s employees at the Plant works were given reminders of past glories as well as evidence of the more sophisticated developments characteristic of the second half of the twentieth century. A businessman of Blyth, Mr Alan F. Pegler, bought **The Flying Scotsman** for its scrap value of £3000 and had it overhauled at the Plant in the winter of 1962–3. On Monday, 18 February 1963 the famous engine, with Mr Pegler on the footplate, and hauling a 750 seat train of twelve coaches, made a round trip to Peterborough and back. On returning to the Plant works it was repainted in its original LNER apple-green livery before being used in April to take enthusiasts from many parts of the country to the Festiniog Society's annual meeting at Port Madoc.[22] News of this veteran A4 Pacific performing in various parts of the UK and abroad is to be found in the Doncaster papers for many years afterwards. On May day 1968 it ran once more on its familiar route between King's Cross and Edinburgh.[23] A year later it was in Texas, USA, at the start of an American tour.[24] It was not the only A4 Pacific to demonstrate its prowess in America. Staff at the Plant gave the **Golden Shuttle**, renamed the **Dwight D. Eisenhower**, a complete overhaul and refit before it crossed the Atlantic.[25]

Less glamorous was the breaking up of old locomotives. That part of the Plant works where the big ones were fragmented was well known as the Goliath area. Each week in the autumn and winter of 1962–3 at least four of the giants were cut apart and the bits dispatched to steelworks in Rotherham and Sheffield.[26]

At the same time as the sparks from the acetylene burners could be seen showering out like roman candles in one part of the works, other staff were busy assembling the AL6 electric locomotives, work which was to continue until the last of this type left the works on 17 January 1967. Over three years earlier, on 6 November 1963, there left the works the Pacific type locomotive No.

FROM
BEECHING
TO
BRITISH
RAIL
ENGINEERING
LTD.

61 Pacific locomotive A2 Class Blue Peter in new erecting shop before repair and painting 4 April 1969

62 Smiths' shop, locomotive works 1966

95

60009, **Union of South Africa**, the last steam locomotive to be given a complete overhaul in Doncaster where some 40 000 engines had been overhauled and repaired since the works was opened in 1853. Eighty or so of the staff involved in the work, together with the driver and fireman, posed for a photograph to mark the historic occasion.

Following its General Election victory on 15 October 1964 the Labour Party had a slim majority of four seats over the other parties in the Commons. This made more difficult the implementation of the promise contained in the Queen's speech at the opening of Parliament on 9 November that 'legislation would be introduced to remove statutory limitations impeding the proper use of the manu-

63 Thompson locomotive being broken up in the 'Goliath' area, early 1960

64 Last steam locomotive repair, 1963

facturing resources of the nationalized industries'. Under Section 13 of Ernest Marples' Transport Act of 1962 the railway workshops were forbidden to manufacture any articles for private firms. In addition, throughout the 1950s Ministers of Transport had urged the BTC to place orders for equipment with 'outside' firms. The result was that whereas in 1957 75 per cent of new locomotives were built in BRB workshops, only 39 per cent were so built in 1962. At the same time the railway workshops were hamstrung from taking orders from 'outside' firms in an endeavour to offset the decline in their work for BR. Unfortunately in the Parliament of 1964–6 the Labour Party in the Commons proved too weak to carry through the necessary legislation in the face of the fierce and persistent opposition of the CBI.

With the much more substantial majority of ninety-seven secured by Labour in the General Election of 31 March 1966 there was now a much better opportunity of carrying out the changes envisaged in the Queen's speech of 1965. Under Barbara Castle's massive Transport Act of 25 October 1968 the workshops were given power to engage in the manufacture and sale of their products, not only to the nationalized industries but also to private customers at home or abroad. They could even sell petrol and repair motor vehicles in their own car parks.

Within a year of the passing of the Act the management of the Plant works secured a contract worth £1 million for the construction/assembly of three 1350 h.p. Bo Bo type diesel engines for the Northern Ireland Railways. This was a co-operative venture with the Hunslet Engine Company of Leeds providing the superstructures, Associated Electrical Industries (AEI) the power units and the Plant works providing the mechanical engineering parts, such as the underframes and the bogies.[26] In May 1970, five months after the BR Workshops Division had become British Rail Engineering Ltd (BREL) under the Transport Act 1968, completion of the three locomotives was delcared to have been 'bang on the button'. The maroon and gold liveried locomotives, the first of which was named 'Eagle', enabled the Nothern Ireland Railways to initiate four journeys a day express services between Belfast and Dublin. The success of the consortium of three companies led to a wave of optimism about future prospects. Mr John Alcock, the chairman of the 105 year old Hunslet Company, declared that 'We could now go out and really bid for orders overseas which we could not have tackled on our own'.[27]

There were seasonal variations in the level of employment in the Plant works. In winter time employment on wagon repairs was generally less than it was in the months of more daylight hours. But the winter of 1962–3 was one of the most severe of the century. About a hundred men employed in wagon repairing were on a four day week from 26 October 1962 to the end of January 1963.[28]

By contrast, in May and June 1963 those employed in the locomotive works were working overtime, mainly at weekends, to cope with the backlog of repair work. On the Eastern region passenger traffic was now more important than the movement of freight, so that at the beginning of summer there was greater activity getting the rolling stock in tip-top condition ready for the busy season.[29] The level of employment in the workshops also depended on fluctuations in the national economy. Britain's balance of payments deteriorated sharply in the early months of 1966 and on 14 July Harold Wilson, the Prime Minister, announced drastic measures to curtail government expenditure. An employees' side meeting of the RSNC held at Congress House, the TUC's headquarters, on 24 August gave consideration to two letters from H.O. Houchen, General Manager of the Workshops Division of BR. He warned that, as a result of government cuts, restrictions had had to be imposed on the amount of repair work being undertaken in the main workshops.[30]

Redundancy was also a continuing problem at the Plant, though on nothing like the scale in many workshop towns. In Doncaster there was anticipation, based on statements from BR, that there would be a total of up to 260 jobs lost in the course of 1965. Mercifully, R.J. Oakes, of the Doncaster railway sub-committee of the confederation of craft unions, was able to inform the **Doncaster Gazette** in June that it was unlikely there would be more than a hundred jobs lost.[31]

In the course of the 1960s there was a substantial reduction of the working week of all railway employees, including shop workers. In 1961 the RSNC agreed to the reduction in the standard weekly hours of duty from forty-four to forty-two. This reduction came into effect on 30 October 1961.[32] At a meeting of the RSNC lasting over the two days 29–30 May 1965 it was agreed that a further reduction from forty-two to forty hours a week should take effect from the first full pay period in April 1966.[33] Acceptance of the change to the forty hour week was made easier for the employer's side through the fact that little overtime work was in prospect during the economic recession. Shortening the working week could reduce the number of redundancies and redundancy payments.

It took hard bargaining between management and the representatives of the unions to secure an increase in the number of paid days leave to which workshop staff were entitled. In 1965–6 the unions put in a claim for one week's additional holiday. Management countered by suggesting that a maximum of three days additional leave should only be granted to those who had completed ten years' service. In the belief that this concession was the most that could be expected in the circumstances, the NUR was for acceptance. The confederation unions, on the other hand, considered that an additional two days after five years service – a proposal that had been mentioned in the discussions – was a better proposition. As there was a deadlock the NUR executive decided to instruct Sidney Greene to write to management suggesting that as the NUR represented a large majority of the staff employed in the shops, the General Manager, BR workshops, should impose the three days solution. This he did.[34]

Work discipline at the Plant was generally good in the late 1950s and early 1960s. Mr James C. 'Ned' Sparks who was in charge of the locomotive, carriage and wagon departments from 1958 to the end of 1962 before moving to become works manager at Crewe, was described as 'the best works manager' by Stan Lewin, a qualified joiner at the Plant. Though the men were 'frightened to death of him' because his standards were high, they respected him because he knew his job. He was not too 'high and mighty' to jump into an engine pit and demonstrate how a job was done.[35]

Making progress on the issue of protective clothing to workshop staff was an uphill task. Not untypically, the meeting of the RSNC on 21–22 May 1966 considered four different resolutions on protective clothing. The strongest feeling was expressed in favour of the issue of two sets of overalls per worker each year, and the issue of steel-toed boots. A delegate stressed that 'an enormous number of man hours were lost through accidents to feet'. In the 1960s the Workshops Division of British Railways was not persuaded to meet these demands and in any case responsibility in these matters passd to the BREL from 1 January 1970.

REORGANIZATION AND PRIVATIZATION, 1970-90

In the twenty years after 1970 there was a complete transformation of the railway workshop industry in Britain. Swindon works, which formerly employed more staff than any similar establishment, was closed down. This was also the fate of Caerphilly, Ashford, Darlington, Shildon, Cowlais and others. Total railway workshop employment in Britain fell from 55 000 in 1970 to 30 000 in 1988.[1] Doncaster's Plant works suffered from cut-backs less seriously than most. Its work force fell from 2634 persons in 1970 to 1891 in 1986.[2]

Among the causes of the decline in railway workshop activity were the huge expansion of road motor transport; the sharp fall in railway freight traffic; technological advances in the design and performance of locomotives and rolling stock, greatly increasing the productivity of railway labour, and the failure of governments to give financial and legislative support to the railway system comparable in scale to that given in most other European states.

The number of motor vehicles registered in Great Britain rose from 15 million in 1970 to 22 million in 1987. Of the 1987 figure some 17½ million were private cars. What is surprising is that this impressive growth in personal and family car ownership did not cause bigger inroads into the volume of rail passenger travel. In fact the number of passenger kilometres travelled by rail fell slightly from 30.4 billion in 1970 to 27.2 billion in 1982 but then rose appreciably to 32.2 billion in 1987.[3] This improvement in the volume of rail travel was the result of BR's imaginative marketing policy in offering reduced fares for special classes of passengers e.g. Awayaday, Senior Citizen tickets, etc. From the viewpoint of the railway workshops, however, this increase in rail passenger travel did not increase the demand for labour in the coach-building and repair side of the industry. Although the number of people travelling by train was increasing, the number of railway carriages in service fell from 18 678 in 1970 to 13 013 in 1987.[4] Steel, a far more durable material, to a large extent replaced wood in the superstructure of the vehicles, thus reducing the frequency and duration of repair and maintenance. Journey times were faster, thus providing the opportunity for carrying more people per day in every vehicle in service. Especially in the later 1980s, BR was under increasing financial restraints through the reduction of the Public Service Obligation (PSO) grant. One result of this pressure was the overcrowding of trains, not only on the commuter services of South East England but also at peak periods of travel elsewhere on the rail network. The Central Transport Consultative Committee — the 'Watchdog' representing the interests of railway passengers — in its report for 1988–89 deplored the growing overcrowding of trains in the Provincial Sector of BR, due to the fact that it had suffered the largest cut-back in passenger vehicles in service.[5]

All these indications point to no net increase in the carriage building and repair side of the industry. The chances of the Plant works ever recovering this part of its output seem remote.

The decline in rail freight traffic over the two decades was far more serious than was the state of passenger travel. In 1970 19.4 per cent of freight movement, measured in tonne-kilometres, was by rail and 61.5 per cent by road. In other words, well under one third of the work of freight movement was done by rail and two thirds by road transport. By 1987/8 the rail share had fallen to only 9.0 per cent. Road transport's share had fallen slightly to 58 per cent, due to the rise of water and pipe line transport, but it was now doing approximately six times the work of the railways compared with only about three times in 1970.[6] Among the influences which brought about this dramatic change were the extension of the motorway network from 687 miles in 1970 to nearly 3000 miles in 1988 and the relaxation of the licensing rules for heavy goods vehicles. Before 1983 the largest trucks allowed on the roads were of 32.5 tons on four axles. But in that year 38 tonners, on five axles, were allowed for the first time. By the end of the 1980s over 80 per cent of these heavy vehicles' journeys were made on the motorways. The speed limit of 70 m.p.h. was difficult to enforce.

BR endeavoured to meet the growing challenge of road freight transport by improving its freight services. In October 1972 the Speedlink scheme was inaugurated guaranteeing overnight delivery in wagon loads or train loads. Two years later the Total Operations Processing System (TOPS) was applied to half the network, preparatory to its nationwide extension in 1985. This computerized organization made it possible to determine, within seconds, the location of any wagon. For parcels traffic the 'Red Star' service guaranteed delivery within twenty-four hours. But these innovations could do no more than staunch, for a while, the haemorrhage of traffic to the roads.

The decline in rail freight traffic would, on its own, have reduced the demand for wagons. The number of wagons needed was still further reduced by other circumstances. Newly built wagons were of a larger capacity, air braked, and often designed for specialized traffic. Among the new types which were being constructed in this period were two-axle coal wagons of 21 tons capacity, two-axle covered vans of 29 tons capacity and open wagons of 31 tons capacity. There were even larger wagons of 75 tons capacity, specially designed for carrying steel.[7] One consequence of this trend in new building, combined with the scrapping of smaller wagons, was an impressive increase in average wagon capacity. In 1970 the average wagon load was 17.95 tonnes. This had increased to 24.88 tonnes by 1978 and to 33.1 tonnes by 1988. In addition the number of train miles covered per wagon increased by over 50 per cent in the 1980s, the consequence of higher running speeds, air braking and more train-load operation. The combined effect of all these changes was that the number of BR owned wagons in service in 1987–8 at 28 884, was under 9 per cent of what it had been in 1970. Inevitably there was a greatly reduced demand for labour to manufacture, maintain and repair railway wagons.

Fewer carriages and wagons on the rails, but running at faster speeds, meant a reduced demand for locomotive power. BR's policy for locomotive power in the post-steam era fluctuated according to prevailing government directions regarding the encouragement or restraint of railway investment. As an example of the fickleness of government policy, the decisions made in 1972–3 may be cited. In BR's **Annual Report** for 1973 Richard Marsh, BR Chairman, wrote:

Within three weeks of the announcement that investment in British Rail for five years would total £891 million (November 1973), a 20 per cent reduction in the investment in the first year was imposed as part of a general cutback in the public sector.[8]

In consequence of such fluctuations of government directive, BR's locomotive policy was of a hesitant and stop-gap character. Given more positive and consistent directives from Whitehall it is probable that BR management would have been more confident to order longer runs of locomotive orders from its own workshops. In the event, orders for DMU's, for example, were placed in relatively small quantities and split between BREL and the private manufacturing companies. Vic Wyman, railway correspondent of **The Engineer**, wrote that:

> On past experience and bearing in mind the timescale BR is working to, it is conceivable that by the next century there will still be no clear cut UK train policy.

He suggested that, because of the variety of locomotive types and the relatively short production runs, 'at least the train spotters will be happy'.[9]

The outcome was a decline in the total locomotive stock shown below:

	1970	1988
Diesel	4126	2040
Electric	323	230
High Speed Train power units	–	197
Advanced Passenger Trains	–	2
Total	4459	2469

There was certainly no guarantee that these locomotives would be built or maintained and repaired in the railway workshops. For as long as the history of railways there had always been private manufacturers of locomotives, as well as of carriages and wagons. However, during the years of the Railway Executive the Workshops Department of BR and the early life of BREL after 1970, the placing of orders for locomotives and rolling stock with outside companies had been marginal compared with the volume of work allocated to the railways' own workshops. After 1979, with a government unsympathetic to state-owned industries, the Railway Industry Association, with its headquarters in Whitehall in close proximity to Parliament, received a more sympathetic hearing for its lobbying in favour of more orders going to private manufacturers of railway equipment.

The private builders gained from the 100 per cent capital allowances which they could offset against corporation tax. The savings which the equipment manufacturers make from capital allowances are passed, in part, to the leasing customers in the form of lower repayment terms. By contrast BREL could

REORGANIZATION AND PRIVATIZATION, 1970–90

not claim these tax allowances and its power to borrow capital was restricted by the government-imposed external financing limit (EFL). At the same time there are no limits imposed on private manufacturers' borrowings.

Less than three months after the new organization BREL came into existence on 1 January 1970, Sir Henry Johnson, Chairman of BR, visited the Plant works. He assured management and staff that there would be no fear of redundancies under the new arrangements and that, in particular, the electrification of the line between Crewe and Glasgow would help to provide Doncaster with plenty of work.[10] Later that year the optimism of the Chairman seemed justified. In August it was revealed that BREL was awarded a contract worth £500 000 to £750 000 for the modification and refurbishment of twenty-five electric locomotives withdrawn from service between two and three years previously. A number of these locomotives were in the process of being dismantled at the Plant when the announcement was made.[11]

In September 1970 the merger of the Hull and Doncaster divisions of the Eastern Region was announced. The merged divisions were to be known as the Doncaster division. This increased the number of administrative and clerical staff employed in Doncaster to 400 by June 1971.[12]

In the summer of 1971 the workers at the Plant were busy carrying out modifications to the Deltic locomotive fleet. Faults in the cylinder liner seals were rectified and modifications were made to make possible air conditioning in the trains.[13]

Confidence in the future role of the Plant works was shown through the introduction of a soundproof test hall for diesel electric locomotives in order to eliminate the menace of noise in the environment. One of the latest tyre reproofing machines, which eliminated the need for the removal of the wheels, was introduced in November. Robert Reid, later Chairman of BR, who was at the time responsible for workshops in the Eastern Region, said that this innovation enabled a main-line locomotive to be serviced in a matter of hours as against the three to four days required in the past.[14]

In the mid 1970s there was sufficient work on locomotive repairs to keep the staff in the machine shop fully employed, though rarely with overtime. The main activity in 1974 was the construction of eleven locomotives for the London Transport Executive. In the wagon shops the main work was the construction of 174 cement wagons which were completed between August and December. In 1975–6 six class 56 diesel electric locomotives were built augmenting the more 'bread and butter' work of repairs and maintenance. New construction of eighteen of the class 56 locomotives continued in 1977–8. But prospects for the end of the 1970s and early 1980s were not so good. Virtually no overtime was worked in 1980 and there was talk of possible redundancies.[15]

More work in the late 1970s and early 1980s was provided by the removal of asbestos from locomotives. Dick Sargeant started work at the Plant in October 1926 at the age of sixteen and retired in 1974. For thirty-eight years he was working with asbestos. The 140 square feet 'crinolines' which were wrapped round the boilers of locomotives were unwrapped and laid out on the shop floor during major repairs. Sargeant worked in an atmosphere so thick with asbestos dust that it was sometimes difficult to see his mate working only a few feet away. In 1980, six years after his retirement, he was in hospital with a chest complaint which was eventually diagnosed as 'bronchitis aggravated with asbestosis'. For twenty years or more staff suffered from these harmful working conditions because there was a general ignorance about asbestosis as a specific industrial disease. In consequence lots of former employees had 'cancer' written on their death certificates where 'asbestosis' should have been stated.[16]

65 Women employed in fitting asbestos crinoline to a boiler barrel in the Second World War

In 1982 the Department of Transport and the Health and Safety Executive issued a joint ruling that asbestos should be removed from all trains by 1987.[17] This was a very belated decision. As early as 1969 the Ministry of Health had advised against the use of asbestos because of its danger to the lungs. In the autumn of that year the Workshops Division of BR responded by authorizing expenditure of £40 000 for the erection of new buildings at the Plant with extraction equipment designed to protect workshop staff and, indirectly, the travelling public, from the dangers of asbestos dust.[18] From then onwards workers resembling 'spacemen' in appearance could be seen entering and leaving the special buildings.

Although BREL authorized a programme of asbestos stripping in the summer of 1982, by November that year, as a result of financial pressures, it downgraded the repairs from Category C1 to Category C3. This involved partial, rather than complete, stripping of the asbestos from the Diesel Multiple Unit (DMU) fleet. The result of this decision was that the full protection of the staff and passengers from this risk to their health was delayed and that 164 wages staff and seventeen salaried staff at Doncaster were made redundant.[19]

By 1982 the affairs of BREL were in a state of crisis. At a meeting of the Rail Council held on 15 April 1982 the representatives of the BR Board informed the unions of a manpower surplus of 5000 staff in BREL and spoke of the consequent need to close two or three main works. They said that the prospect was of a continuing decrease in fleet requirements up to 1986 with a parallel decline in build and maintenance requirements. A week later at a meeting of the Rail Shopmen's Informal Liaison Committee, management of BREL presented the unions with two papers. The first showed the theoretical basis upon which all workshops could be retained by means of a reorganization of the traditional allocation of work load. This would mean a reduction of the surplus manpower from 5000 to 3500. But, even so, the Shildon wagon works would have 900 surplus staff and it would be uneconomic for it to continue in operation.

The second BREL paper proposed more drastic action. It involved the complete closure of Shildon Works by 30 May 1983 with 2285 redundancies; the closure, except for the foundry and spring shop, of the Horwich works by the end of 1982 and the semi-closure of Swindon works by December 1983 with the loss of 1300 jobs. In the reallocation of work consequent upon these closures some of the remaining workshops, including Doncaster, Crewe, Glasgow and Wolverton would have their work load increased.

BREL's assessment of the workshops situation was made in the context of the Thatcher government's transport policy. It was not an independent survey based on the need for a balanced transport policy, but rather one in which the state of BR's finances was an uppermost consideration.

The real needs of the railway were spelt out by Sir Peter Parker, Chairman of BR, in his Annual Reports of the Board. In 1979 he wrote:

> Only 16 locomotives were built in 1979, out of a total fleet of 2,000 which needed replacement ... Unless our investment levels are lifted by some 30 per cent just to replace worn out assets, the consequences will be lower standards of speed, frequency, comfort and reliability on rail services.[20]

In 1981 he warned that:

> 66 per cent of our fleet of electric and diesel multiple unit trains – the work horses of the commuter and rural services – is between 20 and 30 years old.

Their replacement had not been possible on the scale needed because BR's spending over the four years had been cut by increasing amounts in order to stay within increasingly stringent financial limits set by the government.[21]

Some scaling down of the work force in wagon building and repair was no doubt inevitable; but had the needs of the railway been met as stressed by Sir Peter Parker, there could have been plenty of work in other branches of railway engineering and the drastic slashing of workshop activities could have been avoided.

One result of the meeting of the Informal Liaison Committee of 22 April 1982 was the visit of a joint working party to each of the main workshops to assess their future needs for labour. Doncaster's turn came on Thursday 25 November that year. The visiting party compared the estimated manpower requirements at the end of 1983 with the current levels of staffing. It found that Category 4 staff, the skilled blue-collar workers, would be 209 persons below the necessary strength and Categories 1–3 119 over strength at the end of 1983. This would seem to suggest that there was no cause for undue concern in 1983 and 1984. However, over the period 1 October 1982 to 31 December 1984, 231 apprentices were due to complete their training and to be included in Category 4 staff. This resulted in an overall surplus of the highest qualified workers.[22]

The sad aftermath of these assessments was the decision of BREL in February 1984 to end the century-old tradition of the Plant works recruiting an annual intake of apprentices. No new recruits would be enrolled in 1985. In September that year there was a further blow when BREL revealed it was closing down the training school at Doncaster, along with three others. The training

66 Apprentices' training school, 1966

schools at Derby, Glasgow, Swindon and York were being kept as they were supported by government-sponsored youth training schemes. On this decision the comment of the secretary of the Doncaster No. 3 branch of the NUR was:

> We are concerned because apprentices are an insurance for the future. It is a crying shame as Doncaster has a reputation second to none for training youngsters.[23]

A further consequence of BREL's plans to introduce cuts in the railway workshops' labour force was the acceptance by the unions of the Relaxation Agreement of 2 November 1982. This was an arrangement whereby those Category 4 craftsmen who were surplus to requirements undertook to do work generally performed by Categories 1 and 2 staff. The understanding was that it was a temporary agreement which would be abolished in the event of a national agreement being reached.[24] This was followed by a reconsideration of working practices in a trade union side meeting of the RSNC in September 1985. The unions agreed to the formation of composite work groups containing individuals with a core skill, but willing and able to carry out a range of tasks with maximum efficiency. 'Measured work' a form of payment by results, was widely adopted. Bonus payments for those taking part in group working were based on the principles laid down in a procedural agreement reached between BREL and the unions on 22 February 1978.[25] Clearly the unions were acting very realistically in an endeavour to secure the livelihoods of their members.

In view of the Government's failure to produce a clear strategy for BR in the context of the transport needs of the country, the Board asked the Secretary of State for Transport for 'a form of Contract for a Social Railway' which would give it 'a clear sense of direction and a workable financing framework'. The result was the appointment on 2 May 1982 of a Committee of Inquiry chaired by Sir David Serpell. Although the terms of reference of the inquiry were:

> To examine the finances of the railway and associated operations in the light of all relevant considerations, and to report on options for alternative policies, and their related objectives, designed to secure improved financial results in an efficiently run railway in Great Britain over the next 20 years.

in September 1982, David Howell wrote to Serpell directing him to give priority to suggestions for cutting railway operational costs over the next five years.[26]

The Committee found that in comparison with prices of US and Japanese manufacturers the prices charged by BREL for coaches and EMUs were competitive. It also found that, with the exception of locomotives, there was 'no *prima facie* evidence that the new build costs were excessive'.[27] Nevertheless, more competitive tendering, both within Britain and overseas, was advocated. At the same time it declared BREL workshops were 'seriously under utilized'.[28]

Although the Serpell Report was severely criticized and flawed in many of its findings, the Government, BR and BREL sought to implement many of the recommendations. In October 1983 the Secretary of State for Transport, Nicholas Ridley, wrote to Robert Reid, the recently appointed Chairman of the BR Board, directing him to reduce excess capacity within BREL; review the options for the future of BREL, including the possibility of privatization; obtain rolling stock wherever possible by competitive tendering and generally to seek greater private sector participation in the future development of the railway.[29]

Following this directive, in the course of 1983 BREL announced for 1984 the complete closure of the Temple Mills Wagon Works with the loss of 400 jobs, the run down of work at Horwich and the closure of Shildon Works with 1200 redundancies. The unions were assured that the situation would then be stable, at least until 1986. When Mr James Urquhart, BREL Chairman, met the union leaders on 24 November 1983 he gave no indication of further redundancies. A few days later the unions were perturbed to read newspaper articles predicting hundreds more job losses in 1984. When Mr Urquhart was questioned about these reports he admitted that the situation was 'disquieting' but he was 'unable to give any assurances on the future of BREL'.[30]

In the case of Doncaster 140 jobs went in the first two months of 1984. The impact of the cuts was not as serious as it was at Shildon, since enough volunteers for voluntary redundancy came forward to cover the staff reductions. The Plant also had new construction work in hand on Class 58 DML locomotives for BR and repair work on DML locomotives and shunting locomotives.

67 Class 58 locomotive no. 58020 Doncaster Works, 1984

68 Railfreight Class 58 locomotive, early 1980

104

REORGANIZATION AND PRIVATIZATION, 1970–90

Throughout the 1980s the railway unions resisted plans to close workshops and to make drastic reductions in staffing levels. It must be admitted that their efforts in this direction were largely ineffective; but hard work in negotiating redundancy payments brought results. In the workshops the NUR recruited about two thirds of the blue collar staff while the CS & EU recruited the remainder. At Doncaster in September 1970 the NUR had 1690 members and the CS & EU 865. In the engineering depots where there was a lower proportion of skilled craftsmen the NUR preponderance was greater. Since the NUR members' jobs were more at risk it is not surprising that that union took the lead in proposals for industrial action in opposition to the policy of workshop closures.

The unions organizing blue collar staff in the railway workshops were concerned about BREL's policy for ordering new equipment as well as about the massive job losses of the period 1982–4.[31] Following the recommendations of the Serpell Committee Report, more emphasis was given by BR to placing orders with private firms. In 1984 one third of the requirement of seventy-five lightweight DMUs (Railbuses) was placed with the private contractors, Walter Alexander, Coachbuilders Ltd., although this firm had no previous experience in building railway rolling stock and could not deliver the order in the requested contract time. The price quoted was reported to be 0.5 per cent lower than that quoted by BREL.[32] A further order, this time for a hundred medium-density DMUs, was split between BREL and the Birmingham firm of Metro-Cammell. Jimmy Knapp, General Secretary of the NUR, claimed that the BREL price beat its competitor's 'hands down', his evidence for the claim being a leaked Metro-Cammel telex. The managers of the private firm impressed on Nicholas Ridley, the Secretary of State for Transport, that it needed the order to keep it in business, the foreign market having slumped.[33]

These developments helped to persuade the executive of the NUR to call a one day strike of its workshop members on 10 August 1984 and to organize a demonstration in the town of Derby that day. The union hired a number of special trains to take its members to the demonstration and some of the 1500 members of the Doncaster No.3 branch boarded a train from Edinburgh which stopped at Doncaster station at 10.34 a.m.[34] The contingent following the branch banner is shown in figure 69.

The reductions in workshop staffing were bad enough in the period 1982–4. There was even worse news to follow in the spring and summer of 1986. Union representatives met leading managers of both BR and BREL on 20 June that year. They were informed of proposed staff reductions of 6279 within BREL and a further 1400 in the regions, making a total of 7679 over the next three years. In the executive of the NUR the opinion was unanimous that the time was right to conduct a ballot of the union's workshop members in accordance with the terms of the Trade Union Act, 1984, to discover whether they would support strike action. The result of the ballot was declared on 8 July 1986 and it showed that 5956 members supported the executive's recommendation for strike action whereas 11 715 – nearly twice as many – were opposed. Redundancy payments which many regarded as 'acceptable' if not over-generous, weakened the resolve of many of the older workers.[35]

In the later 1980s the rates of pay of BREL shopmen were slightly above the very low wages of the traffic staff of BR. Thus, from 11 April 1989 Category 1 shopmen were on a weekly rate of £111.75 while those in Category 4 were paid at a weekly rate of £139.30. By comparison the starting grade of 'Railman' was on a basic rate of no more than £95.80 a week, while trackmen started at £105.10 and signalmen at £107.45. However, following the introduction of the Relaxation Agreement in November 1982, shopmen who were qualified tradesmen but who worked 'on the fringes' of other trades, e.g. qualified electricians who had some training as fitters and did the more repetitive work, were entitled to a bonus of £8.20 weekly, although at the same time their hourly rates were slightly reduced. Also most workshop staff were members of gangs which were assigned particular tasks to be completed in a given time. A price was paid for the completion of the task and the rewards shared by the members of the gang. It was a far more flexible, if also more complicated, system of wage payment than was traditional in the industry.[36]

69 Demonstration against workshop cuts, Derby, 10 August 1984

In 1982 the Doncaster works employed forty-four women office cleaners, nine of whom were full-time workers, classed as 'female labourers' earning £76.60 for a forty hour week. The thirty-five part-time cleaners were only allowed to work a total of eighteen hours, made up of three hours on each of six mornings. For this labour they received £23.50. F. Linney, a shopman member of the Doncaster No.3 branch of the NUR, pleaded with the union's AGM delegates on 7 July 1982 to press BREL to alter the basis of payment of the part-time women. He questioned 'how many delegates... would have their wives get up at 5.30 a.m. for six mornings out of seven for that mere pittance?' He pointed out that the part-time cleaners did the same kind of work as did those employed full time and that they should be paid at least the same rate as the full timers, *pro rata* to the hours worked. The AGM endorsed this appeal by a majority of sixty-four to thirteen but BREL would not agree to the change urged by the union.[37]

One indication of the increasing financial restraints imposed on BREL was the phasing out of the annual works' outing to the seaside. In the

70 BRITISH RAIL ENGINEERING WORKS DONCASTER 1987 JUST BEFORE BEING SPLIT UP.

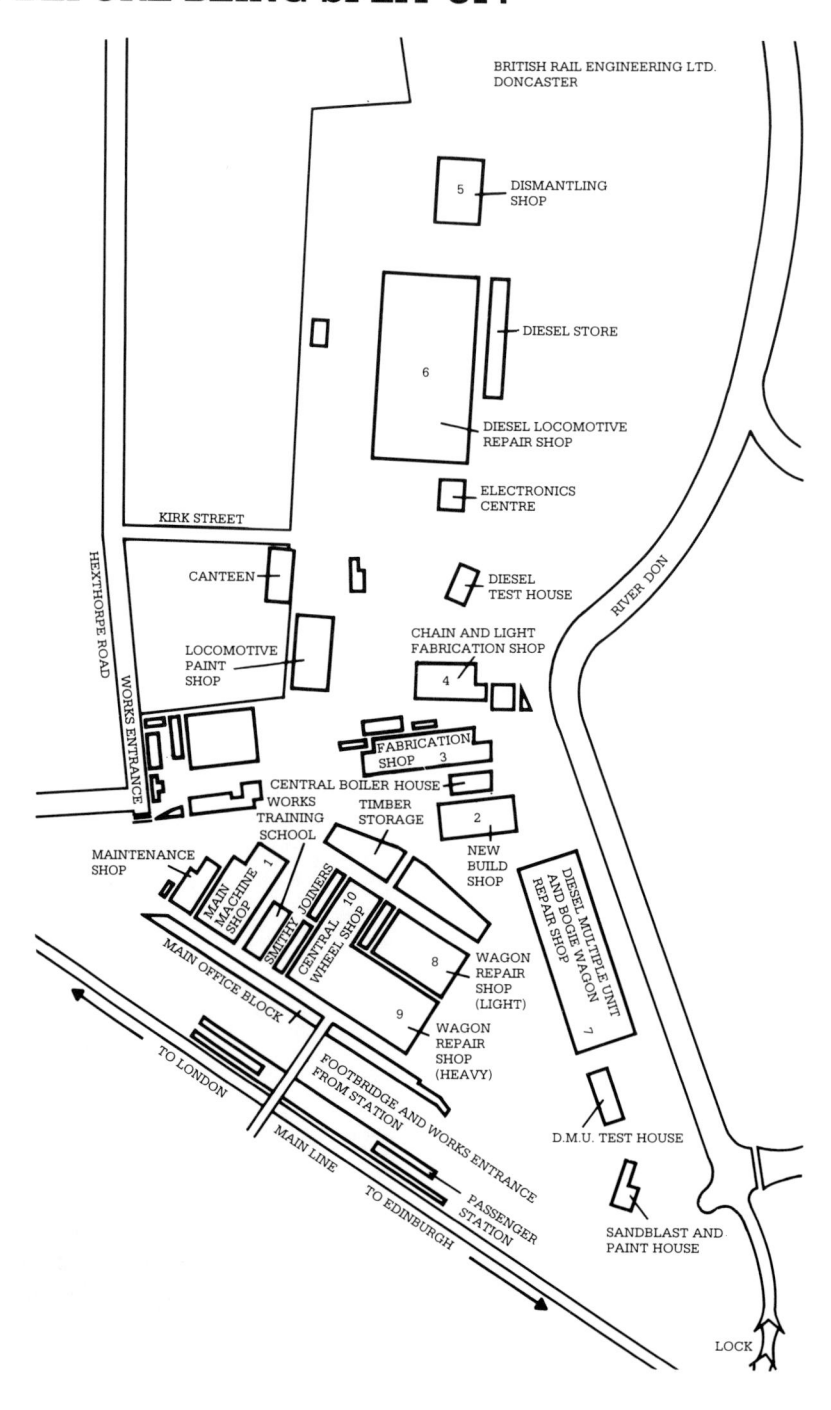

paternalistic days of the GNR and LNER several train loads of workers and their children were carried free on the outward and return journeys to and from the coastal resorts. As late as 1965 two trains were provided free by BR to take the families to Skegness and back. In 1967 a charge of £110 was made for the hire of the trains. In 1971 hard bargaining with BREL was needed to bring the charge down from £325 to £300. Thereafter the more than century-long tradition of an annual works' outing to the seaside came to an end.[38]

Another more recently established tradition was the annual presentation ceremony for long-serving employees on their retirement. BR prepared a catalogue of possible presentation gifts, such as mantel clocks, televisions, etc. from which the employee was invited to choose. A coach party would then visit a place of historic interest, a special meal would be laid on and the presentations made. The last such outing was held in 1988 when a visit was made to Harewood House. After this, the huge reductions in staff numbers and the division of the old works into three separate undertakings meant that the numbers retiring from any one of the establishments in any one year was too small to justify a special outing.[39]

In the 1970s members of the Works Committee became more safety conscious. The first Safety Committee was established in 1971. Monthly meetings were held and a 'Black Museum' was set up in two railway passenger coaches with some 600 exhibits showing dangers arising from the misuse of equipment and the ways to avoid accidents in the Works and in the home.[40] At the same time union activists pressed for better provision for protective clothing. By February 1985 BREL management agreed to some categories of workshop staff being given a subsidy of two-thirds of the cost of up to two pairs of BR-approved safety boots in the first year of the scheme with, thereafter, 'as required', up to two pairs per annum.[41]

At a meeting of the Rail Council held on 21 January 1986 the BR Board tabled a new Manufacturing and Maintenance Policy. BREL Ltd was to be split into two distinct business groups from April 1986. The New Build and Repair Group, comprising Crewe; Derby Litchurch Lane and Derby Loco; York and Horwich Foundry, would concentrate on new build, heavy overhaul and component repairs and would be financially independent of BR. The other group known as BR Maintenance Ltd (BRML) would comprise the Works at Wolverton, Doncaster, Eastleigh and Glasgow and would be under the direct control of BR. It was also announced that from April 1987 the Board would take over from BREL responsibility for providing new materials' stores based on a site at Doncaster occupying a part of the old Plant works area.

The effect of these radical changes on Doncaster was to split the works into three parts. The BRML Doncaster Depot on the western side of the old works complex with its various shops is shown in the diagram. The National Store, under direct BR control, and holding the spares for the entire BR network, occupy several buildings near the river Don side of the old Plant works area. The third part, nearest the Doncaster Central railway station and containing wagon construction and repair shops, was sold to RFS Industries, a consortium financed by several banks, on 16 October 1987.[42] In April 1990 the total number of staff employed on the three sites was over 1600, with 673 waged and 98 salaried staff employed by BRML, approximately 250 working in the National Store and some 600 employed by RFS Industries.

In the Doncaster BRML Depot a large variety of locomotives, mainly DMUs, including classes 31, 37, 47, 56 and 58; power units of Inter-City 125s; shunting engines and class 20 unclassified locomotives were maintained and all but class 47 overhauled. The bogies of all class locomotives except 47 were maintained. The watchword at this Depot was 'Cost Effective Maintenance', the speedy turn-round of vehicles achieved, in part, by a policy of 'component exchange'. Although the staff were generally fully capable of undertaking repairs, the practice was to exchange the damaged or worn-out component for a new one, to minimize delays. DMUs brought into the shops one day were frequently maintained by the night shift working in gangs and made ready for service again on the following morning. The staff, stunned by heavy job losses in the middle 1980s, responded to the Depot

71 DONCASTER DEPOT

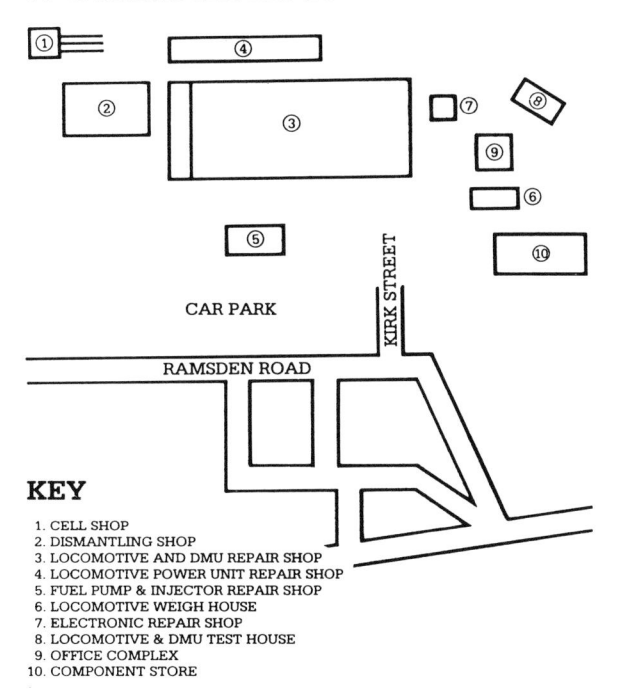

KEY
1. CELL SHOP
2. DISMANTLING SHOP
3. LOCOMOTIVE AND DMU REPAIR SHOP
4. LOCOMOTIVE POWER UNIT REPAIR SHOP
5. FUEL PUMP & INJECTOR REPAIR SHOP
6. LOCOMOTIVE WEIGH HOUSE
7. ELECTRONIC REPAIR SHOP
8. LOCOMOTIVE & DMU TEST HOUSE
9. OFFICE COMPLEX
10. COMPONENT STORE

Manager's policy of joint consultation with the staff on all aspects of production. There were regular official meetings with the Depot Committee of eight but there was an 'open door' to management to ensure that, as far as possible, no grievance festered. The feeling among both management and staff was that if only they were spared more organizational changes imposed by government, there was prospect of a more secure future.[43]

Those planning the establishment of the National Stores miscalculated the amount of space which would be needed for a central depot and more buildings, including the fabrication shop and the chain and light fabrication shop, had to be taken over. Stores to the value of £2½ million were dispatched from Doncaster each week. It would naturally be expected that these would be sent by rail, since all stores went to railway centres. Freightliner Ltd did make a bid for the work but the contract went to Swift Transport Services of Wakefield. BR Freight and Parcels sectors were not invited to tender. The unions believed that Mr Tidmarsh, the electronics industry entrepreneur and leading board member of the LEP Company, had a large hand in ensuring that the contract went to the firm of Swift which had recently been acquired by LEP.

Meanwhile RFS industries was well supplied with wagon construction and repair work. In April 1990 it was awarded a contract for the construction of large capacity coal wagons worth £20 million, the kind or order that the wagon department of BREL's, still-in-one-piece, Doncaster works would love to have secured only a few months earlier.[44]

72 Visit of BR Chairman to Doncaster Depot, 10 March 1989

108

CONCLUSIONS

When the nineteenth-century growth of Doncaster is compared with that of other important railway manufacturing towns such as Crewe, Derby and Swindon, it is clear that all had the common characteristic of being well placed geographically for the railway networks they served. The dependence of Crewe on its railway workshops was more complete than was the case with any of the others. In 1841 there was no place called Crewe mentioned in the population census of that year. The two parishes of Monks Copenhall and Church Copenhall, later to become the site of the new railway town, had a combined population of only 741 persons.[1] Derby, by contrast, was an old market town with an already well-established pottery industry when the recently formed Midland Railway set up its workshops there in 1844. Old Swindon was like Doncaster in that at the time of the arrival of the Great Western Railway there in 1840 it was a market town with a wide catchment area but without an industrial base.

In the case of Doncaster there is no doubt that the arrival of the GNR in the town in 1849 and, more importantly, the establishment of the Plant works there in 1853 were the outstanding causes for the more than doubling of its population from 12 005 in 1851 to 25 933 in 1891. The railway workshops were the principal source of both employment and wealth in the town in the second half of the century. As late as 1932 the LNER paid nearly half the wages of all who lived in the Doncaster district and that company was the largest single ratepayer in the borough. It is true that the opening up of the South Yorkshire coalfield in the first two decades of the new century and the expansion of general engineering from the later 1930s onwards challenged the Plant works' predominance, but it was not until the later 1950s and after that the sharp decline in BR's railway workshop activity set in.

The erection of a tall chimney at the works in 1855 was a visible sign that Doncaster was becoming industrialized. The completion of the tall spires of the Plant Church (St James') and the Parish Church of St George in 1858 was evidence that the establishment of the GNR workshops in the town was also influencing its spiritual and cultural development. Edmund Denison, the Chairman of the GNR, raised subscriptions for the building of St James' and was also an active sponsor in the rebuilding of St George's after its destruction by fire in 1853. The initiative for the building of a number of nonconformist churches and chapels in the middle 1850s came mainly from better off employees of the works.

From 1854 when the GNR Board voted £1000 towards the establishment of a school for the children of the Plant works' employees, until 1903, when the company decided to sell one of its two schools to the Local Education Authority and to let out the other on a twenty-one year lease, it made an important contribution to the development of primary education in the town. Nor was the provision of adult education neglected. The Great Northern Doncaster Mechanics Institute was founded in the same year as the Plant works began operation. In 1863 the company provided a recreation ground for the use of its employees and by the 1880s each department had its own cricket team. Nigel Gresley was particularly keen to sponsor sporting activities and in 1920 he and other directors were present at the official opening of the LNER's Eden Grove Playing Fields in Hexthorpe. He donated the Gresley Cup for which there was keen competition between the departmental cricket teams.[2]

The link between the Plant works and the Doncaster Rovers football team, founded in 1879, was very close. 'Tich' Pearce, who retired from employment at the Plant in 1933, started as a trainer for the Rovers in 1903 and helped them win the Sheffield Challenge Cup in 1912. At that time the team had its ground on the Intake. A big problem in those days was filling the big zinc bath which held 500 gallons of water and could hold up to eight men. After a match all the players made a concerted rush for the bath where they were paid. Pearce recalled that possibly the first eight men would be given their wages, but those who turned up later would be told by the secretary that it had been a wet day, the gate had been poor and they would therefore have to wait until the following week to be paid. In 1922 the club moved to the Belle Vue ground.

The presence of the Plant works' brass bands on

ceremonial occasions and on the works' outings to the seaside was an indication that the musical life of the town was flourishing.

Employees of the Plant works and those based at the railway station at Doncaster played a distinguished part in the politics and local government of the district. As Appendix B demonstrates, nineteen of the Mayors of Doncaster who held office between 1910 and 1987 inclusive, were railway workers. Eight of these were skilled craftsmen from the workshops, six were railway clerks, four were from the traffic grades and one was a retired supervisor. Those who achieved the distinction of the mayoralty were only the tip of the iceberg compared with the many more who served as councillors from the time Doncaster had a town council in 1902 and then became a county borough in 1927.

Doncaster men played a significant part in the growth of trade unionism both locally and nationlly and, through their trade unions, influenced national political developments. Within three years of the foundation of the Amalgamated Society of Railway Servants (ASRS) in 1872 the Doncaster branch of the Society had 108 members.[3] Between 1880 and 1898 three of its members were elected to the National Executive Committee of the Union, W. Hoyes in 1880, D.V. Cooper in 1884 and 1890–1 and T.R. Steels in 1897–8.[4] At that time the branch met at the Good Woman Inn, St Sepulcre Gate.[5] It was there in March 1899 that T.R. Steels moved the adoption of the famous resolution which J. Holmes proposed at the Plymouth Congress of the TUC in September of the same year. Its adoption by Congress led to the creation of the Labour Representation Committee (LRC) in 1900, an organization which changed its name to 'The Labour Party' in 1906. Steels, who was a member of the Independent Labour Party (ILP), stood as an LRC candidate in a municipal by-election in South Ward Doncaster in July 1903. He defeated W.C. Wright, a grocer of Catherine Street, by 222 votes to 218.[6] He was the first Labour member of the council.

If it can be claimed that actions of workers employed by the railway had some impact on local and national politics, it is much more the case that the actions of MPs at Westminster were often decisive in shaping the history of Doncaster's railway workshops. Edmund Denison's influence as MP for the West Riding division of Yorkshire from 1841–7 and 1848–59 was decisive in two respects. Between 1844 and 1846 he fought prolonged battles in Parliamentary Committees to secure the adoption of the London and York through route to the North and Scotland rather than George Hudson's plans for alternative routes either through the Fens or through the Midland counties. Had Hudson's plan for a route via Leicester and Rotherham been adopted Doncaster would have been by-passed and it would not have been a possible option for the location of the GNR's main workshops.[7]

Denison's second decisive intervention was to persuade the GNR Board to reject the recommendation of Archibald Sturrock, the Chief Mechanical Engineer, that Peterborough should be selected as the most suitable location for the company's workshops. Denison's skilful delaying tactics eventually paid off when the Board decided in favour of Doncaster on 3 June 1851.

Political influences were of less significance for the development of the Plant works in the period before the First World War. In 1914, however, in order to secure the most economical use of the nation's transport resources the individual railway companies were placed under the directon of the Railway Executive Committee and its Railway War Production Sub-Committee. The structure of the work performed at the Plant was changed through the virtual cessation of new carriage building and the limitation of new wagon building to essential replacements. More importantly the experience of war and a large degree of unified working under government direction paved the way for the consolidation of ownership under just four main-line companies under the Railways Act of 1921.

The grouping of the railways under the 1921 Act was a political decision made by Sir Eric Geddes, the Minister of Transport, who was influenced by the lobbying of group interests and a judgment about future industrial and commercial developments. The assumption that the economy of the North East, based on the coal, iron and steel and shipbuilding industries, would continue to prosper after the conclusion of the war proved ill-founded. In many of the inter-war years, and not just in the slump years of 1929–32, the heavy industries were severely depressed. The LNER's mineral traffic in 1932 was only half of what it had been in 1924; but in the relatively prosperous year of 1938 it was still only 69 per cent of the 1924 volume. Inevitably the Plant works felt the repercussions of this situation with severe fluctuations in the demand for both locomotives and rolling stock.

The decision to declare war on Germany on 3 September 1939 had even more profound effects on railway engineering than did Britain's involvement in the First World War. As early as May 1941 more than one fifth of the staff employed by the LNER were engaged in war work. At Doncaster, as in other workshop towns, there soon developed a severe shortage of labour. At the Plant this was in large measure met by the extensive employment of women. They were engaged in a greater variety of tasks than their predecessors of 1914–18 had been.

Even during the immediate aftermath of the First World War Lloyd George's Coalition government gave serious consideration to plans for the nationalization of the railways as the advantages of unified wartime control were appreciated. As a result of an even longer experience of the advantages of unified control of railways in the Second World War 'some form of public ownership or control was inevitable whatever the political party in power at the time'.[8] The record majority achieved by the Labour Party in the General Election of 5 July 1945 ensured that the railways, along with canals, buses and a substantial fraction of road freight haulage, would be placed under public ownership.

The Plant works were fully occupied after the passing of the Transport Act of 1947 in making good the arrears of construction and maintenance which had accumulated during the war years. A political decision of the Attlee government, confronted with the ending of Lend Lease in August 1945, was to give priority in steel allocations to export industries, thus limiting the new build programme in the workshops.

The Attlee government's aim in placing the main forms of surface transport under public control through the British Transport Commission was to co-ordinate and integrate all the principal forms of freight and passenger transport. Before 1939 the main-line railway companies had diversified their activities to include, inter alia, shipping, docks, road haulage and hotel services. The profits from these subsidiary undertakings were used to cross-subsidize the railways. In the same way in the early years of the BTC the growing surpluses of the Road Haulage Executive between 1949 and 1953 helped to keep solvent the finances of the BTC and therefore helped to sustain full activity in the railway workshops.

The return of the Conservatives to power following their General Election victory on 25 October 1951 led to a major change in direction in transport policy. Under the Transport Act of 1953 all attempts at establishing an integrated transport system were abandoned. The painstaking work of bringing together 2900 separate road haulage undertakings into one large and increasingly profitable business over the years 1949–53 was destroyed through the privatization of the Road Haulage Executive after 1953. Henceforward the possibility of the cross-subsidization of the profits of the road haulage industry to the railways was lost. At the same time the programme of standardization of design of locomotives and rolling stock which had begun under R.A. Riddles' direction in the Railway Executive was largely abandoned when responsibility for the workshops was transferred to the regions. Opportunities for specialization and economies of scale were then lost.

Great Britain lacked a comprehensive transport policy in the second half of the twentieth century. Its European partners worked on the assumption that large scale investment in the railways was essential for the maintenance of an efficient transport infrastructure for their economies. In Great Britain there was no consensus between the main political parties on the imperative need for a national railway system adequately financed from public funds, where necessary, in order to ensure the full potential of railway transport.

Whenever there was a balance of payments crisis or a downturn in economic activity, as in 1955, 1967–8, 1973–4 and 1979–80, railway investment suffered. Plans for new construction of locomotives and rolling stock were cut. The lack of confidence in government support for railways led to small runs of orders, inhibiting economies of scale. It was a 'stop-go' situation for railway workshop activity.

For a decade from 1979 railway investment was still further squeezed as the Public Service Obligation (PSO) grants were slashed and BR's External Financing Limit greatly reduced. In this era there occurred the closure of some of the leading workshops of Britain. In Doncaster the Plant works staff was reduced by over 1500 in the mid 1980s.

How was it that Doncaster's railway workshops survived – albeit on a much diminished scale – while others such as those at Swindon, Ashford and Inverurie did not? The Plant works' survival was no doubt partly due to its convenient situation in the heart of the North Eastern region. But the works had a reputation second to none for the skilled and dedicated workmanship of its staff. The Plant works had been in business for fifty years when the Inverurie works was opened in 1903. It therefore had a longer tradition of local people's attachment to a particular place of employment. By the 1980s it was very common for fourth generation men to be at work in the various shops which made up the Plant. This was the case with Jack Lovell, who retired, aged 63, on 11 August 1984 after 49 years service, mainly as a coachbuilder. His great-grandfather was a fitter who lived in one of the terraced houses built specially for craftsmen when the Plant opened in 1853. His father, like him, was a coachbuilder.[9] This kind of experience was common among Doncaster families, but admittedly not unique to the town.

What *was* unique was Doncaster's achievement in locomotive design and construction over many decades. **Mallard's** record of 126 m.p.h., gained in 1938, has not been beaten by any other steam locomotive, and the **Flying Scotsman** and **Silver Jubilee** are household words among train lovers. It would have been widely regarded as a national scandal if a works which had such an outstanding record – in carriage and rolling stock building as well as locomotive building – had been closed down completely. However, when the steam age passed the employees proved very adaptable to change. Steam traction ended on BR in 1968. In the 1970s the unions discussed 'group working' and 'measured work' in the light of the more sophisticated machinery by then in use in the factories and the decline in importance of the individual craftsman working on his own.[10] The Relaxation Agreement of 2 November marked the formal recognition of the need for changes in working practices. As is noted in chapter thirteen, Plant workers were rewarded for devising new inventions or methods of working. The workers at Doncaster found good reasons for supporting nationally organized demonstrations against workshop closures, but industrial relations at the Plant were generally good because of the willingness of management and staff representatives to settle problems by discussion wherever possible. This persuaded BR to allocate to Doncaster an important role in maintenance of locomotives and rolling stock.

What are the prospects for Doncaster's continuing involvement in railway engineering? Just as the works' past history has depended on the level of importance attached to rail transport by government and the electorate, so future policy decisions will determine whether or not the railway workshops will have an assured future. The immediate prospects for tipping the balance of transport investment more towards railways seem bleak. The passenger grant from central government to BR (the PSO) was cut by 40 per cent between 1986–90 at the same time as investment in roads increased. In 1989 West Germany's annual subsidy to railways was six times that given by local and national government to BR. The French government was committed to spending £4.5 billion on new high speed lines while the British government was reluctant to spend any money on the high speed rail link between the Channel Tunnel and London. In the longer term, however, prospects for railways in Britain may be brighter.

There is a growing awareness that the 'free market' policy for transport provision results in intolerable costs in the destruction of the environment through atmospheric pollution, noise and traffic congestion. In 1989 an Institution of Civil Engineers' report **Congestion**, noting that large parts of the road network had 'become choked for many hours' each day, concluded that 'the market for transportation, where it can be said to exist, is inefficient and distorted'. The report advocates increased taxes on heavy goods vehicles, the abolition of company car tax allowances, tax concessions on rail season tickets and increased capital expenditure on the rail infrastructure. Earlier policies of the CBI emphasized the need for more expenditure on roads, but its November 1989 publication, **Trade routes to the future**, which estimated the cost of road congestion to the nation at £15 billion annually, advocated that 'the external benefits of rail investment should be recognized by Government through environmental grants'. A central government strategic planning body was needed to work for a more balanced transport policy. It was the expectation that 'the Channel Tunnel fixed rail link will call forth a railway renaissance'. Reaching a larger readership, the **Observer Magazine** theme on 15 April 1990 – 'Choked! Britain's Transport Crisis' – used economic, environmental and social arguments for a greater investment in the rail network and a substantial improvement in BR's services.

If the policies advocated in these three publications are followed then the prospects for the railway workshops at Doncaster may well be brighter in the 1990s than they were in the 1980s.

APPENDIX A: CHIEF MECHANICAL ENGINEERS OF THE GNR AND THE LNER

Joseph Locke	May–September 1844
William Cubitt	1844–1848
Edward Bury	1848–1850
Archibald Sturrock	1850–1866
Patrick Stirling	1866–1895
Henry A. Ivatt	1895–1911
Sir Nigel Gresley	1911–1941
Edward Thompson	1941–1946
Arthur H. Peppercorn	1947

APPENDIX B: MAYORS OF DONCASTER EMPLOYED AT THE RAILWAY/PLANT

1910–11	Charles Wightman	Railway blacksmith
1913–14	Patrick Stirling	Engineer
1929–30	Walter James Crookes	Locomotive engine driver
1933–34	George Herbert Ranyard	Railway signalman
1934–35	Harry Herbert Bone	Painter and decorator (railway)
1937–38	Willie Corbett	Foreman brass finisher (railway)
1944–45	Frederick Charles Trotter	Railway clerk
1946–47	Harry Llewelyn Gee	Metal machinist (railway)
1947–May 1949	Percy Judd	Railway clerk

(Mayoral Election Day altered from November to May)

1953–54	Albert Edward Cammidge	Foundry foreman (railway)
1957–58	William Chappell	Fitter, motive power (railway)
1958–59	Arthur Harvey	Railway clerk
1959–60	Fred Ogden	Locomotive engine driver
1961–62	Thomas Henry Wright	Erecting shop foreman (railway)
1964–65	Stanley Claude Holbrook	Railway clerk
1968–69	William Hubert Kelly	Railway clerk
1973–74	Arthur Heaven	Railway clerk
1974–75	Albert Edward Cammidge	Retired railway supervisor
1986–87	Edward Gardner	Railway guard

NOTES AND REFERENCES

CHAPTER 1

1. J. Tomlinson, **Doncaster from the Roman Occupation to the Present Time** (1887 Doncaster, pub. by author), 214
2. Statement made by Councillor G. Watson when opening an exhibition of 'Old Doncaster', **Doncaster Chronicle**, 23 November 1933
3. **Doncaster Chronicle** Supplement, issued with the Centenary Edition of the paper, 12 March 1936
4. J. Murray, **The impact on Doncaster of the arrival of the GNR and its workshops, 1850–1870**. Typescript in Doncaster Public Library
5. **Doncaster Chronicle** Supplement, 12 March 1936
6. J. Murray, op. cit., 9

CHAPTER 2

1. R. Hough, **Six Great Railwaymen** (Hamish Hamilton 1958), 88
2. Hough, op. cit., 89
3. O.S. Nock, **The Great Northern Railway** (Ian Allan 1958), 3
4. Advertisement in **The Times**, 10 September 1844
5. C.H. Grinling, **The History of the Great Northern Railway** (1966 edn.), 23
6. H.G. Lewin, **The Railway Mania and its Aftermath, 1845–52** (David & Charles 1968), 16
7. Grinling, op. cit., 32
8. Minutes of the Board of the Great Northern Railway, PRO RAIL, 236/14
9. **Doncaster, Nottingham and Lincoln Gazette**, 7 September 1849
10. P. Ferriday, **Lord Grimthorpe, 1816–1905** (John Murray 1957), 4–5
11. PRO RAIL, 236/12
12. PRO RAIL, 236/14
13. ibid.
14. Grinling, op. cit., 211
15. PRO RAIL 236/13
16. Ferriday, op. cit., 4
17. J.E. Day, **History of the Doncaster Plant Works**, Typescript in Doncaster Public Library (1953), 1
18. PRO RAIL 236/14 and 15
19. Minutes of the Executive Committee of the GNR, PRO RAIL, 236/71. See Also Sturrock's strong recommendation of Peterborough to the directors in PRO RAIL 236/16
20. GNR Board Minutes, 14 May 1851, PRO RAIL 236/16
21. ibid.
22. E.J. and J.G. Larkin, **The Railway Workshops of Britain, 1823–1986** (1988), 75
23. **Doncaster, Nottingham and Lincoln Gazette**, 6 June 1851

CHAPTER 3

1. Day, op. cit., 1
2. ibid., 3
3. Reports to the Directors from Joseph Cubitt, Engineer, PRO RAIL 236/275/2
4. Report from A. Sturrock to the executive committee of the GNR, 8 November 1851, PRO RAIL 236/206
5. GNR, Minutes of the Board of Directors, 4 January and 25 February 1853, PRO RAIL 236/18
6. ibid., 15 February 1853
7. Grinling, op. cit., 137
8. **Doncaster Chronicle**, 19 July 1861
9. **Doncaster, Nottingham and Lincoln Gazette**, 6 August 1852 and 5 July 1853
10. C.W. Hatfield, **Historical Notices of Doncaster, September 26th 1862–December 22nd 1865**, cited in Murray, op. cit., 60
11. Grinling, op. cit., 138
12. **Doncaster, Nottingham and Lincoln Gazette**, 4 March 1853
13. Hough, op. cit., 108–9
14. Ferriday, op. cit., 33–4
15. Nock, op. cit., 22. GNR, Report of the Directors to the 25th half yearly ordinary general meeting of the proprietors 19 February 1859, Appendix: St James' Church, Doncaster, PRO RAIL 236/24
16. Report from E.B. Denison to the Board of the GNR, 19 February 1859, PRO RAIL 236/14
17. **Doncaster, Nottingham and Lincoln Gazette**, 29 February 1856
18. Report from E. B. Denison to the Board of the GNR 19 February 1859, PRO RAIL 236/14
19. **Doncaster, Nottingham and Lincoln Gazette**, 3 March 1854
20. **Doncaster, Nottingham and Lincoln Gazette**, 17 March and 20 October 1854
21. **Doncaster, Nottingham and Lincoln Gazette**, 1 August 1856
22. **Doncaster, Nottingham and Lincoln Gazette**, 12 June 1857
23. **Doncaster, Nottingham and Lincoln Gazette**, 2 June and 29 December 1854
24. GNR, Minutes of the Board of Directors, 8 August 1855, PRO RAIL 236/21
25. **Doncaster, Nottingham and Lincoln Gazette**, 14 December 1855
26. GNR, Minutes of the Board of Directors, 7 February 1859, PRO RAIL 236/21
27. Statement of the working of the Great Northern Mechanics Institute, read at the close of the lecture on 'The Cultivation of Literature', given by the Mayor on 24 October 1856
28. **Doncaster, Nottingham and Lincoln Gazette**, 9 December 1853
29. GNR, Minutes of the Board of Directors, 12 June 1855, PRO RAIL 236/20 and 10 August 1855, PRO RAIL 236/21
30. **Doncaster Gazette** 25 January 1940
31. Day, op. cit., 6
32. GNR, Minutes of the Board of Directors, 6 October 1851, PRO RAIL 236/17

CHAPTER 4

1. Grinling, op. cit., 453
2. Day, op. cit., 21
3. T.C. Barker and M. Robbins, **A History of London Transport**, vol. 1 (1975), 122–3, Day, op. cit., 23
4. Day, op. cit., 39
5. Grinling, op. cit., 72
6. Day, op. cit., 39
7. Grinling, op. cit., 412
8. J. Wrottesley, **The Great Northern Railway**, Vol. 1 (1979), 190
9. **Doncaster Chronicle** 21 September 1866
10. Larkin, op. cit., 76
11. **Doncaster Gazette** 25 May 1923, '70 Years of the Doncaster Plant'
12. PRO RAIL 236/288/1 and 236/288/11, 11 May 1863
13. **Doncaster Chronicle**, 1 July 1864
14. **Doncaster Chronicle**, 21 February 1873
15. **Doncaster Chronicle**, 1 February 1861
16. **Doncaster Chronicle**, 18 January 1861
17. **Doncaster Chronicle**, 22 July 1864
18. **Doncaster, Nottingham and Lincoln Gazette**, 16 June 1854
19. **Doncaster Chronicle**, 9 July 1869
20. **Doncaster Chronicle**, 6 March 1868
21. **Doncaster Chronicle**, 5 May 1877
22. **Doncaster Chronicle**, 8 November 1861
23. **Doncaster Chronicle**, 10 October 1862
24. **Doncaster Chronicle**, 15 August 1862
25. **Doncaster, Nottingham and Lincoln Gazette**, 14 October 1859
26. **Doncaster Chronicle**, 12 July 1861
27. PRO RAIL 236/30, 22 July 1862
28. Wrottesley, op. cit., Vol. 1, 154
29. Hough, op. cit., 132–3, **Doncaster Chronicle**, 29 May 1974
30. Wrottesley, op. cit., Vol. 1, 239

CHAPTER 5

1. This account of Patrick Stirling is based on Day, op. cit., 24, 27
2. O.S. Nock, **Steam Locomotive: a restrospect of the work of eight great locomotive engineers**, British Railways Board (1964), 17–18
3. Grinling, op. cit., 364, 380, 423
4. Day, op. cit., 26–7
5. **GNR Rolling Stock: Report by the General Manager to the Board**, 8 November 1877 PRO RAIL 236/327. **GNR Rolling Stock: Report of the Locomotive Engineer**, 17 December 1877, PRO RAIL 236/43
6. J. Simmons, **The Railway in England and Wales, 1830–1914**, Vol. 1 (Leicester University Press 1978), 210.
7. **GNR Rolling Stock, Report of the Locomotive Engineer**, 17 December 1877, 10. PRO RAIL 236/43
8. Simmons, op. cit., 205
9. GNR Rolling Stock Reports, 8 November and 17 December, as above
10. ibid., and Reports of Messrs Fletcher and Co. Public Accountants, and of Mr James Ramsbottom, the engineer referred to in the Directors Report to the GNR Shareholders, August 1878, PRO RAIL 236/44
11. GNR Board Minutes, 7 October 1882, PRO RAIL 236/46 and 2 April 1886 and 2 November 1888, PRO RAIL 236/60
12. Minutes of GNR Board, 6 December 1889, PRO RAIL 236/52
13. GNR Traffic Committee decision on recommendation of H. Oakley, General Manager, 14 July 1884, PRO RAIL 236/354/7
14. Simmons, op. cit., 209
15. P.S. Bagwell, **The Railway Clearing House**, (Allen & Unwin 1968), 201–8
16. Simmons, op. cit., 198
17. Simmons, op. cit., 196
18. Letter from H. Oakley, General Manager to the Board of the GNR, 26 October 1872, PRO RAIL 236/313/23
19. GNR Board, 4 December 1874, PRO RAIL 236/315/23
20. F.A.S. Brown, **Great Northern Locomotive Engineers**, Vol. 1, **1846–1881** (Allen & Unwin 1966), 184, 186
21. A.H. Ahrons, **Locomotive and Train Working in the later part of the Nineteenth Century**, Vol. 1 (Cambridge, Heffer 1951), 1
22. Wrottesley, op. cit., Vol. 2 (1979), 184
23. GNR Board, 19 November 1875, PRO RAIL 236/41
24. GNR Board, 28 January 1878, PRO RAIL 236/327/4
25. GNR Board, 25 October and 22 November 1979, PRO RAIL 236/44
26. **Doncaster Chronicle**, 24 October and 28 November 1879
27. Day, op. cit., 41
28. GNR Board, 4 October 1892, PRO RAIL 236/373/2
29. GNR Board, 4 October 1895 and 17 June 1896, PRO RAIL 236/376 Pt. 1
30. GNR Board, 31 March 1885, PRO RAIL 236/49 and 16 March 1893 PRO RAIL 236/375/7
31. Grinling, op. cit., 307–9
32. GNR Board, 9 April 1875, PRO RAIL 236/41
33. Patrick Stirling, Letter to H. Oakley, 31 July 1872, PRO RAIL 236/313/20
34. Grinling, op. cit., 348–9
35. Grinling, op. cit., 381
36. GNR Board, 1 April, 6 May and 11 August 1887, PRO RAIL 236/50
37. GNR Board, 17 October 1873, PRO RAIL 236/39
38. GNR, Report from Patrick Stirling to the Board, 17 December 1877, PRO RAIL 236/327/11
39. GNR Board, 21 December 1877, PRO RAIL 236/357/13
40. GNR Board, 4 November 1881, PRO RAIL 236/46
41. GNR Board, 28 October 1881, PRO RAIL 236/338/4
42. GNR Board, 2 February 1882, PRO RAIL 236/46
43. GNR Board, 5 October 1883, PRO RAIL 236/47
44. GNR Board, 2 March 1888, PRO RAIL 236/51. Wrottesley, op. cit., Vol. 2, 68
45. GNR Board, 6 December 1889, PRO RAIL 236/52
46. 'The Great Northern Railway Works, Doncaster', **The Engineer**, 16 December 1892, 515. A.J. Brickwell, 'The Great Northern Railway Works at Doncaster', in 'Various Authors', **Round the Works of our Great Railways** (London, Arnold 1894), 77
47. Larkin, op. cit., 76. Brickwell, op. cit., 77
48. **Doncaster Chronicle**, 10 July 1868
49. **Doncaster Chronicle**, 8 July 1870
50. **Doncaster Chronicle**, 7 July 1871
51. **Doncaster Chronicle**, 13 July 1877
52. **Doncaster Chronicle**, 5 July 1895
53. **Doncaster Chronicle**, 8 October 1880, 11 January and 11 October 1895
54. **Doncaster Chronicle**, 22 February 1895

CHAPTER 6

1. J.E. Day, op. cit., 28
2. O.S. Nock, **Great Northern 4–4–2 Atlantics** (Ian Allan 1984), 9
3. ibid., 10
4. ibid., 9
5. **Railway Magazine**, December 1898
6. Wrottesley, op. cit., Vol. 3 181. Day, op. cit., 29
7. G.F. Bird, **The Locomotives of the Great Northern Railway, 1847–1910** (London Locomotive Publishing Company 1910), 161
8. Day, op. cit., 31
9. Nock, op. cit., 54
10. Day, op. cit., 31
11. GNR, Locomotive Committee Report, 28 September 1891, PRO RAIL 236/370/3
12. Day, op. cit., 41. Nock, op. cit., 41
13. **The Railway Gazette**, 25 September 1953, 363
14. J. Armstrong, 'The role of coastal shipping in UK transport. An estimate of comparative movements in 1910', **The Journal of Transport History**, 3rd Ser. Vol. 8 No. 2, September 1987, 164–178.
15. Bird, op. cit., 179
16. Minutes of the GNR Board, 6 December 1901 and 3 July 1903 PRO RAIL 236/60 and 236/61
17. Minutes of the GNR Board, 3 October 1902. PRO RAIL 236/60
18. Minutes of the GNR Board, 6 March 1908 and 5 March 1909 PRO RAIL 236/63
19. C.E. Lee, **Passenger Class Distinctions** (London Railway Gazette 1946) 45
20. C.J. Allen, **Great Northern** (Ian Allan 1961) 35
21. Grinling, op. cit., 429
22. Allen, ibid.
23. D.N. Smith, **The Railway and its Passengers. A Social History** (David & Charles 1988) 130
24. Letter filed with GNR Board Minutes. PRO RAIL 236/62 C.H. Montgomery **Railway Car Lighting** (1907) 167 Horwich Railway Mechanics Instutute Meeting, PRO reference Z LIB 5/89
25. Minutes of the GNR Board, 1 December 1905. PRO RAIL 236/62
26. Minutes of the GNR Board, 8 January 1897. PRO RAIL 236/57
27. Minutes of the GNR Board, 4 March 1898, PRO RAIL 236/58
28. Minutes of the GNR Board, 7 July 1899, 2 November 1900 and 1 February 1901. PRO RAIL 236/58 and 59
29. Minutes of the GNR Board, 1 February 1901. PRO RAIL 236/59
30. Minutes of the GNR Board, 5 December 1902. PRO RAIL 236/60
31. Minutes of the GNR Board, 1 December 1905, 29 June and 7 December 1906. PRO RAIL 236/62
32. Minutes of the GNR Board, 3 November 1905 and 7 July 1911. PRO RAIL 236/62 and 64
33. Minutes of the GNR Board, 1 December 1895. PRO RAIL 236/56
34. Minutes of the GNR Board, 2 November 1874. PRO RAIL 236/375/2
35. Minutes of the GNR Board, 29 January 1896. PRO RAIL 236/56
36. Minutes of the GNR Board, 9 January 1903. PRO RAIL 236/61
37. Minutes of the GNR Board, 12 June 1903. PRO RAIL 236/61
38. **Doncaster Chronicle**, 11 October 1895 and 5 October 1911

CHAPTER 7

1. PRO RAIL 236/302/5
2. Wage rates, for the fortnight to 15 October 1870, included in the above
3. H.A. Clegg, A. Fox and A.F. Thompson, **A History of British Trade Unions since 1889** (Oxford, Clarendon Press 1964), 138
4. Locomotive Department, Report to the Board of the GNR, 22 January 1870, PRO RAIL 236/332
5. Minutes of the GNR Board, 26 August and 23 October 1979, PRO RAIL 236/332
6. R.D. Steward, **Edwardian Doncaster, 1900–1914**, (Typescript in Doncaster Public Library), 20
7. **Doncaster Chronicle**, 22 March 1895
8. Steward, op. cit., 21
9. **Doncaster Gazette**, 31 January 1908
10. F.A.S. Brown, **Great Northern Locomotive Engineers**, Vol. 1, 1846–81 (Allen & Unwin 1965), 90, 108
11. **Doncaster Chronicle**, 27 October 1871
12. Minutes of the GNR Board, 3 November 1871, PRO RAIL 236/31
13. **Doncaster Chronicle**, 17 November 1871. In 1872 similar concessions to those made at Doncaster were granted at Crewe, Swindon and Derby. For further details of these changes see W.H. Chaloner, **The Social and Economic Development of Crewe, 1780–1923**, (1953), 76. A. Williams, **Life in a Railway Factory**, (David & Charles 1969), 8, 307–8, and Amalgamated Society of Railway Servants, **Jubilee Souvenir**, (London ASRS 1901), 60–1
14. Report of the General Manager to the GNR Board, 17 September 1877, PRO RAIL 236/327/1
15. Minutes of the Board of the GNR, 21 July 1871 and 12 January 1872, PRO RAIL 236/38
16. A. Williams, op. cit., 29
17. **Doncaster, Nottingham and Lincoln Gazette,** 5 October and 2 November 1855 and 21 November 1856
18. Letter from Patrick Stirling to A. Forbes, Assistant Secretary of the GNR, 1 October 1867. PRO RAIL 236/299/10
19. **Doncaster Chronicle**, 29 January 1864
20. **Doncaster Chronicle**, 4 December 1868
21. **Doncaster Chronicle**, 9 May, 19 September and 21 November 1902
22. **Doncaster, Nottingham and Lincoln Gazette**, 26 May 1854
23. **Doncaster, Nottingham and Lincoln Gazette**, 12 January 1855
24. **Doncaster Chronicle**, 17 May 1861
25. **Doncaster Chronicle**, 13 March 1868
26. **Doncaster Chronicle**, 25 July 1902
27. **Doncaster Chronicle**, 14 July 1871
28. **Doncaster Chronicle**, 6 June 1902
29. **Doncaster, Nottingham and Lincoln Gazette**, 5 September 1856
30. **Doncaster Chronicle**, 2 June 1865
31. Memorandum from Henry Oakley to the GNR Board, 9 April 1888, PRO RAIL 236/362/7
32. **Doncaster Evening Post**, 10 December 1981
33. Interview with Frank Cresswell, 14 October 1987
34. Williams, op. cit., 32–3
35. W.F. Burks, **The Development of Trade Unionism within the Crewe Locomotive Works between 1843 and 1880** Thesis approved for Ruskin College Labour Studies Diploma, (1976), 18. Mr Burks' source was the LNWR Board minutes
36. Minutes of the Board of Directors LNER, 27 July and 28 September 1944
37. Railway Executive, Joint Administrative Council on Welfare and BTC Minute 1/899 of 19 October 1948
38. Minuts of the GNR Board, 14 July 1868, PRO RAIL 236/36
39. P.L. Scowcroft, 'Road Excursions from Doncaster in the late nineteenth century', **Journal**. Railway and Canal Historical Society, Vol. XXIX, Part 2, No. 136, July 1987
40. Minutes of the GNR Board, PRO RAIL 236/376 Part 2/14
41. Minutes of the GNR Board, 4 April 1913, PRO RAIL 236/64
42. Minutes of the GNR Board, 7 April 1911, PRO RAIL 236/64
43. Minutes of the GNR Board, 5 May 1911, PRO RAIL 236/64
44. Minutes of the GNR Board, 6 June 1913 and 2 October 1914, PRO RAIL 236/65
45. B.R. Mitchell and P. Deane, **Abstract of British Historical Statistics** (Cambridge University Press 1962), 476–7
46. GNR, Comparative statements of Capital and Revenue, PRO RAIL 1110/172
47. **Doncaster Chronicle**, 16 August 1861
48. **Doncaster Chronicle**, 14 February 1862
49. **Doncaster Chronicle**, 2 April 1875
50. **Doncaster Chronicle**, 7 December 1877

NOTES

51 Steward, op. cit., 35. **Doncaster Gazette**, 5 November 1909. In 1913 the **Doncaster Gazette** printed a series of articles drawing attention to the town's worst slums. See **Doncaster Gazette**, 11 April 1913
52 P.S. Bagwell, **The Railwaymen** (Allen & Unwin 1963), 184
53 Steward, op. cit., 22. **Doncaster Gazette**, 20 May 1913

CHAPTER 8

1. Cited in P.W. Kingsford, **Victorian Railwaymen** (London, Frank Cass 1970) 152
2. Evidence given to the Select Committee on Railway Companies, Law of Compensation, 1870
3. Kingsford op. cit., 162
4. 'End of the Line for Old Society', Doncaster **Evening Post**, 10 December 1981
5. Minutes of the GNR Board 6 October 1851, PRO RAIL 236/17 and 23 May 1853 PRO RAIL 236/276/9
6. GNR Locomotive Sick Society (GNRLSS) Archives Document D59/9/20–6
7. **Doncaster Chronicle** 14 June 1861
8. As in the case of C.J. Beckford on 24 June 1895. An injury to one of his eyes had 'rendered him incapable of following his employment'. DS9/1/3
9. e.g. Decisions of Management Committee on 12 January 1870 and 20 February 1872 DS9/1/3
10. **Doncaster Chronicle** 14 June 1861
11. Management Committee Minutes 5 and 27 October 1868. DS9/1/1
12. ibid., 26 August 1874
13. ibid., 27 August 1873
14. ibid., 30 August 1874
15. ibid., 26 July 1897
16. ibid., 29 November 1904
17. ibid., 23 April 1898
18. ibid., 19 December 1938 DS8/1/6
19. ibid., 28 April 1878
20. D59/9/17
21. D59/4/35 43 and Valuation Report 31 December 1919 D59/9/20–26
22. Announcement by the Chairman of the Management Committee 29 July 1874
23. Doncaster **Evening Post** 10 December 1981
24. Monthly figures in DS1/9/5
25. Doncaster **Evening Post** 10 December 1981
26. Management Committee Minutes 28 January 1935 DS8/1/6
27. ibid., 22 December 1941 DS8/1/6
28. Management Committee Minutes 6 May 1946 DS8/1/6
29. D59/9/52
30. 99th Annual Report to 31 December 1950
31. 101st Annual Report to 31 December 1952
32. Figures taken from the Annual Reports
33. 121st Annual Report 1971
34. Doncaster **Evening Post** 10 December 1981

CHAPTER 9

1. F.A.S. Brown, **Nigel Gresley; Locomotive Engineer** (Ian Allan 1961) 9–14
2. O.S. Nock, **Great Northern: Pre-Grouping Railway Scene, No. 2**, (Ian Allan 1979), 8
3. GNR Executive Committee, Memorandum to Directors 10 September 1914, PRO RAIL 236/408/2
4. **Doncaster Gazette**, 25 September 1914
5. **Doncaster Gazette**, 28 August 1914
6. GNR General Manager's report to the Directors 9 September 1914
7. **Railway Review** 30 October 1914
8. This account, and the details of the war work undertaken at Doncaster, are in **A Report of the Munitions made at Doncaster during the Great War 1914–19** GNR Board meeting 10 January 1919, PRO RAIL 236/442
9. Census 1911 Vol. IX, Table 15 (b), 456
10. **Report on the Munitions made at Doncaster**, p.4
11. ibid., 5
12. NUR, Executive Committee Minutes, June 1915 and Special Executive Meeting Minutes 31 July 1915
13. Minutes of the Board of Directors of the GNR 5 June 1915. PRO RAIL 236/66
14. Minutes of the Board of Directors of the GNR 3 November 1915. PRO RAIL 236/66
15. G.D.H. Cole, **Trade Unionism on the Railways**, London (1917), 103–4
16. P.S. Bagwell, **The Railwaymen** (Allen & Unwin 1963), 357
17. Cole, op. cit., 104
18. Minutes of the Board of Directors of the GNR, 3 November 1916. PRO RAIL 236/65
19. Minutes of the Board of Directors of the GNR, 3 March 1916. PRO RAIL 236/66
20. R.J. Essery, D.P. Rowland and W.O. Steel, **British Goods Wagons from 1887 to the Present Day** (David & Charles 1970), 22–24
21. **Report of the Select Committee on Transport, 1918** HC130/136
22. GNR Summary of Financial Results 1913–22 PRO RAIL 1110/174
23. Speech of Albert Bellamy at the TUC annual conference at Bristol, September 1915, reported in **Railway Review** 17 September 1915. Series of articles on workshop organization **Railway Review** 4 March 1921 and five subsequent weeks
24. **Railway Review** 17 September 1915
25. **Railway Review** 7 April 1916
26. **Railway Review** 8 April 1921, reporting meetings at the TUC on 17 April, 9 and 22 May, 26 June and 20 July 1917

CHAPTER 10

1. **Railway Gazette** 22 June 1917 726
2. **Outline of Proposals as to the Future Organization of Transport Undertakings in Great Britain and their relation to the State**, Cmd 787 (1920)
3. M.R. Bonavia, **The Four Great Railways** (David & Charles 1980), 63
4. D.H. Aldcroft, **British Railways in Transition** (Macmillan 1968), 54
5. LNER Locomotive Committee Minutes 4 June 1925, PRO RAIL 390/30
6. LNER Locomotive Committee Minutes 2 June 1927, PRO RAIL 390/31
7. LNER Memorandum of CME to the Board 5 January 1933, PRO RAIL 390/14
8. LNER Minute 80 Locomotive Committee 29 November 1934, PRO RAIL 390/14
9. LNER, Memorandum of the CME 20 July 1936. Locomotive Committee Minute 99 of 7 January 1937
10. LNER, **Short time working**. Reports to Railway Staff Conference 1939 PRO RAIL 1172/44
11. LNER Locomotive Committee Minutes, 22 February 1923. PRO RAIL 390/30
12. LNER Minute 62 of the Board of Directors 23 February 1923. PRO RAIL 310/6
13. LNER Minutes 1688 of the Board of Directors, 26 January 1934. PRO RAIL 930/8
14. C.J. Allen, **The London and North Eastern Railway** (Ian Allan 1966) 113
15. ibid., 11–123
16. ibid., 127
17. O.S. Nock, **The Locomotives of Sir Nigel Gresley** (Longman 1945), 125. C.J. Allen, op. cit., 133
18. C. Lorenz, 'Bugatti's railway revolution', **Financial Times, Weekend FT**. 4/5 June 1988. H. Conway, **Bugatti** (Haynes 1949)
19. J.E. Day, **A History of the Doncaster Plant Works**, Doncaster (1953) 37
20. Interview at Doncaster, 14 October 1987
21. O.S. Nock, op. cit., 115–125
22. ibid., 104–5
23. R.A. Thom, 'Repairs to Locomotives at Doncaster Works', **London and North Eastern Railway Magazine**, Vol. 20, No. 11, November 1930
24. Interview at Doncaster, 18 November 1988
25. LNER Locomotive Committee, Minute 1063, 25 July 1929, PRO RAIL 930/31
26. LNER Locomotive Committee, Minute 1154, 9 January 1930, PRO RAIL 930/31
27. M. Harris, **Gresley's Coaches, Coaches built for the GNR, ECJS and LNER, 1905-53** (David & Charles 1973) 11
28. C.J. Allen, op. cit., 182. LNER Locomotive Committee Minutes 22 February 1923. PRO RAIL 390/30
29. Harris op. cit., 22
30. J.F. Lewis, 'Train lighting and heating', Supplement to the **Railway Carriage and Wagon Review**, 1925, PRO reference: Z Lib 5/269.
31. Harris, op. cit., 23
32. LNER, Locomotive Committee, minute 2703, Memorandum from the Chief Mechanical Engineer, 28 May 1939. PRO RAIL 390/33
33. **Doncaster Gazette**, 1 January 1932. LNER Special Committee Minutes 29 November 1928. Authority given for the construction of twelve third class sleeping cars. PRO RAIL 390/14
34. LNER Special Committee report 26 October 1933, Minute 70, PRO RAIL 390/14
35. LNER Special Committee report 4 January 1934, Minute 74, PRO RAIL 390/14
36. LNER Special Committee report 25 October 1934, Minute 78. PRO RAIL 390/14
37. Interview at Doncaster, 14 October 1987
38. LNER, Minute 331 of the Locmotive Committee, 19 February 1925. PRO RAIL 390/14
39. LNER Report from Sir Vincent L. Raven to the Locomotive Committee, 22 February 1923. PRO RAIL 390/30
40. LNER, Locomotive Committee Minutes 18 February 1923, PRO RAIL 390/30
41. LNER, Minutes of the Board of Directors 30 October 1925, PRO RAIL 930/7
42. LNER, Minutes of the Joint Locomotive and Traffic Committee, 6 January 1927, PRO RAIL 390/14
43. LNER, Minutes of the Joint Locomotive and Traffic Committee, 24 October 1929. PRO RAIL 390/14
44. ibid., 23 October 1930
45. ibid., 22 October 1931
46. LNER Special Committee Minutes 26 October 1933. PRO RAIL 390/16
47. LNER Special Committee Minutes 21 February 1935 and 25 June 1936 PRO RAIL 390/14
48. ibid., 25 June 1936
49. ibid., 7 January 1937
50. D.L. Munby, **Inland Transport Statistics Great Britain**, Vol. 1 (Clarendon Press 1978), 134–5

NOTES

51 Interview 14 October 1987
52 LNER, Special Committee Minutes 5 January 1928, PRO RAIL 390/14
53 ibid., 28 January 1932
54 ibid., 25 October 1934
55 ibid., 24 January 1935
56 **Doncaster Gazette**, 3 October 1919. P.S. Bagwell, **The Railwaymen** (Allen & Unwin 1963), 375–403
57 Railway Shopmen's Arbitration 1921–2, PRO RAIL 1025/97
58 **Doncaster Gazette** 3 August 1923. Bagwell, op. cit., 428
59 **Doncaster Gazette**, 7 May 1926
60 Bagwell, op. cit., 485
61 **Doncaster Gazette**, 14 May 1926
62 C.J. Allen, op. cit., 80
63 Railway Shopmen's National Council (NRSC) 10 August 1928. PRO RAIL 1026/20
64 ibid., 18 October 1929
65 ibid., 18 March 1931
66 ibid., 11 October and 9 November 1932
67 ibid., 13 June 1934, 28 September 1934, 29 June 136 and 16 August 1937
68 **Doncaster Chronicle**, 2 November 1933
69 **Doncaster Gazette**, 29 April 1932
70 A.V. Morrish, **Our Doncaster** (Doncaster Public Library 1987), 2
71 **Doncaster Gazette**, 27 October 1932
72 Railway Shopmen's National Council, 26 January 1931 and 10 August 1937 PRO RAIL 1026/20

CHAPTER 11

1. M.R. Bonavia, **The Four Great Railways**, David & Charles 1980), 185
2. D.H. Aldcroft, **British Railways in Transition**, London (1968), 94–8
3. Railway Executive Committee (REC) Minute 8530 of 18 April 1945, PRO AN 3/8
4. Bonavia, op. cit., 190
5. REC Minute 375 of 2 September 1939 and Minutes of a meeting held at the Ministry of Transport on 24 August 1939. PRO AN 3/1 PRO RAIL 1026/20
6. Minute 264 of the Railway Shopmen's National Council, 30 April 1943 PRO RAIL 1026/20
7. British Railways Press Office, **British Railways in Peace and War**, London (1944), 19, 43
8. REC Minute of 22 November 1939, PRO AN 3/2
9. REC Minute 391 of 12 September 1939.
10. REC Minute of 20 December 1939 Appendix B
11. **Doncaster Chronicle**, 10 April 1941. C.J. Allen, **The London and North Eastern Railway** (Ian Allan 1966), 138
12. **Doncaster Chronicle**, 6 June 1946
13. Allen op. cit., 139
14. ibid., 140
15. REC Minute 6225 of 13 April 1943, PRO AN3/5
16. REC Minute 1375 of 20 March 1940, PRO AN3/5
17. REC Letter from Ministry of Transport dated 5 April 1940, PRO AN3/3
18. Interview at Doncaster 14 October 1987
19. LNER Locomotive Committee Minute 2840 of 30 May 1940, PRO 390/34
20. Bonavia, op. cit., 189
21. REC Minute 2378 of 5 November 1940, PRO AN3/4
22. REC Minutes 1697, 2378, 6169 and 7208 in PRO AN3/4, AN3/5, AN3/7
23. REC Minute 8530 of 18 April 1945, PRO AN3/8, Bonavia, op. cit., 191–2. BR Press Office, **British Railways in Peace and War** (1944), 63
24. REC Minute 447 of 16 September 1939 PRO AN3/1
25. REC Minute 568 of 2 October 1939
26. British Railways Press Office. **It can now be revealed** (1945) 7
27. REC Minute 2440 of 19 November 1940 PRO AN 3/4
28. British Railways Press Office op. cit., 15
29. REC Minute 1853 of 3 July 1940, PRO AN 3/4, Larkin and Larkin op. cit., 178
30. H.R. Wormald, **Modern Doncaster, progress and development of the borough 1836-1973** (Doncaster Borough 1973), 77. LNER Board Minute 3107 G2 29 October 1942 PRO RAIL 390/10
31. REC Minute 3451 of 24 June 1941
32. RSNC Minute 138 of 20 August 1940 PRO RAIL 1026/20
33. Minute 3078 of the LNER Board 27 August 1942. PRO RAIL 390/10
34. **Doncaster Gazette**, 16 November 1944
35. Minute 3078 of the LNER Board 27 August 1942. PRO RAIL 390/10
36. Minute 325 B (7) of the LNER Board 27 May 1943 PRO RAIL 390/11
37. Exchange of correspondence between the REC and the Ministry of War Transport, PRO AN2/455
38. File number 548/87/3 in PRO AN2 465
39. Minute 138 of the RSNC 20 August 1940, PRO RAIL 1026/20
40. NUR, General Secretary's Report to the AGM 1942, 29
41. NUR, General Secretary's Report to the AGM 1943, 20
42. REC Minutes 589 and 648, 5 October and 13 November 1939 PRO AN3/2
43. REC Minutes 2238 and 2290 30 September and 18 October 1940 PRO AN3/4
44. Information kindly supplied in a letter from Harry Procter 22 February 1990. See also A.V. Morrish (ed.) **Our Doncaster** Doncaster, (1988), 75 and A. Darfield, **No Sugar in the Tea**, (Doncaster 1989), 18
45. **Doncaster Chronicle**, 7 January 1943
46. Darfield, op. cit., 45–6
47. REC Minute 6346 19 May 1943 PRO AN3/5
48. **Doncaster Chronicle**, 28 June 1945

NOTES

CHAPTER 12

1. REC reports to the Ministry of Transport included in BTC Board minute 35 PRO AN 85/17
2. C.I. Savage, **Inland Transport**, (1957) 639
3. REC reports to the Ministry of Transport 26 August 1947, PRO AN 85/17
4. LNER, **Doncaster Locomotive and Carriage 'Plant' Works and Carr Wagon Shops**, October 1946, unnumbered bound typescript with illustrations, PRO ZLIB 6/310
5. LNER Minute 3691 of the Board of Directors, 21 February 1946. PRO RAIL 390/34
6. LNER Joint Locomotive and Traffic Committee, Minutes 3285 and 3333 (a). PRO RAIL 390/34
7. Railway Executive (RE) Memorandum to the British Transport Commission (BTC) 11 June 1948. PRO AN 58/20
8. T.R. Gourvish, **British Railways 1948–73**, (1986), 8–10
9. The Railway Executive: British Railways first **Annual Report** 1948, 40
10. E.J. Larkin and J.G. Larkin, **The Railway Workshops of Britain 1823–1986** (Macmillan 1988), 239
11. LNER Locomotive Committe minute 3093 of 26 September 1946. PRO RAIL 390/34
12. LNER, **Doncaster Locomotive and Carriage Plant Works**, etc. PRO ZLib 6/310
13. Cited in Gourvish, op. cit., 27–8
14. Larkin and Larkin, op. cit., Table A 10, 239–40
15. PEP, **Locomotives: A Report on the Industry** (1951) 16 Larkin and Larkin ibid. RE Memorandum to BTC Board September 1949, PRO AN 95/26
16. PEP, ibid.
17. Larkin and Larkin, op. cit., 244. S.J. Woods and P. Tuffrey, **Doncaster Plant Works**, (Doncaster, Bond Publications 1987) 67
18. Memorandum from the RE to the BTC, 9 December 1950, PRO AN 85/30
19. Memorandum from the RE to the BTC, 25 January 1949 PRO AN 85/23
20. J. Johnson and R.A. Long, **British Railways Engineering, 1948–80** (Bury St Edmunds, Mechanical Engineering Publications 1981) 512
21. REC Report to the Minister of Transport 26 August 1947. PRO AN 85/17
22. Memorandum from Miles Beevor, Secretary to the BTC, to the Minister of Transport 25 February 1948. PRO AN 85/19
23. British Railways, Report of the all regions productive efficiency committee on the Carriage and Wagon Engineers Department, Eastern Regions No 7 January 1956 PRO AN 8/126
24. RE, **First Annual Repot**, 1948, 17
25. Larkin and Larkin, op. cit., 239
26. British Railways, op. cit., 26
27. RE, **Annual Report**, 1949. 52
28. Woods and Tuffrey, op. cit., 66
29. Memorandum from RE to BTC 6 March 1951. PRO AN 85/31/4/187
30. RE, **Annual Report**, 1959 62–3
31. ibid., 61
32. RE, Annual Report 1952, 35
33. Report from Mr H.B. Taylor to RE, September 1954. PRO AN7/22
34. RE **Annual Report**, 1949, 54–7
35. Johnson and Long, op. cit., 58
36. D.H. Aldcroft, **British Railways in Transition** (Macmillan 1968), 153
37. **Report outlining the anticipated effect on the main locomotive carriage and wagon works and carriage and wagon outdoor depots of the Modernisation and Re-equipment Plan**, PRO AN 8/9
38. Gourvish, op. cit., 275
39. ibid., 281
40. **Report of the all regions productive efficiency committee on the Carriage and Wagon Engineers Department, Eastern and North Eastern Regions**, number 7, January 1956. PRO AN8/126, 29
41. ibid., 44
42. Report of a Court of Enquiry under Mr C.W. Guillebaud, Cmd 7161 of 1947. Arrangements negotiated in implementing the Report are recounted in Bagwell, op. cit., 607–8
43. Productive efficiency Report, 1956, 23 PRO AN8/126
44. NUR, General Secretary's Report to the AGM, 1946. Railway Shopmen's National Council (RSNC). Agreement of 24 August 1945
45. British Railways, **Annual Report,** 1952, 32
46. NUR, AGM 4 July 1957, **Verbatim Report**
47. NUR AGM 1957, **Agenda and Decisions**, 100
48. NUR, AGM 9 July 1958. **Verbatim Report**
49. Interview at Doncaster 18 November 1988
50. RSNC Minute 902 of 21 January 1953

CHAPTER 13

1. T.R. Gourvish, **British Railways 1948–73. A business history**, (Cambridge University Press 1986), 299
2. J. Johnson and R. Long, **British Railways Engineering 1948–80**. (Bury St Edmunds, Mechanical Engineering Publications 1981), 530–8
3. **The Times**, 23 August 1962. **Doncaster Chronicle** 23 August 1963
4. **Doncaster Chronicle**, 4 October 1962
5. **Doncaster Chronicle**, 20 September 1962
6. **Doncaster Chronicle**, 4 October 1962
7. E. Wistrich **The Politics of Transport** (Longman 1983), 32–7
8. P.L. Cook, **Railway Workshops: the Problems of Contraction**, (Cambridge University Press 1964), 58
9. ibid., 52
10. ibid., 55
11. **Doncaster Chronicle**, 19 April 1962
12. **Doncaster Gazette and Chronicle**, 28 November 1963
13. BRB, **Annual Report and Accounts**, 1965, 56
14. **Doncaster Gazette**, 12 August 1965
15. BRB, **Annual Report and Accounts**, 1965, 56
16. **Doncaster Gazette**, 10 April 1969
17. **Doncaster Gazette**, 6 March 1969
18. **Doncaster Gazette**, 13 November 1969
19. NUR, General Secretary's Report to the AGM, July 1969, 30
20. BRB, **Annual Report and Accounts**, 1968, 49
21. **Doncaster Gazette**, 31 July 1969
22. **Doncaster Gazette**, 21 February 1963
23. **Doncaster Gazette**, 19 April 1968
24. **Doncaster Gazette**, 7 September 1970
25. **Doncaster Chronicle**, 8 August 1963
26. **Doncaster Gazette**, 30 October 1969
27. **Doncaster Gazette**, 14 May 1970
28. **Doncaster Gazette**, 24 January 1963
29. **Doncaster Gazette**, 30 May 1963
30. NUR, Executive Committee, September 1966, Appendix S61, 205–6
31. **Doncaster Gazette**, 17 June 1965
32. **NUR, General Secretary's Report to the AGM**, July 1966, 19–20
33. Minutes of the RSNC. 29–30 May 1965
34. NUR, **General Secretary's Report to the AGM**, July 1966, 19–20
35. Interview with Stan Lewins 14 October 1987 **Doncaster Gazette**, 6 December 1962
36. Minutes of the RSNC 21–22 May 1966

CHAPTER 14

1. Department of Transport, Welsh Office and Scottish Development Department, **Transport Statistics Great Britain, 1968-1978**, (1979) 114, and **Transport Statistics Great Britain 1977–1987** (1988) 148
2. **NUR News: Workshops**, September 1970. Information provided by Albert Meredith
3. **Transport Statistics Great Britain, 1977–87**, 143
4. ibid., 149
5. Central Transport Consultative Committee, **Annual Report 1988–89**, 10
6. **Transport Statistics Great Britain, 1968–78**, 28 and 1977–1987, 28
7. J. Johnson and R.A. Long, **British Railways Engineering 1948–80**, (Bury St Edmunds, Mechanical Engineering Publications 1981), 308
8. Cited in Gourvish, op. cit., 510
9. V. Wyman, 'Railway Bizarre', **The Engineer**, 15 March 1984, 18–20
10. **Doncaster Gazette**, 26 March 1970
11. **The Engineer**, 20 August 1970
12. ibid., 17 June 1971
13. ibid., 24 June 1971
14. ibid., 25 December 1971
15. **NUR News: Workshops**, Nos 16–61, April 1974-December 1980
16. Interview with Dick Sargeant at Doncaster, 14 October 1987
17. **The Engineer**, 27 May 1982
18. A. Clegg, 'Geared for New Role at the Plant', **Doncaster Gazette**, 13 November 1969
19. **NUR News: Workshops** No. 81, January 1983
20. BRB, **Annual Report and Accounts, 1979**
21. BRB, **Annual Report and Accounts**, 1981, 9
22. Minutes, Railway Shopmen's Informal Liaison Committee, (ILC), 22 December 1982
23. **Doncaster Star**, 4 September 1984
24. Minutes, ILC, 22 December 1982
25. NUR Branch circular, 23 September 1985
26. House of Commons Transport Committee **Second Report**, Session 1982–3, Sir David Serpell's answer to Question 1
27. Department of Transport, **Railway Finances** (Serpell Report) (H.M.S.O. 1983) paras. 7.9 and 7.10, 37
28. ibid., paras. 7.25 and 7.27 39
29. NUR Research Department, **Workshop Closures and Redundancies**, (London, NUR 1986), 5
30. ILC Minutes, 11 January 1984, British Railways Board **Corporate Plan, 1981–5**, 23
31. ILC Minutes, 11 January 1984
32. **The Engineer**, 14 November 1985, 32
33. ibid.
34. **Doncaster Star**, 10 August 1984
35. NUR Executive Committee Minutes, 18 July 1986
36. The expression 'on the fringes' is that of Ron Price, Depot Manager, Doncaster BRML. Interview at the Works 18 April 1990
37. NUR, AGM 7 July 1982 Verbatim report of item 134
38. **Doncaster Gazette**, 8 July 1971. Information supplied by Ron Price, 18 April 1990
39. Information supplied by Albert Meredith, 21 April 1990
40. Interview with Stan Lewins, Doncaster 14 October 1987
41. NUR Branch circular, 11 February 1985
42. BRE Shopmen's National Council, 16 October 1987
43. Information supplied by Ron Price, 18 April 1990
44. **Financial Times**, 11 December 1986. **Doncaster Star**, 15 December 1986

CHAPTER 15

1. W.H. Chaloner, **The Social and Economic Development of Crewe, 1780–1823** (Manchester University Press 1950), passim. D. Drummond, 'Building a locomotive: Skill and the work force in Crewe locomotive works, 1843–1914', **The Journal of Transport History**, Third series, Vol. 8 Number 1, March, 1987
2. P.L. Scowcraft, **Lines to Doncaster**, Doncaster (1986), 40
3. G.W. Alcock, **Fifty years of Railway Trade Unionism** (London Co-operative Press 1922), Appendix A
4. ibid., 620–1
5. 'Labour Party born in a Doncaster Inn', an article based on research by Dr E.A.P. Duffy and Councillor R.W. Bowes, **Doncaster Chronicle**, 6 May 1965
6. **Doncaster Chronicle**, 23 July 1903
7. A full account of these struggles is given in C.H. Grinling's **The History of the Great Northern Railway** (Allen & Unwin 1966), Chapters 2 and 3
8. D.H. Aldcroft, **British Railways in Transition** (Macmillan 1968), 106
9. **Doncaster Star**, 16 August 1984
10. Appendix A 51 of the meeting of the RSNC held on 3 May 1973

SELECT BIBLIOGRAPHY

PRIMARY SOURCES

The records of the Great Northern Railway, London and North Eastern Railway, the Railway Executive Committees which controlled railway services during the two World Wars and the Railway Executive of the British Transport Commission are all housed in the Public Record Office at Kew.

The Great Northern Railway records are classified under RAIL 236. Under this general classification the most useful items are:

The Minutes of the Board of Directors RAIL 236/13–68

Executive Committee Minutes: RAIL 236/69–142

Locomotive Committee Minutes: RAIL 236/207–219

There are also some special reports which influenced key decisions of the company, such as Joseph Locke's proposals concerning the London-York Railway in 1844, included in RAIL 236/266.

The Railway Executive Committee minutes are to be found in the classification AN. For example, the important decisions of the REC between September 1938 and December 1947 are in AN3/1–9.

The records of the London and North Eastern Railway, which functioned from 1923–1948, are to be found under the general classifications RAIL 390 to 401, with the Board Minutes included in RAIL 390/6–13 and the Locomotive Committee Minutes in RAIL 390/30–34.

The Railway Executive of the British Transport Commission, which was in business from 1 January 1948 to 10 October 1953, kept records which are preserved in AN4/1–8. Reports of decisions made after 1960 are not available (under the thirty year rule) but AN7 contains statistics concerning British Railways locomotives and rolling stock.

Miscellaneous reports concerning workshops are to be found under other Public Record Office classifications RAIL 1057/3280, for example, gives figures of the women employed on 30 June 1942 by all the four main-line companies, classified by the jobs they performed.

For more detailed information on sources readers are referred to D.L. Munby's, **Inland Transport Statistics Great Britain 1900–1970** (Oxford, 1978) 9–16.

British Railways Board **Reports and Accounts** 1963 – include summary figures of the numbers of locomotives, carriages and freight vehicles in service. They also give indication of the trends in BR policy and voice the concerns of the BR Board. The BRB's annually published **Corporate Plan** should also be consulted.

The Department of Transport's **Transport Statistics Great Britain**, published annually from 1976, are invaluable for their wide coverage and occasional special articles.

For a critical appraisal of effects of the government's and BR's policies, the Central Transport Consultative Committee's **Annual Reports** (from 1949 to the present) help to explain the decline in railway workshop activity over the years.

BOOKS

A.H. Ahrons, **Locomotive and train working in the latter part of the nineteenth century** 6 vols (Cambridge, Heffers 1951–4)

G.W. Alcock, **50 Years of Railway Trade Unionism** (Co-operative Printing Soc. London, 1922)

D.H. Aldcroft, **British Railways in Transition** London (1968) 'Innovation on the Railways: the lag in Diesel and Electric Traction', in **Studies in British Transport History, 1870–1970** (David & Charles 1974)

C.J. Allen, **The Locomotive Exchanges**, 1870–1948 (Ian Allan 1949)

_____**The Gresley Pacifics of the LNER** (Ian Allen 1950)

_____**Great Northern** (Ian Allen, 1961)

_____**The London and North Eastern Railway** (Ian Allan 1966)

P.S. Bagwell, **The Railwaymen** Vol. 1 (Allen & Unwin 1963)

_____Vol. 2 (Allen & Unwin 1982)

_____**End of the Line?** (Verso 1984)

_____**The Transport Revolution from 1770** (Routledge 2nd Ed. 1988)

B.T. Bayliss and S.L. Edwards, **Industrial Demand for Transport** (HMSO 1970)

T.C. Barker and C.I. Savage, **An Economic History of Transport in Britain** (Hutchinson 1974)

R. Bell **History of British Railways during the War 1939–45** (Railway Gazette 1945)

G.F. Bird **The Locomotives of the Great Northern Railway 1847–1902** (London, Locomotive Publishing Co. 1903)

M.R. Bonavia, **The Four Great Railways** (David & Charles 1980)

_____**The Nationalisation of British Transport** (Macmillan, 1987)

A.J. Brickwell, 'The Great Northern Railway Works at Doncaster' in **Round the Works of our Great Railways** (London, Arnold 1893)

BRB, **The Reshaping of British Railways** (London, 1963)

_____**A Study of the relative true costs of Rail and Road Freight Transport over Trunk Routes** (London, 1964)

British Railways Press Office, **British Railways in Peace and War** (London, 1944)

_____**It can now be revealed** (London, 1945)

BRB and Institute for Transport Studies, University of Leeds, **A Comparative Study of European Rail Performance** (London, BRB 1979)

BTC, **Modernisation and Re-equipment of British Railways** (London, 1955)

F.A.S. Brown, **Nigel Gresley, Locomotive Engineer** (Ian Allan 1961)

_____**Great Northern Locomotive Engineers, 1846–1881** (Allen & Unwin 1966)

_____**From Stirling to Gresley, 1882–1922** (Oxford Publishing Co. 1974)

C.D. Campbell, **British Railways in Boom and Depression** (London, P.S. King & Son 1932)

W.H. Chaloner, **The social and economic development of Crewe, 1780–1923** (Manchester University Press 1950)

G. Charlesworth, **A History of British Motorways** (London, Telford 1984)

P.L. Cook, **Railway Workshops: the Problems of Contraction** (Cambridge University Press 1964)

E.S. Cox **British Railways' Standard Steam Locomotives** (HMSO 1966)

J.E. Day **Doncaster Plant Works** (Unpublished Typescript in Doncaster Public Library, 1953)

Department of Transport, **Railway Finances, Report of Committee Chaired by Sir David Serpell** (HMSO 1983)

Doncaster Chronicle Supplement, 12 March 1936

H.J. Dyos and D.H. Aldcroft, **British Transport: an economic survey from the 17th to the 20th centuries** (Leicester University Press 1969)

R.J. Essery, D.P. Rowland and W.O. Steel, **British Goods Wagons from 1887 to the Present Day** (David & Charles 1970)

C.D. Foster, **The Transport Problem** (Croom Helm 1975)

M.J. Freeman and D.H. Aldcroft, **An Atlas of British Railway History** (Croom Helm 1985)

T.R. Gourvish, **British Railways 1948–73. A Business History**, (Cambridge University Press 1987)

L.V. Grinsell, **Studies in the History of Swindon** (Shire Publications 1953)

K.M. Gwilliam, **Transport and Public Policy** (Allen & Unwin 1964)

M. Harris, **Gresley's Coaches. Coaches built for the GNR, ECJS and LNER** (David & Charles 1973)

C.W. Hatfield **Historical Notices of Doncaster September 26th 1862–December 22nd 1865** (Doncaster, privately printed)

G.R. Hawke, **Railways and Economic Growth in England and Wales**, 1840–1870 (Clarendon Press 1970)

M. Hillman and A. Whalley, **The Social Consequences of Rail Closures** (London, Policy Studies Institute 1980)

BIBLIOGRAPHY

K. Hoole, **North East England** Vol. 4 in D. St. J. Thomas (ed.) **A Regional History of the Railways of Great Britain** (David & Charles 1965)

R. Hough, **Six Great Railwaymen** (Hamish Hamilton 1955)

J.R.T. Hughes, **Fluctuations in Trade Industry and Finance** (Oxford Univeristy Press 1960)

G. Hutchinson and M. O'Neill, **British Railways Engineering 1948–80** (Bury St Edmunds, Mechanical Engineering Publications 1981)

S. Joy, **The Train that Ran Away: A Business History of British Railways** (Ian Allan 1973)

P.W. Kingsford, **Victorian Railwaymen 1830–1870** (Frank Cass 1970)

R.S. Lambert, **The Railway King 1800–1871** (Allen & Unwin 1934)

E.J. and J.G. Larkin, **The Railway Workshops of Britain 1823–1986** (Macmillan 1988)

C.F. Lee, **Passenger Class Distinctions** (London, Railway Gazette 1946)

R. Marsh, **On and off the Rails:** An Autobiography (Weidenfeld & Nicolson 1978)

C.H. Montgomery, **Railway Car Lighting** (London, 1907 PRO ref Z Lib 5/89;)

A.V. Morrish, **Our Doncaster** (Doncaster Public Library 1988)

E.R. Mountford, **Caerphilly Works, 1901–1964** (Hatch End, Roundhouse Books 1965)

B. Murphy, **ASLEF 1880–1980** (London, ASLEF 1980)

NUR, **Planning Transport for You** (London NUR 1959)

O.S. Nock, **Locomotives of Sir Nigel Gresley** (Longmans 1945)

_____**Steam Locomotives: a retrospect of the work of eight great locomotive engineers** (London, British Transport Commission 1955)

_____**Great Northern 4–4–2 Atlantics** (Wellingborough, Patrick Stephens 1984)

P. Parker, **For Starters** (Jonathan Cape 1989)

P.E.P., **Locomotives:** A report on the industry London (1951)

S. Plowden, **Taming Traffic** (André Deutsch 1980)

H. Pollins, **Britain's Railways: An Industrial History** (David & Charles 1971)

J.B. Radford, **Derby Works and Midland Locomotives** (Ian Allan 1971)

_____**A Century of Progress: Centenary brochure of the Derby Carriage and Wagon Works** (Derby, British Rail Engineering 1978)

Railway Companies' Association, **Britain's Railways and the Future** (London, The Association 1946)

C.I. Savage, **Inland Transport** (HMSO 1957)

P. Scowcroft, **Lines to Doncaster** (Doncaster Public Library 1986)

J. Thomas, **The Springburn Story: The History of the Scottish Railway Metropolis** (David & Charles 1964)

J. Tomlinson, **Doncaster from the Roman occupation to the present time** (Doncaster, privately printed by author 1887)

R.M. Tufnell, **The Diesel Impact on British Rail** (Bury St Edmunds, Mechanical Engineering Publications 1979)

W.A. Tuplin, **Great Northern Steam** (Ian Allan 1976)

J.C.H. Warren, **A Century of Locomotive Building by Robert Stephenson & Co. 1823–1923** (Newcastle-on-Tyne A. Reid & Co. 1923)

D. Wedderburn, **Redundancy and the Railwaymen** (Cambridge University Press 1965)

A. Williams, **Life in a Railway Factory** (David & Charles 1969)

E. Wistrich, **The Politics of Transport** (Longmans 1983)

S.J. Woods and P. Tuffrey, **Doncaster Plant Works** (Doncaster, Bond Publications 1987)

H.R. Wormald, **Modern Doncaster, the progress and development of the Borough 1836–1973** (Doncaster Borough 1973)

ARTICLES

J. Armstrong, 'The role of coastal shipping in UK transport: an estimate of comparative traffic movements in 1910', **The Journal of Transport History** 3rd Ser. Vol. 8 No. 2 (September 1987), 164–178

―――――'Freight pricing policy in the coastal liner companies before the First World War', **The Journal of Transport History** 3rd Ser. Vol. 10 No. 2 September 1989, 180–197

B. Barber, 'The Concept of the Railway Town and the Growth of Darlington 1801–1911: a Note', **Transport History** Vol. 3 (No. 3 November 1970), 283–289

R. Bell, 'The London and North Eastern Railway: Sixteen Years 1923–38', **Journal of Transport History** Vol. 5 No. 3 (May 1962), 133–9

W.F. Burks, 'The development of trade unions within the Crewe locomotive works between 1843 and 1880', Ruskin College Oxford, Labour Studies Diploma (1976)

P. Butterfield, 'Grouping, pooling and competition: the passenger policy of the LNER, 1923–39', **Journal of Transport History** 3rd Ser. Vol. 7 No. 2 (September 1986) 1–20

D. Drummond, 'Building a locomotive'. 'Skill and the workforce in the Crewe locomotive works 1843–1914'. **Journal of Transport History** 3rd Ser. Vol. 8 No. 1 (March 1987) 1–29

P.K. Else and M. Howe, 'Cost-Benefit Analysis and the withdrawal of railway services', **Journal of Transport Economics and Policy** Vol. III (May 1969)

D.E.C. Eversley, 'The Great Western Railway and the Swindon Works in the Great Depression', **University of Birmingham Historical Journal** Vol. 5 No. 2 (1957)

The Engineer, 'The Great Northern Railway Works Doncaster', (16 December 1892)

P.S. Gupta, 'Railway Trade Unionism c. 1889–1920' **Economic History Review** Vol. XIX 1966

C.R. Hawke and M.C. Reid, 'Railway Capital in the UK in the 19th Century' **Economic History Review** Vol. XXII (1969)

K. Hudson, 'The early years of the railway community in Swindon', **Transport History** Vol. 1 No. 6 (July 1968) 130–165

R.J. Irving, 'British Railway Investment and Innovation 1900–1914', **Business History** Vol. XIII (1971)

A.G. Kenwood, 'Railway Investment in Britain, 1825–75', **Economica** Vol. XXXII (1965)

C. Lorenz, 'Bugatti's railway revolution', **Financial Times** (weekend edition 4–5 June 1988)

R.C.S. Low, 'The Re-organisation of British Railway Workshops', **Journal of the Institute of Locomotive Engineers** (1967)

J. Murray, 'The Impact on Doncaster of the Arrival of the GNR and its Workshops' Thesis for the Dorset Institute of Higher Education May 1980. Typescript in Doncaster Public Library.

H. Pollins, 'Railway Contractors and the Finance of Railway Development in Britain', **Journal of Transport History** Vol. III (1957–8)

S.B. Saul, 'The Market and the Development of the Engineering Industry in Britain 1860–1914', **Economic History Review** Vol. XX (1967)

P.L. Scowcroft, 'Road Excursions from Doncaster in the Nineteenth Century', **Journal of the Railway and Canal Historical Society** Vol. XXIX Pt. 2 No. 136 (July 1987) 78–84

R.D. Steward, 'Edwardian Doncaster, 1900–1914' Typescript in Doncaster Public Library

R. Sugden, 'Cost Benefit Analysis and the Withdrawal of Railway Services', **Yorkshire Bulletin of Economic Research** Vol. XXIV (May 1972)

R.A. Thom, 'Repairs to Locomotives at Doncaster works' **LNER Magazine** Vol. 20 No. 11 (November 1931)

V. Wyman, 'Railway Bizarre' **The Engineer** (15 March 1984)

INDEX

Accidents, railway 24, 28
    in Plant works 38–9, 46
Acts of Parliament
    Railways 1844 12
    Town Improvements Clauses 1847 10
    Factory Acts Extension 1867 38
    Regulation of the Forces 1871 47
    Public Health, 1875 26
    Employers' Liability 1880 39
    Education 1902 33
    Industrial Courts 1919 62
    Railways 1921 53, 55, 62, 110
    National Insurance 1946 45
    Transport 1947 74, 77
    Transport 1953 86, 111
    Transport 1962 91, 92
    Transport 1968 97
Apprenticeship 37, 49, 102–3
Arnold and Sons, Builders 32, 33
Asbestos 101–2
Aspinal, J.A.F. 27, 28
Association of Private Owners of Wagon Stock 21
Atlantic type engines 28

Baines, Eric 45
Balby 8
Baxter, Robert 4, 5, 6, 14
Baxter, Rose and Norton, Solicitors 5
Beeching, Dr Richard 91
Beeching Report 89, 93
Board of Trade 4, 52
Boston 3, 7, 8, 42
Brakes
    Air 100
    Automatic continuous 24
    Smith's Vacuum 24
Brakesmen 24
Brassey, Thomas 6
Briggs Motor Bodies Ltd 68
British Empire Exhibition, 1924 55
BR Maintenance Ltd 107
British Railways 91, 107
British Rail Engineering Ltd (BREL) 100–101, 102–3
British Transport Commission 78, 86, 91, 111
    General Staff Plan (the Wansbrough-Jones Report, 1959) 91
Bugatti, Ettore 56
Bury, Edward 5–6

Campion, Revd J. 9, 10, 14
Carr, the 21, 25, 62, 67, 77, 85, 88, 94
    new wagon shops at 25, 39
CBI 112
Channel Tunnel 112
Clarke, Seymour 6
Coal trade 17, 50, 58, 61
Coastal shipping 30
Cockshott, F.S. 23, 24
Common user scheme 51–2, 59
Containerization 62
Co-operation 14, 25, 26, 34
Cost of living 41, 64
Crewe 39. 93, 107, 109
Crimpsall 7, 19, 25, 32
Cubitt, William 3

Darlington 93, 99
Denison, Edmund 3, 4, 5, 6, 110
    and churches 8
    and GN Rifle Corps 14
    and schools 8–9, 10
    illness and retirement 15
    death 15
Derby 93, 105, 107, 109
Donaldson, Sir Francis 47
Doncaster

Angel Hotel 13
Charter 1
Churches 8–9, 109
Death rate 13, 23
Hospitals 10, 44
housing 8, 13
inns 1, 13
libraries 1
Lyceum 1
markets 1
mayors 110, 113
Mechanics Institute 10
municipal elections 14
Plant works (see separate heading)
population 1, 8, 9, 48
public health 2, 10
railways 3, 4
relief kitchens 13
St Leger 1, 5, 32
Schools 1, 8, 10, 33–4, 109
sport 14, 109
station 4
workhouse 32
Doncaster Co-operative and Industrial Society 13–14, 25, 34
Doncaster Depot 107, *107*
Doncaster Rovers 109
Dukinfield 59, 68
Dunn, Dr, GNR Surgeon 10

Eastleigh 107
External Financing Limit 101, 111

Faverdale 61
Fenton, James 6
Fenton, Myles 12
'Flying Hamburger' 56
Freight traffic 20, 30, 53, 61, 99
    Red Star parcels 100
    Speedlink 100
    TOPS 100
Frith, J.A. 89–90

General Board of Health 10
General Strike, 1926 63
Glasgow 102, 107
Gooch, Daniel 12, 42
Great Northern Railway 3, 4
    dividends 5
    Board and location of engineering works 6
    and Mechanics Institute 10
    and Metropolitan Railway 12
    and passenger carriages 12, 13, 23, 24, 32
    and passenger traffic 24
    petitions to 10, 37
    and St James' Church 8
    and school 8, 9, 10, 33–4
    and staff cuts 36
    and wagon policy 30
    working expenses 40
    works extension 23
Great Northern Railway Locomotive Sick Society 42 ff.
    benefits 43, 45
    diseases of members 44
    dissolution of 45
    foundation 42
    General Secretaries 44
    membership 44, 45
    rules 43–4
    Savings Bank 40
Greene, Sidney (Lord Greene) 94
Gresley, Sir Nigel
    biography 46
    carriages of 58
    CME of LNER 54
    death 66

    locomotives of 46
    and overseas railways 56
    and Railway Executive Committee 65
    salary 54
    wagon building policy 61
Griffiths, John 13

Hexthorpe 7, 8
Holme, A. and G., Contractors 7
Holmes, James 41
Horwich 102, 104, 107
Hospital 10
Hudson, George 3, 4, 110

Illustrated London News 4
Imperial Chemical Industries (ICI) 67
Independent Labour Party (ILP) 41
Industrial relations 37, 39, 41, 50, 52
    Arbitration Court Award 727 (1922) 62–3
    National Railway Shopmen's Council 62
    negotiating machinery 62
    Railway Conciliation Scheme, 1907 52
    strikes
        1919 62
        General Strike, 1926 63
        3 October 1962 93
        10 August 1984 105
        ballot 1985 105

International Harvester 94
Ivatt H.A.
    biography 27–28, 34
    Atlantics 28
    and freight traffic 30
    locomotive policy 28

Kerr, Kenelm 54–5
King's Cross–Edinburgh route 12, 55

Labour Party 41, 74, 85–6, 96
Labour Representation Committee 41
Leeds 51
Lloyd George, David 49, 111
Locke, Joseph 3
Locomotives
    efficiency 28–9
    numbers in service 58
    private contractors and 12, 81, 87, 97, 100
    repair of 11, 19, 74, 83
    standardization 75, 77, 81
    streamlining of 56–7
    types
        APTs 100
        diesel 56, 86, 87, 94, 97, 100, 107
        electric 86, 94, 100
        High Speed Train power units 100
        steam
            compound 30
            oil burning 76
            superheating 30
    types
        8 foot singles 18, 28
        Atlantics 28
        Pacifics 55, 111
    named
        Caerphilly Castle 55
        Cock o' the North 58
        Dwight D. Eisenhower 96
        Flying Scotsman 94
        Golden Shuttle 94
        Henry Oakley 28, 30
        Mallard 57, 111
        Pendennis Castle 55
        Silver Link 30, 57, 111
        Silver Jubilee 57, 111
        Union of South Africa 96
        Victor Wilde 55

Manufacturing and Maintenance Policy
    1987 107
Marples, Ernest 91, 97
Marsh, Richard 100
Measured work 103
Mechanics Institute 10
Missenden, Sir Eustace 77
Mitchell, Steuart 92
    Workshop Plan 92, 93
Modernization Plan, 1955 86–7
Motorways 99

Nasmyth, James 6
National Railway Shopmen's Council 62
National Stores 107, 108
    Swift Transport Ltd and 108
National Union of Railwaymen (NUR) 41, 81, 90
    Doncaster No. 3 Branch 89, 90, 105, *105*
North British Locomotive Company 81

Oakley, Sir Henry 23, 24, 25, 27, 38, 39, 40
The Observer 112
Overcrowding 59, 66, 99

Paris–Deauville railcar 56
Parker, F. 6, 8
Parker, Sir Peter 102
Passenger carriages 12, 13, 74, 77, 86–7, 99
    brake coaches 24
    corridor coaches 24, 27, 31
    design 22
    dining-cars 24, 27, 31, 58, 68, 84
    heating of 58
    lighting of 13, 32, 58
    Post Office sorting vans 77, 84
    Pullman cars 22, 24, 32
    repairs 84
    royal 13, 22
    second class 24
    sleeping cars 27, 59
    third class 21, 31
Passenger traffic 65, 66, 99
Peppercorn, A.H. 74–5
Peterborough 3, 6, 42
Plant Centenarian Excursion, 1953 30
Plant works
    area 25
    building of 7
    clock 8
    extension of 13, 25, 32–3, 93
    fire, 1940 77
    gas supply 8
    'Goliath' area 94
    importance to Doncaster life, 1932 64
    land for 5
    machinery 7, 33, 58
    plans of 7, 79, 106, 107
    pollution and 10
Plant works staff
    accidents 38–9
    apprentices 37, 102–3
    ARP 72–3
    discipline 37
    holidays 64, 98
    hours 37, 89, 97
    improvement classes 40
    numbers employed 7, 13, 25, 35, 78, 81, 84, 88–91, 93, 97, 99, 107
    recreation 40
    sanitary arrangements 39
    skilled and unskilled component 36, 67
    short time working 36–37, 44, 47, 54, 64, 97
    wages 36, 37, 52, 63, 105
    women workers 48, 50, 105
    works' outings 14, 25–26, 106–7
Price, Ron 107–8

Productivity 62, 87, 90, 94, 99, 100
Protective clothing 72, 90, 98
Public Service Obligation (PSO) grant 99, 111, 112
Pullman cars 22, 24

Rail Council 107
Rail Shopmen's Informal Liaison
    Committee 102
Railway Benevolent Institution 42, 66
Railway Clearing House 51
Railway companies
    Eastern Counties 4
    Glasgow and South Western 53
    Great Central 53
    Great Eastern 53
    Great North of Scotland 53
    Great Northern 3
    Great Western 42
    Hull and Barnsley 53
    London and North Eastern 53, 54–62
    London and North Western 24
    London and York 3, 4
    Manchester, Sheffield and Lincolnshire 19
    Metropolitan 12
    Midland 4, 21, 24
    North British 53
    North Eastern 53
    Pennsylvania 32, 56
    Philadelphia and Reading 56
Railway Executive 76, 81, 84
    Ideal Stocks Committee, 1950 84
Railway Executive Committee 53, 65, 74
Railway Industry Association 10
Railway races 17
Ramsbottom Report, 1878 20
Raven Report, 1923 59, 61
Red Star parcels 100
Redundancies 92–3, 94, 97, 102, 104, 105
Reid, Sir Robert 104
Relaxation Agreement, 1982 103, 112
Relief kitchens 13, 26, 37
RFS Industries 107, 108
Riddles, R.A. 76, 77, 83, 111
Ridley, Nicholas 104, 105
Road Haulage Executive 91, 111
Road transport competition 61, 62, 88, 99, 112
Robert Stephenson and Co. 81
Rotary Club 64

St Leger 1, 5, 32
Schmidt, Wilhelm 30
Select Committee on Transport, 1918 53
Serpell Inquiry 103–4
Shildon 88, 99, 102, 104
Speedlink 100
Stedeford, Sir Ivan 91
Steel shortages 83, 85
Steels, T.R. 41
Stirling, Patrick
    biography 16–17
    8 foot singles 18, 28
    goods engines 19
    passenger carriages 23, 24
    and staff 37
    works extension 23
Stratford 93
Strikes
    1919 62
    General Strike, 1926 63
    3 October 1962 93
    10 August 1984 105
    ballot, 1986 105
Sturrock, Archibald 5, 6, 7, 11, 37, 42
    and environmental pollution 10
    locomotive policy 12

and passenger carriages 13
and Metropolitan Railway 12
retirement and death 15
Swindon 6, 11, 38, 39, 99, 102, 109

Temple Mills 104
Thomas J.H. 53
Thompson, Edward
    biography 66
    antipathy to Gresley 66–7
    Austerity locomotives 66
TOPS 100
Trade cycles 30, 36, 53, 111
Trade unions 40–1, 51, 62, 112
    Amalgamated Society of Carpenters
        and Joiners 40
    Amalgamated Society of Engineers 40
    Amalgamated Society of Railway Servants
        (ASRS) 40
    Associated Society of Locomotive Engineers
        and Firemen (ASLEF) 52
    Boilermakers Society 40, 52
    National Union of Railwaymen (NUR) 51, 72
    Railway Clerks' Association 51
    Yorkshire Miners' Association 41
Train speeds 18
Transport, Ministry of 83
Transport policy 53, 91, 93, 102, 111
    France 112
    Germany 112
Transport Users' Consultative Committee 99
TUC 41

Unemployment 47, 54, 59, 64, 92
USA
    influence on British railway practice 31–32

Victoria, Queen 13

Wagons
    Association of Private Owners of Wagons 21
    capacity 20–21, 30, 61, 87, 100
    common user scheme 51–2, 59, 67
    continuous brakes 21, 84, 87
    design of 21, 84–5
    private manufacture and ownership of 21, 61, 62, 76, 85
    shortages 61, 65, 67, 76
    stock of 12, 20, 30, 51, 61, 65, 74, 87, 89, 100
Wagon Repairs Committee 76
Walkden, Evelyn 74
Walker, Sir Herbert 53
Walter Alexander Coachmakers Ltd 101
Wedgwood, R.L. 63, 68
White Paper on Transport, 1920 53
Williams, Alfred 38, 39
Wilson, E.B. 6
Wolverton 102, 107
Women's employment 48–9, 51. 68–72, 106
    campaign for equal pay 72
World War I 46 ff.
    dependents' allowances 47
    war work at Plant 47–9
    women's employment 48–9, 51
World War II 65 ff.
    Air Raid Precautions 73
    locomotive programme 66–7
    passenger and freight traffic 66
    rolling stock shortages 67
    war work at Plant 68
    women's employment 68–72
Work study schemes 90, 94

York 3, 4, 32, 59, 84, 88, 107